Some Comments About the Book

"Your book reminds us of the basic principles that have contributed to Steelcase's success."

>Larry Sparks
>Director, Corporate Sales Support and Aviation
>Steelcase, Inc.

"Dr. Yager's book contains a wealth of advice which is invaluable for anyone."

>Dorothea Johnson
>Protocol Consultant
>to the World Trade Center Washington DC

"***Business Protocol*** will help some of us to understand why we may have fallen short of our present career goals, and should help all of us achieve our future expectations."

>J. Douglas Phillips
>Senior Director, Corporate Planning
>Merck & Co., Inc.

"Nothing short of great. Handles a complex subject in simple, direct language that is refreshing reading. Truly a distinguished accomplishment."

>Kenneth A. Snella
>Vice President, Administration
>Berkshire Electric Cable

"***Business Protocol*** is great. Tells you how, then shows you how."

>William Thourlby
>Author of *Passport to Power*

"Jan Yager's book deserves a permanent spot on your reference shelf. Indeed, the country-by-country etiquette review is by itself worth the price of admission."

>Laurence J. Stybel
>President
>Stybel Peabody & Associates

(continued)

"Basic consideration for others is the key to communicating effectively in business. Jan Yager primes her readers with important information that makes the road ahead smoother for ambitious executives."

Camille Lavington
International Communications Consultant

Other Books by Jan Yager, Ph.D.

Making Your Office Work for You

Creative Time Management

How to Write Like a Professional

Friendship: A Selected, Annotated Bibliography

The Help Book

Single in America

Victims

The Vegetable Passion: A History of the Vegetarian State of Mind

Business Protocol

How to Survive and Succeed in Business

Jan Yager, Ph.D.

John Wiley & Sons, Inc.
New York • Chichester • Brisbane • Toronto • Singapore

To my husband

Fred

and our children

Scott *and* **Jeffrey**

In recognition of the importance of preserving what has been written, it is a policy of John Wiley & Sons, Inc. to have books of enduring value published in the United States printed on acid-free paper, and we exert our best efforts to that end.

Library of Congress Cataloging in Publication Data

Yager, Jan, 1948–
    Business protocol : how to survive and succeed in business by Jan Yager.
        p.   cm.
    Includes bibliographical references and index.
    ISBN 0-471-54259-8 (cloth)   ISBN 0-471-51234-6 (paper)
    1. Business etiquette.   2. Business entertaining.   I. Title.
HF5389.Y34   1991
395'.52—dc20   90-45859

Printed in the United States of America
91 92 10 9 8 7 6 5 4 3 2 1

Acknowledgments

This book, like every nonfiction book, is dependent upon countless others for helping it develop from an idea to a published entity. I want to extend special thanks to such corporate observers as: Harold Burson, Chairman, Burson-Marsteller; Charles Peebler, CEO, Bozell Inc.; J. Douglas Phillips, Senior Director, Corporate Planning, Merck & Co., Inc.; Sharon Peake Williamson, Manager of Public Information, Mead Corporation; Nella Barkley, President, Crystal/Barkley Corporation; Mark Goines, Vice President, Product Development, Charles Schwab & Co., Inc.; William R. Cox, Executive Vice President and Managing Director, Dentsu Burson-Marsteller; Gary Root, Vice President of Marketing, Johnson & Johnson Consumer Products, Inc.; Carol Meyers, AT&T telemarketing consultant; Thomas R. Horton, Chairman and CEO, American Management Association; Trudi Gallagher, Houlihan-Lawrence, Inc.; Rosemary Xiques, Chris Markatos Associates; Regula Noetzli; The Charlotte Sheedy Agency; Ellen Gendel, Brown-Fowler; Glen Lewis; Judith Berkowitz, Merritt Associates; John S. Sturges, President, Siebrand-Wilton Associates, Inc.; Larry Stybel and Maryann Peabody, Stybel, Peabody & Associates; Edward I. Koch; Neil Allison, Sales Manager, Eastern U.S.A. and Canada, Australian Airlines; Julie Phelan, The Gersh Agency Inc.; Martin Poll; Bob Bly; Dan E. Burner, Associate Director of Personnel Administration, VALIC; David Carradine; Gail Jenssen; Nancy Creshkoff; Jeffrey R. Epstein; Nancy Howe; Nana Greller; Patti Breitmen; Don Hauptman; Robert M. Hecht; Bob Kalian; Larry Marshall, President & CEO, Marshall Consultants, Inc.; Donna McCarthy; Peter Jeff and Larry Sparks, Steelcase, Inc.; Lydia Schindler, Director of Communications, Ethics Resource Center, Inc.; Sara McWilliams, Personnel Director, Tallix; Carl Sautter; Ginny Dembner, Prudential Connecticut Realty; Carl Schupp, Director of Human Resources, Dowty Aerospace Corporation; Howard Seligmann; Diana Simkin, Director, Family Focus; Kenneth A. Snella, Vice President, Berkshire Electric Cable; Ann West; Dorothy Paleologos, Aetna; Richard Zeif; John Artise, Drake Beam Morin, Inc.; Irene Cohen, Irene Cohen Personnel Services; Paul Critchlow, Bill Clark, Bobbie Collins, and Claudia Kahn of Merrill Lynch; Toni Clark; Marcia Pear; Annette C. Doran; Howard S. Freedman, Korn/Ferry International; Jacqueline Thompson; and etiquette and image experts Letitia Baldrige, Dorothea Johnson, Randi Freidig, Judi Kaufman, Linda Phillips, Camille Lavington, Susan Bixler, William Thourlby, Diana Rowland, and Barbara Chizmas. Others whose assistance was valuable to this project include Nancy Bren, Linda Harnett, Thomas W. Cheney, and Dana Kyle.

I also want to thank my dedicated and enthusiastic editor at John Wiley & Sons, Inc., Mike Hamilton, who originally asked me to write this book. Mike's encouragement and involvement in this project were very helpful to me. I also want to thank Deborah Wiley, Mike's assistant Elena Paperny, Terry Zak, Margie Shustak, Maureen Heffernan, and the rest of the Wiley staff who oversaw this project from proposal to published book. Mike Hamilton commissioned two outside reviewers to read earlier drafts of the manuscript; their comments were extremely helpful to me.

Friends and family who were especially supportive during the time I spent researching and writing this book include Marcia and Marty Hoffenberg, Gail Tuchman, Leslie Rusgo, Mary Ellen Ostrander, Nona Aguilar, Mary Tierney Kelly, Roz Bindman, Sharon Fisher, Sharon Hymer, Karen McMahon, Monica Sharma, Judy Cohn Pooler, Carol Ann Finkelstein Shoretz, Joyce Guy Patton, Shelia Conner, Mary Jane Haymond, Kate Kelly, Joyce Bronstein, Phyllis Wexler, Sally Wendkos Olds, my parents, Dr. and Mrs. William Barkas, my in-laws, Mary and the late William Yager, Elsie Forbes, and my sister Eileen and her husband Dick. Most of all I want to thank my dedicated husband Fred and our young children Scott and Jeffrey, who put up with all the hours—sometimes most of entire evenings or weekends—when I was less available because I had to work on "the book." I could not possibly manage to accomplish all that I do without Fred's help, guidance, editorial genius, and, most of all, love.

In addition to my graduate training and teaching experiences in sociology, and an earlier brief course in etiquette at John Robert Powers School, this book is an outgrowth of my field work and consulting in business over the last ten years. This book is also based on extensive research specifically on business etiquette, including an analysis of a survey on etiquette completed by 108 randomly selected members of the Society for Human Resource Management, working at a wide range of companies throughout the country, as well as dozens of follow-up phone and in-person interviews with that sample, other executives, or etiquette experts. Some of those survey respondents, executives, or experts are quoted by name in this book. However, all who participated in my survey or with whom I spoke played a pivotal role in helping this book become a reality. I thank everyone for their generous time and input into this business etiquette study. Katherine Compton, Public Relations Associate at the Society for Human Resource Management (formerly the American Society for Personnel Administration), was extremely helpful to me in the distribution of my business etiquette survey to a sample of the society's members. Her cooperation was essential to my research project; her help made a formidable task much easier to complete.

Jan Yager

Contents

Introduction

Business Protocol: How to Survive and Succeed in Business is based on the principle that as the world becomes more competitive, appropriate behavior or proper business protocol plays a more important role in the success or failure not only of individuals but of corporations as well.

This book views protocol as a business strategy and provides etiquette guidelines that can help advance your career.

In 1936, Dale Carnegie wrote, "about 15 percent of one's financial success is due to one's technical knowledge and about 85 percent is due to skill in human engineering."

It's hard to estimate the amount of money lost every year or the numbers of careers that are ruined because of inappropriate behavior or bad manners. Acknowledging the potential liabilities, the Japanese spend hundreds of millions of dollars a year on etiquette training and consulting.

Business Protocol is designed not only to help you understand the importance of acting appropriately but also to offer the skills and knowledge necessary to address most business situations.

Going beyond the basic principles, I also explore some of the deeper

1

and perhaps more important underlying elements of etiquette, such as interpersonal skills.

"In most organizations, the success of the organization is based entirely on the ability of the individuals in the organization to work together toward a common goal," says William R. Cox, Executive Vice President and Managing Director of Dentsu Burson-Marsteller, a firm that provides public relations for Japanese clients who work in the United States.

"Concern for others is a paramount requirement for people to even begin to do that," Cox adds. "It comes before skills, experience, or talent."

The etiquette principles discussed in this book are based on scores of interviews with top executives as well as a survey of 108 human resources managers across the country at a variety of companies.

As a sociologist and management consultant, I have been studying the rules of proper business protocol, and writing about corporate America, for the past decade.

A common theme expressed to me during those years was the growing importance of protocol or etiquette within the business world, and how often the topic would come up at business strategy sessions.

BusinessWeek magazine has labeled the 1990s "the decade of the customer," noting that successful companies will be those who provide not only the best service, but who make the customer or client feel welcome and cared for. Proper etiquette or protocol and appropriate behavior are two key elements to quality service.

The opening chapter of this book provides an overview including the six basic business protocol principles. The following chapters deal with issues such as image, being on time, table manners, speech, relationships at work, executive communication, appropriate office settings, international etiquette, business meals, executive entertaining, personality types and how to deal with them effectively, gift-giving and receiving, leisure time, changing jobs, and the connection between etiquette and ethics.

I hope that by reading this book and applying its protocol principles your business will grow and your career will thrive, and that as these principles and concern for others spread, the sometimes harsh and cutthroat world of business, will, to paraphrase President Bush, become a kinder, gentler place.

Chapter 1

How Etiquette Can Make or Break Your Career

One thing is certain about the 1990s—there will be numerous changes in the workplace. As companies restructure and downsize, some industries will contract while others expand. As the competition becomes fiercer, getting or keeping a job, or being promoted, will hinge not only on how qualified you are—for there are hundreds of others with similar qualifications—but how *appropriately* you behave, and how much you look and act the part for that particular position.

Opinions are formed within the first five minutes of a job interview; people tend to hire candidates they find likeable, and to promote those who make them feel comfortable. Good manners, like saying "Thank you," being polite and considerate, using appropriate language, and dressing the right way for a certain job are some of the traits that generally make workers likeable or likely to succeed.

Etiquette, or behaving in an appropriate manner, has become a key strategy to getting ahead—and staying ahead—in the business world.

Whether we like it or not, getting to the top, and staying there, can sometimes be a matter of saying the right thing at the right time, or avoiding such career-damaging situations like revealing too much at the water cooler; drinking too much at the Christmas party; breaching the etiquette of when to arrive at the office, based on the arrival time of subordinates or superiors. Good judgment needs to be shown by appropriate gift-giving; socializing with the right people at the annual holiday party; behaving correctly at power breakfasts, lunches, or dinners, and deciding who picks up the tab; choosing the right words to say if a colleague is fired; being aware of the etiquette of male–female relationships at work and behaving accordingly; conversing properly over the phone, in person, or by mail; effectively conducting seminars, meetings, or conferences; creating and replying to invitations; and arranging business entertaining that reflects well on you and your company.

The premise of this book is that proper business protocol offers you another strategy for getting to the top and staying there.

Rules change not only from industry to industry but from company to company. In order to get ahead, you have to know what those rules are at any particular time. In terms of dress, for example, there is an expected way of dressing if you work as an executive in a financial services institution, compared to a publishing company. Furthermore, whether you work in the creative versus the administrative area of a company may influence dress, speech, or written communications and related behaviors. Even within an industry, rules change depending upon the persons with whom you come in contact; the creative types at an advertising agency dress one way, and those who meet with clients usually dress to fit the industry the client represents. For example, someone in advertising whose clients are in the financial services sector would dress like a Wall Street executive.

Proper etiquette has always been a key element to the smooth operations of a successful business. Now, as businesses become global in their research, etiquette plays an even greater role. Japanese executives recognize the importance of etiquette probably more than those in any other industrialized nation. According to Diana Rowland, a California-based international business consultant, the Japanese spend an estimated $700 million a year in proper etiquette training and consulting for their employees.

Improper etiquette costs companies billions and billions of dollars in lost business sales and deals and hiring and training costs. Executive recruiter Larry Marshall placed two executives to head communications for a Japanese consumer electronics corporation based in New Jersey. Says Marshall: "One lasted a week. The other lasted fifteen years. The first one kept sending memos that they've got to do this immediately. But with the Japanese, you never tell them this is an emergency and act on it immediately. The second said, 'I think we should think about these options,' and he's been there ever since."

Improper etiquette may also prevent you from getting the job. An executive at a conservative financial services institution shared with me why one man, who was otherwise very qualified, did not get an executive position. "He wore loud suits, a diamond pinky ring, and a gold bracelet on his wrist. He was so good that it almost made me go against my own instincts and hire him. But I knew he would have trouble establishing himself in this business because of that style of dress."

Here are some additional true-life examples of how etiquette violations hampered someone's advancement in business as well as caused countless lost hours in training dismissed employees and hiring new ones. Although a few of the examples may seem somewhat outlandish, they are all real situations that could have happened to you:

- Mark is an interviewer with a software development company. His boss has been sitting in on the interviews to "see how management is presenting the company." While Mark is interviewing a job candidate, he puts his feet up on the desk. "It's terrible," says Mark's boss.

- Donna, a real estate broker, cancels a business appointment because she is ill. However, she fails to make a new appointment immediately. Although she is well within a day, she lets two weeks go by before she again calls her clients. By then they have found a new broker, one whom they hope will be more responsive to them.

- Sandra, a thirty-five-year-old consultant, gives a seminar to executives at one of the major television networks. The human resources executive who hired Sandra is shocked that Sandra conducted the seminar in a sweater and pants, rather than in a business suit. To make matters worse, when Sandra is reprimanded over the phone, she loses control, and in her anger shouts the four-letter *s* word at the woman who hired her.

- Sam, who earns over $200,000 a year, has written a "kiss-and-tell" book about his experiences at his last job. Should he submit the manuscript to his current employer, even though it has nothing to do with his present company? He decides to show it to his employee, who says it is okay. When the book is published, however, and Sam's admissions of wrongdoings in his last job become public, his current employer does not take so kindly to such attention-getting negative publicity and Sam is soon looking for another job.

- After a department Christmas party, Molly, a marketing executive earning about $60,000 a year, accepts a ride home from her male boss. She gets out of the car but inadvertently leaves her attaché case in his trunk along with the keys to her apartment. Slightly tipsy and upset,

Molly goes to the nearby apartment of another executive who was at the party, and who had been in the same car earlier with her and her boss. Once in his apartment, she starts cursing at the top of her lungs about the situation.

- Bob, an assistant to a vice president in corporate communications, always arrives half an hour before everyone else in his department, including his boss. Bob finds it hard to understand why his boss is displeased by his early arrival and wonders if he should get a transfer to another department, or if he should start coming in at the same time as, or later than, his boss. Bob also has started to answer phone inquiries without consulting his boss even though he does not have the experience, nor has he been given the authority, to do so.

Mark, Donna, Sandra, Sam, Molly, and Bob are just six businesspersons and executives trying to work their way up the ladder, whose future may hinge on how well they know business etiquette and the "rules of the game." Let us look at what happened to these six because of the way they handled business etiquette issues:

Mark was reprimanded for his overly casual style. He is now taking more seriously how he represents his company during these job interviews by studying the do's and don'ts of the etiquette tip sheet that his boss has put together.

Donna learned you should always reschedule a business appointment at the same time you have to cancel it, and that some of her customers require more frequent phone contact so they feel their needs matter to her.

Sandra learned her lesson and dressed more appropriately when she conducted future seminars. She also learned to control her temper and her language in all business situations, even when criticized.

Molly, by failing to get her behavior in line, lost her job a year later, but first she got her male boss fired on trumped-up charges of sexual harassment. Whether or not the sexual harassment charges were true, her married boss also lost his job because he had been indiscrete with his female employee—meeting her for dinner on more than one occasion.

Sam lost his job because he admitted wrongdoings at his last job, which led his current employers to distrust how he was currently performing. They also feared he might write another kiss-and-tell book about them once he moved on again.

Bob figured out that by upstaging his boss he was risking his own job. So he began arriving later and made sure he was clear on what questions from callers he should answer.

Like Bob, Mark, Donna, Sandra, Sam, and Molly, rising executives need guidance on etiquette (protocol), or the proper way of doing things. This book is designed to provide that guidance.

In addition to universally accepted rules of behavior, we will examine how etiquette varies, not only from industry to industry, but from company to company within the same area. Each firm has its own corporate culture, and even within large corporations there are subtle degrees of differences.

At Merrill Lynch, for example, for many years there were actually two companies. One was devoted to the retail brokerage business catering to individual investors, while the other provided investment banking services to large institutional clients and government agencies. Each had its own rules of etiquette tailored to the vastly different worlds of the more informal consumer retail market and the more formal and strict protocol-laden arena of capital markets. Recently this changed as the company attempted to integrate these two cultures into one cohesive firm.

This book will also point out how some of the rules are changing as women achieve higher positions of authority. For example, it is becoming more common for men to report incidents of sexual harassment.

As a sociologist and management consultant, I have been researching and writing about appropriate business practices since the early 1980s. For this book on business etiquette I also conducted original field work, including interviews and observations with rising and top executives in a variety of professions and at a wide range of companies throughout the country, as well as an analysis of a survey on business etiquette completed by 108 members of the Society for Human Resource Management (SHRM)—human resources or personnel administrators at companies who know about etiquette and what breaching it can mean. (See Appendix I for a copy of the cover letter and final etiquette survey that were distributed to SHRM members.) Although the questionnaire was anonymous, 30 respondents voluntarily provided their names and phone numbers for possible follow-up. The 108 who completed questionnaires represent a broad range of companies, from manufacturing, consulting, telecommunications, insurance, and health care to research, high tech, beverage distribution, and computer software, among others. The companies are located throughout the United States, in Raleigh, North Carolina, Archbold, Ohio, Richmond, Virginia, Huntsville, Alabama, Montgomery, Minnesota, and Cranford, New Jersey, to name just a few areas. In addition to that survey, I did additional interviews with dozens of executives, such as Harold Burson, Chairman of Burson-Marsteller; Charles Peebler, CEO, Bozell Inc.; and J. Douglas Phillips, Senior Director, Corporate Planning, Merck & Co., Inc.

WHAT IS YOUR BEQ (Business Etiquette Quotient)?

Before we evaluate what the research found, you have an opportunity to do some evaluating of your own. The following quiz will measure your BEQ, or Business Etiquette Quotient.

Pick the answer that accurately reflects what you usually do (*not what you wish to do*) in the following situations:

1. When I am invited to a business function, I always RSVP (respond) within the week.
   a. Yes _____ b. No_____ c. Sometimes _____
2. I always return a phone call the same day I receive a message.
   a. Yes _____ b. No _____ c. Sometimes _____
3. I never use curse words at work or at home.
   a. Yes _____ b. No _____ c. Sometimes _____
4. I always write thank-you notes (or make a thank-you phone call) for meals, gifts, or any kind of extra kindness extended to me.
   a. Yes _____ b. No _____ c. Sometimes _____
5. My table manners are superb.
   a. Yes _____ b. No _____ c. Sometimes _____
6. I see myself as part of a team, rather than a lone corporate player mainly seeking praise for my individual efforts.
   a. Yes _____ b. No _____ c. Sometimes _____
7. I answer important letters immediately and take care of the rest of the mail within a week.
   a. Yes _____ b. No _____ c. Sometimes _____
8. Before dealing with someone from another culture, I take the time to find out the proper etiquette unique to that person's culture so I do not offend anyone.
   a. Yes _____ b. No _____ c. Sometimes _____
9. I give verbal or written credit where credit is due.
   a. Yes _____ b. No _____ c. Sometimes _____
10. I send holiday cards to my most highly valued business relationships.
    a. Yes _____ b. No _____ c. Sometimes _____

Give yourself a 3 for each *yes* or *a* answer; a 2 for each *c* or *sometimes*; and a 1 for each *b* or *no*. Add up your score. If you rated a score of 28–30, your BEQ is excellent. If you got 25–27, you have a good BEQ. If your score is 20–24, your BEQ is fair. If your score is 10–19, you have a poor BEQ.

Now reconsider your answers. Pat yourself on the back for all your "yeses" and make special note of your "no's." Those are just some of the areas you have to work on. Your "sometimes" answers indicate you know the right thing to do, but you need to be more consistent in doing it. All ten issues raised in the previous self-evaluation are discussed in this book. By improving your BEQ you will also give yourself another winning strategy to assure your rise to the corporate top. If you are self-employed, you may find you will retain more clients or customers if you have a superior BEQ. Those holiday cards that you send at the end of the year are not just a tradition; they are a way of telling your co-workers, employees, clients, customers, or suppliers that you think enough of them to take the time to send a card and spread good cheer.

SIX BASIC PRINCIPLES OF BUSINESS ETIQUETTE

The six basic etiquette principles set forth below are backed up by statistics as well as specific anecdotes based on the results of the business etiquette survey completed by 108 human resources managers; my observations and additional interviews in the etiquette area reinforce those survey findings. However, it is up to you to modify any information to fit the company setting in which you find yourself currently employed. The general guidelines will remain the same; just the details will change. Understanding these universal rules will benefit you at all levels—from administrative assistant to manager to vice president to CEO—as well as whatever company setting you find yourself in—from a small company of less than twenty employees to a corporation of 35,000 employees to a business of your own that you run from your home. These six key etiquette rules will improve your BEQ and help you get ahead in whatever job you do, or aspire to.

1. Be on Time

Be sensitive to the people around you in matters of common courtesy, such as being on time, being punctual, scheduling of appointments. It's just the little things that add up.

   —*Harold Burson*
   Chairman
   Burson-Marsteller

Lateness, since it often impedes the company's operations, is the most obvious tip-off that you are unreliable and not "executive" material. If you are late, your boss may consider you disrespectful. Your advancement at that job would be questionable. (But as we have seen from the example of Bob, being on time may also mean you should not arrive too early and upstage your boss.)

The most important time of the day that you should consistently arrive on time is in the morning. Whether you are expected in at 7:30 A.M. or 9 A.M., be there *every day* at that same time. If a rare occasion occurs where you have to be late, and you know about it in advance, call in and let your secretary or some other key person know so you look like a reliable person.

Being on time also applies to reports or any other tasks you are asked to do. Any kind of lateness requires an explanation, and it makes you look less reliable than someone who gets things in on time. Of course you have good reasons for needing an extension, but that is not what the company cares about! It cares that you get things in on time. So be on time and, if necessary, get more time initially so you will have as much time as you need. Time-management experts suggest you add 25% to whatever length of time you think you will need so you will actually end up with enough time. Remember Murphy's laws: things take longer than you think *and* everything that can go wrong usually does, especially when you have a deadline. So budget extra time for problems that might arise.

Whether or not "being on time" is considered proper etiquette at their company was asked of the respondents on my etiquette survey. A whopping 94% wrote that being on time *is* considered correct etiquette. As human resources manager Nancy Howe, who works at a high-tech company based in Vienna, Virginia, points out, being late at meetings interferes with an efficient business: "When people are late, meetings frequently have to be rescheduled, and the progress of other people who rely on them, such as co-workers whose questions go unanswered, is also held up."

As you will note in the chapter on international etiquette, being on time is relative depending on the business culture of the country you are working in. For example, in Central and South American countries, it is perfectly acceptable to be thirty minutes late; in countries such as Germany, punctuality is expected.

2. Be Discrete

*You have to be extremely discrete, very sensitive
to the impact that information might have on*

those working with it, as well as what the
competition might do if they fall upon it.

> —Mark Goines
> *Vice President, Product Development*
> *Charles Schwab & Co., Inc.*

Being discrete means you keep confidences of a corporate or business as well as a personal nature. You keep to yourself any company secrets, whether that means the design for a unique product, or the fact that there will be massive layoffs in a week. Goines tells the story of someone at Schwab who talked in press interviews about a product in development, a trust account service, that they were not prepared to support. The result? Says Goines: "We didn't have the materials ready for it. They ran the article and we had several thousand requests for information that we couldn't yet provide." It certainly did not help the credibility of the woman who committed the indiscretion.

One hundred percent of the administrators I surveyed at assorted companies around the country wrote that "keeping business confidences" is correct etiquette at their company. "Confidentiality is an issue" explains Donna McCarthy, a corporate personnel manager at a hospital administration company based in Florida.

On the personal side, you should keep to yourself any confessions you hear from co-workers, bosses, or subordinates, whether that means someone has told you his wife asked him to sleep on the living room sofa the night before or their teenager is getting out of another drug rehab program. Be careful also to be discrete about good news! The boss may not thank you for spreading the news that his wife is pregnant—before he has a chance to tell others—or your co-worker may prefer to keep it to herself that she received an award from a professional organization (since she might fear others will be jealous of her).

3. Be Courteous, Pleasant, and Positive

Organizational culture is a composite of the
values and attitudes of those in the
organization. Eventually negative thinking or
actions lead to negative business results. So,
regardless of the pressures on you or your
company, try to remain courteous, pleasant, and
upbeat.

> —J. Douglas Phillips
> *Senior Director, Corporate Planning*
> *Merck & Co., Inc.*

No matter how demanding your clients, customers, co-workers, or employees might be, it is important to be courteous, pleasant, and positive. No one likes to work around a negative, suspicious, or contrary person. What gets you to the top is a friendly manner (but that does not mean becoming best friends with everyone you work with). If everyone says you are *likeable*, you are on the right track. *Saying the right thing* is part of being courteous, pleasant, and positive. You want to be that way in your actions and to reflect it in your own words.

"What is the key business etiquette concern at your company?" I asked on my survey. Those who answered that question, over and over again, whether the respondent was an employee benefits administrator at a manufacturing company in Nashville, Tennessee, or the director of personnel at a nonprofit service organization in Colorado Springs, Colorado, gave the same answer: "overall professionalism in a friendly manner" or "projecting a positive company image." It is important to be courteous, pleasant, and positive at all levels—to fellow employees, subordinates, or superiors, and clients and customers as well—however trying they might be. As Sara McWilliams, Personnel Director of Tallix, a company in Beacon, New York, that casts sculptures for commissioned artists says: "At times the artists can be difficult to work with, but we understand. We don't perceive it as a power struggle or obnoxiousness."

4. Be Concerned with Others, not Just Yourself

I've seen people whose careers were ended, stalled, or reversed because they lacked concern for others. The greatest mistakes are made when we don't have sufficient empathy and understanding of our clients and their needs and their problems.

> —William R. Cox
> Executive Vice President and Managing Director
> Dentsu Burson-Marsteller

Whatever business you are in, the necessity to find out a client's or customer's point of view will help you get ahead in practically every industry—from manufacturing to publishing to health care to telecommunications. "We portray an environment that gives people the feeling they are being treated fairly . . . that we are straightforward and above-board with them," says Dan E. Burner, Associate Director of Personnel Administration, VALIC, The Variable Annuity Life Insurance Company in Houston, Texas. Because new or current clients may have had negative experiences with other insurance companies, or other types of insurance (annuity insurance is different from the more typical death benefits insurance), it is important for the employees at Burner's company to be responsive to the fears or worries that customers might have.

Concern for others should extend beyond just clients or customers to co-workers, superiors, or subordinates as well. Says Cox of Dentsu Burson-Marsteller: "All sorts of evils fly from selfishness or self-centeredness, like hurting your colleagues and others in order to gain the competitive advantage in the job or in the organization."

Be *empathetic* to others' points of view, and be sensitive to where their point of view is coming from. Be open to criticism and suggestions from colleagues, superiors, or subordinates. Avoid defensiveness if your job performance is questioned; show an openness to the ideas and experience of others. Be humble yet self-assured.

It is too easy to fall into the trap of thinking "There are two ways of doing something: the wrong way and *my* way." That type of thinking is counterproductive in most business environments.

5. Dress Appropriately

First impressions are first impressions. You only make one. Look and listen and pick a role model.

> —*Charles Peebler*
> *CEO*
> *Bozell Inc.*

You can read whole books on this topic—most notably John T. Molloy's *New Dress for Success,** as well as Susan Bixler's *The Professional Image*, Alison Lurie's *The Language of Clothes*, or Janet Wallach's *Working Wardrobe*. But the most important tip to remember is that you want to fit into your corporate environment, as well as your level within that environment. Some experts suggest that you dress for the job you want, rather than the one you have, but this is impractical if you consider what it

---

* Cited references have complete bibliographic entries in the Selected Bibliography.

would look like if an executive secretary appeared in a pin-striped business suit carrying an expensive attaché case, or someone in the mailroom started wearing a suit that mirrored the look of the top executives. It would be so obvious that they were bucking for the jobs at the higher level of dress that it might backfire—leading to no job.

You want to "fit in" at whatever level you are currently employed, but you also want to do it in good taste and in colors that suit you so you look your best. Carefully chosen *accessories* can make an enormous impression on others, from well-chosen shoes to attractive and distinctive ties.

If you have a business dinner right after work, especially if it is with someone of the opposite sex, be careful not to change into evening clothes that might give the impression that the dinner is taking on more social, rather than professional, overtones. (If you are going out socially *after* the business dinner, you should make plans to change *after* the dinner, not before.)

When asked "Are employees ever reprimanded for the way they dress?," out of 108 respondents, 60% wrote *occasionally;* 20% wrote *sometimes;* and 19% wrote *never.* Of the 19% that wrote *never,* 43% worked in manufacturing; the remainder in assorted industries (nonprofit, high tech, government, aerospace).

6. Use Proper Written and Spoken Language

People who can express themselves clearly are at an advantage. Poor written and oral communication skills may hold someone back, undermining their other skills.

   —Sharon Peake Williamson
     Manager of Public Information
     Mead Corporation

Using proper written and spoken words means that what you say as well as what you write in your interoffice memos and whatever letters go to others outside the company should be well written, and all names should be spelled correctly. If you need help in the areas of grammar and spelling, and a textbook or computer program is not enough of an aid, seek out someone you trust at your level who might check over your correspondence, memos, or reports. Your company might also have a communications department whose functions include helping executives with their written communications.

Be careful never to use foul language—even in what you think is a personal telephone call that, to your shock and horror, was overheard by someone whose opinion of you means everything—in any situations that are work-related. If, for some reason, you are repeating the foul language that someone else used, by way of example or because you want to be thorough about a situation, do not use the actual word. Even if you are quoting someone else, others will hear that word as if it is part of your vocabulary. (There are discrete ways to indicate that an expletive has been deleted. An article in a major newspaper even used the word *expletive* in place of the actual quoted foul word.) (Five of those surveyed wrote that using foul language [4] or saying the wrong thing [1] had led to employee firings.)

Seattle-based business etiquette expert Randi Freidig comments on the increasing importance of proper written and spoken language: "We have not been polite to each other. We don't have a sense of what offends the other person, and yet we are moving into a decade where that is going to be much more important. We have to be much more sensitive to de-meaning language and gestures. Women in the workplace don't want to be called *girls*. No one wants the putdowns."

In summary, the six basic principles of business protocol or etiquette are:

1. Be on time.

2. Be discrete.

3. Be courteous, pleasant, and positive.

4. Be concerned with others, not just yourself.

5. Dress appropriately.

6. Use proper written and spoken language.

Not only is being gracious in a business situation essential for all of us who want to get ahead, proper business etiquette is a legacy we want to pass on to those youngsters who will be the executives of tomorrow. That more needs to be done in this regard is brought home by Randi Freidig's experience when she gave a lecture on business manners to juniors and seniors in high school. Says Freidig: "We started talking about the word *gracious*, and when you define the word *gracious* it means *polite, considerate, thoughtful*. I asked if they're around someone like that, how do they feel? This audience had nothing but negatives to say. 'It's fake.' 'They're putting on something.' I looked at them and said, 'Well, frankly, you're going to have to change your attitude before you get into the business world. How would you feel if you tried to get a bank loan and the guy treated you like dirt?' One kid stood up and said, 'Well, at least he's honest.' "

Let's hope that that youth's cynical view of being courteous is an unrepresentative one. But it is definitely an attitude to be reckoned with—whether he tries to be a part of the business world or has to deal with businesspersons as a client or customer.

Business etiquette is too valuable a tool for career enhancement for any of us to ignore the importance of learning about it on our own or teaching it at school or at work.

In the next chapter, we will begin our workday etiquette training by looking more closely at the image you should be creating, including the do's and don'ts of business dress, the maxim of being on time, correct table manners, and proper speech, including phone etiquette.

Chapter 2

Good Morning—
Rise and Shine!

Wake up with a smile on your face—or if one is missing, put one there—for
a positive attitude about yourself and your job will make you a joy to be
around. Complainers, loners, foretellers of doom, and just plain negative
folks eventually are weeded out in business. It is those who are positive
and upbeat who have the best chance of advancement. The rules govern-
ing how you conduct yourself at work differ from those that apply in the
informality of your home or in the living room of your best friend. At work,
a smile and a friendly attitude are the correct way to present yourself if
you want others to enjoy working with and around you.

How often have you heard it said about someone who failed to advance
as fast or as far as he should that he had an "attitude problem"? When the
president of one of the major American cereal companies was abruptly
fired after nine months at his high job (but sixteen years with the company), his colleagues explained the action as a combination of poor
business decisions that cost the company money as well as an attitude
problem. He was described as "demanding and abrasive and often unwilling to listen to subordinates."

Greet people with a "Hello," "Good morning," or, if appropriate, a
handshake that is firm but not crushing. "A handshake should not be too

hard," says Barbara B. Chizmas of Chizmas Business Etiquette International in Redlands, California. Says Chizmas: "You shake from the elbow, not from the wrist and not from the shoulder. If you look at your hand, and think of the web, it should meet the other person's web. That's a good way to prevent someone from giving you the little whimpy, fishy handshake. Give a couple of shakes—two, three, four—and look at the person in the eyes as you shake their hand."

IMAGE

Image is the sum total of our appearance, speech, demeanor, and even our people skills. Image is what the noted late sociologist Erving Goffman referred to as *impression management.* There are as many images as there are people, but what we are concerned with is whether or not your business image fits the type of work you have to do and the company you have to do it in. A car company, an industry which has been one of the foundations of the economy in the United States, chose well when it picked Lee Iacocca, someone with a fatherly image, to lead a revitalization of design and production. A major movie studio, when a Japanese company bought it to take it from its "has-been" status and revitalize it as one of the new creative, economic leaders in the field, was wise to pay millions of dollars to put the two hottest independent producers at its helm. Their image of megahits became instantly associated with the new movie studio.

Some aspects of our image we are born with, such as height, bone structure, or facial features. But even those physical aspects of image may be changed by us doing everything from keeping in shape instead of becoming overweight or obese, applying just enough makeup rather than too much or the wrong colors, or even having cosmetic surgery, if necessary. Clothing may definitely enhance or detract from someone's basic physical self. If your taste is questionable, consider a "personal shopper" who, with your corporate image in mind, suggests clothing selections that suit your body type, coloring, and corporate image. An executive in Washington, D. C., for example, never really felt comfortable with her clothing choices for work. Although she was always well dressed, shopping was stressful for her. Since she started using a personal shopper, some of the anxiety has been removed from her business clothes shopping. She is also more likely to update her wardrobe every six months, rather than every couple of years.

Voices may be trained to be more pleasant or softer. Speech may be modified so that specific words or how they are spoken make a better impression. Nails may be cleaned, polished, or colored. Hair may be coiffed, curled, or colored. Just how important nicely done hair is for the executive woman is evidenced by the growing number of 6:00–7:30 A.M. and late-night hairdressers, who cater to professional women, as reported by Deirdre Fanning in the *New York Times*. Executives in all fields, from advertising, law, banking, and interior design, to newscasters, may have their hair done as often as three times during a business week before or after work.

An exercise regime tailored to your current physique, weight, and endurance will give you extra stamina and strength. Not only is being in shape good for your heart, health, and self-esteem, but some companies officially or unofficially discriminate against overweight employees or applicants in terms of advancement or hiring opportunities.

Image consulting is a new field that emerged in the 1980s to fill the needs of corporations and individuals in enhancing their professional appearance. The current biannual *Directory of Personal Image Consultants* compiled by Jacqueline Thompson lists 364 firms that do image consulting with specialization in the areas of speech, etiquette, dress, color, motivation, and career development.

Remember that personal habits that are demonstrated while you are communicating, whether that means inappropriately combing your hair during a business meeting or chewing on celery or gum during a telephone call, are all part of the image we convey. How positive or negative that image is not only reflects on us but on those for whom we work. It may also be a factor in why someone wants to continue to do business with us or our firm, or switches to another executive or professional. (I remember all too well how uncomfortable it was to have an orthodontist with halitosis! An expectant mother told me she was uneasy being treated by an obstetrician with long, dirty nails.)

The theme of a talk by outplacement counselor John Artise at a luncheon meeting of the Sales Association of the Graphic Arts was "Mind Your Manners." Artise stressed how everything—from how you look to sales etiquette over the phone to keeping client confidences—may be the deciding factors in whether a client stays with one salesperson (or service provider) versus another. Advocating a holistic approach to image, Artise said: " 'You should convey the impression that there is a harmony and a balance about you, and that includes everything from the color coordination of your clothes to your grooming, attitude, and demeanor.' "

Unfortunately, it is hard for any of us to assess accurately how we appear to others since research has shown that most people are extremely poor judges of how others see them. If you are unsure what impression you give others, set up a situation outside your job, with friends or acquaintances giving you feedback as to your appearance, self-confidence, and communication skills. If that approach is discomforting to you, consider finding a course or seminar given by an image consultant where part of the session is a stock-taking, with feedback, by your teacher and other students, as to what first impression you are actually making on strangers. You might also ask a friend or relative to videotape you. Then, in the privacy of your home or office, you can review the tape and critique your image. If being videotaped is uncomfortable for you, you might at least have a still photograph taken of you. Even critically studying that photograph will provide evidence of some basics of your image, such as if your shape appears too thin, too fat, or just right. Is your outfit appropriate, striking, or too casual? Are you smiling, sad, inexpressive, or bright and cheerful? Are your accessories coordinated and attractive?

Some businesspersons, or their bosses, are finding that seminars on creating a positive professional image offer valuable basic information, but some employees with problems in this area also need a more individualized approach. To overcome image problems that may be hampering a manager's ability to command authority, ask for and receive a raise, or represent the company in an exemplary way, private image coaches are being hired by companies or by the employees themselves, as discussed in Claudia H. Deutsch's *New York Times* article, "To Get Ahead, Consider a Coach." In addition to videotaping a client to review how he or she actually appears, coaches, who may be management consultants, sociologists, psychologists, psychotherapists, or human resources experts, may role play problem or threatening situations, such as asking for a raise or reprimanding a subordinate, helping the employee to improve his or her mastery of the situation. Written tests may also be given and analyzed to determine the client's strong areas and deficiencies. Co-workers, employers, or employees may be interviewed to give their opinion of the client's corporate/business image, or a coach might observe a client at work to provide data for his or her own opinion of the client's behavior. Videotapes showing ideal behavior, such as effective ways of walking, talking, or interacting with customers, may also be reviewed.

Do you even know what kind of image you project? What will help you succeed as a vice president for a bank based in Richmondville, New York, may not be the image you want as marketing manager for a beverage distributor in Atlanta, Georgia. To help you learn more about your current image, take the image self-evaluation test that follows.

Image Self-Evaluation

Circle the answers that most closely fit your current job situation.

1. When it comes to punctuality, I am on time

   a. all the time   *b.* most of the time   *c.* rarely

2. At my level, dress should be

   a. what I wear   *b.* more formal than   *c.* I am not sure
   what I wear

3. I answer letters

   a. right away   *b.* within a week   *c.* sometimes never

4. My handwriting is

   a. easy to read   *b.* adequate   *c.* illegible

5. I chose my eyeglasses

   a. for appearance   *b.* to correct my   *c.* I did not give my
   and to correct   vision problems   glasses much
   my vision   thought
   problems

6. I go to the hairdresser/barber

   a. as needed   *b.* once every three months   *c.* rarely

7. I think about my image

   a. everyday   *b.* rarely   *c.* never

8. On my last job, my boss said my image was

   a. outstanding   *b.* average   *c.* in need of work

9. In terms of honesty, others would say I am

   a. always honest   *b.* honest most of   *c.* dishonest in business
                             the time   but honest in my
                                                   social life

10. If I am at a business lunch and my hair is out of place, I would

   a. fix it in the   *b.* leave it alone till I   *c.* I probably would not
        restroom   got back to the   even know it was out
                             office   of place

How many *c* answers did you indicate? You need to learn about the basics of creating an image; your *c* responses suggest areas you need to give special attention. Your *a* answers reflect your solid understanding of basic grooming and related image issues. Your *b* answers indicate those areas you might want to work on.

Look over your answers. Which aspects of your image are you pleased with or do you want to change? Work on each change you want to accomplish, one concern at a time, until your image is as professional and flattering as possible. After you finish this book, go back to this self-evaluation and take it again, noting how your image has improved or where changes still need to be made.

How important is image to a rising executive? It should be one of your most vital concerns, that is, if you want to impress a headhunter like Howard S. Freedman, Vice President at Korn/Ferry International, the largest executive search firm in the world. Says Freedman, author of *How to Get a Headhunter to Call*: "People with a touch of class are still the ones who have an edge. It's as simple as that. First impressions, including how you dress and carry yourself, are important."

DO'S AND DON'TS OF BUSINESS DRESS

After having a pleasant and winning attitude and image, how you dress for work ranks as one of the key elements to correct business etiquette. You will first be judged by how you look (next by how you speak, and third by the office you work in). Neat, appropriately dressed rising executives will inspire more confidence than those who are disheveled, inappropriately dressed, or too flamboyant. In some industries, to avoid the element of personal choice which might lead to questionable attire in some cases, the so-called "soft" uniform has been introduced. In those situations, employees are given a range of acceptable outfits that they have to buy and wear, with the result looking more or less like a uniform. (Airline attendants or fast-food restaurant employees have a uniformed look, whereas some bank employees who are actually wearing soft uniforms seem to be wearing mix-and-match sportswear.)

Although most companies do not have the rigid dress codes apparent when "hard" or "soft" uniforms are worn, there are standards of acceptable dress, at each level of the corporation, that you should know about. Some companies may even have a written dress code, although at other companies the code may be a more informal one that requires you to look like others at your level. A manufacturing company based in Buena Park, California, only has a dress code in terms of safety issues, according to its former human resources manager. Some companies may have a "dress down" Friday, when all levels of employees are allowed to dress more casually—but the line is drawn at rubber thongs or shorts. Shirts without ties are okay and executives may even wear jeans.

Says the manager of human resources for a San Diego-based insurance company: "Except for casual Friday (after we get paid), we expect our executives to dress appropriately in professional dress, which means women are to dress professionally with appropriate shoes and nylons. Men should wear dark shoes, dark socks, pressed slacks, pressed shirt, a tie."

As image consultant William Thourlby writes in *Passport to Power* about the importance of our dress: "There is probably no sphere of human activity in which our values and our lifestyles are reflected more openly than in the way we present ourselves to others by the way we dress. . . . The power to inspire, control and even manipulate those with whom we come in contact, lies in the decisions you make regarding how you choose to package yourself."

What dress is expected of you may differ within the same company based on the job you hold, with distinctive looks for secretaries, sales representatives, assembly-line workers, managers, vice presidents, or presidents. There may even be differences among divisions within the same company if division heads are personally allowed to set the standards for their employees.

There may also be differences on acceptable dress depending upon the profession you are in, or whether you are self-employed or working for a small company or a major corporation. Someone who writes screenplays for a television series who is self-employed might dress casually at home when writing scripts, but wears typical business attire when meeting with studio executives. A writer on staff at a small, independent company might wear very casual dress all the time at work, whereas another staff writer, employed at a major network, might dress daily in corporate business attire.

If you work behind the scenes in a television newsroom, for example, it may be perfectly acceptable to wear jeans and a shirt without a tie. But if you work on camera for the same station, a business suit may be required of both men and women. If you work on Wall Street, even if it is behind the scenes, the kind of dress permitted in a newsroom would be considered unconventional, inappropriate, and would garner negative attention.

Dress may differ depending upon what section of the country you work in, and whether you work in a city or a more rural area. East Coast major cities, like New York, Boston, or Philadelphia, may be more conservative than West Coast major cities, like Los Angeles or San Diego. San Francisco may be more like New York than Los Angeles. I remember, years ago, when I was looking for a job in San Francisco at an advertising company, the employment agency I went to told me to change out of my too-flamboyant black opaque stockings and into sheer hose instead. Smaller cities or rural areas may be more casual than larger cities. A suit may still be required if you work in a smaller city or town, but it might not have to be a dark, conservative suit or the latest fashion statement.

Study the type of dress of successful people at your level at the company you work for. For women, what suits or dresses do they wear? What are the most typical styles or colors? How much jewelry is worn, and what type? What types of handbags and other accessories do they wear? What types of attaché cases do they carry? Do they use perfume?

Chairman Harold Burson of the public relations firm Burson-Marsteller notes: "In my experience, people conform fairly well to appropriate dress, or they learn very, very fast."

In Kathleen A. Hughes' *Wall Street Journal* article, "Businesswomen's Broader Latitude In Dress Codes Goes Just So Far," it is pointed out that business-dress researcher John T. Molloy asked managers to describe their employees' style of dress, and then tracked their careers for three years. He found that female office workers whose clothes were labeled "extremely feminine" "were typically paid less and promoted less frequently. The highest-paid women, on the other hand, were those whose dress was described as professional, dull, conservative, non-sexy or non-frilly."

For men, what color and style of suits do they wear at your company?

What pattern and color are their ties? What color and style of shirts? Is white the only acceptable color, or do executives wear blue or even pink shirts? What kind of attaché case do they carry?

Hughes reports that since acceptable business dress is more uniform for men than for women, the mistakes men make in how they dress are less dramatic than those of women, but just as damaging to a rising career nonetheless. She notes in particular that men ". . . are often judged harshly for looking too sloppy, too casual, too quirky or too flashy." (Should you really wear the tie with a huge fish on it that your eight-year-old daughter bought you for Father's Day?)

To avoid looking sloppy, if a man or a woman has to carry additional materials that do not fit into a attaché case, what is the most acceptable carryall? (How often have you seen a distinguished-looking executive carrying a $200 attaché case, only to have extra newspapers or other reading materials in a plastic shopping bag?)

Remember that you should be serious about your business wardrobe. You should not risk your professional image by wearing clothes that are either too cheap, too old (worn-looking, baggy, in need of repair), out of style, or inappropriate for the environment in which you work.

As image consultant Susan Bixler notes in her book, *The Professional Image*: "The best business wardrobes begin with a plan. Just as companies project their income and expenditures, you need to plan specifically how you will invest the next fifty dollars or five hundred dollars or one thousand dollars you spend for your clothing." Bixler suggests you go through your closet and sort your clothes into four piles: useless; marginal; worn regularly and comfortable; and sportswear or formal wear.

Be very careful about what clothing you wear when you interview for a new job, especially if you are changing the kind of work you will be doing, because what clothes work at your current job may be completely out of place at the new one. Dress for the job you are applying for, not the one you already have. This point is illustrated by Wayne, a forty-year-old struggling to support his family on $40,000 a year. He had an opportunity to get a new job, at nearly twice his current salary, but the interview process was grueling. Wayne had been working in the creative end of the entertainment business, at a job that tolerated informal dress—casual pants, even jeans, and knits or shirts without ties—but at his new job, he would need traditional business suits. Because he had only one suit, Wayne hoped the interviews were spaced far enough apart so no one would notice he was wearing the same clothes each time. (His finances were too tight to buy a second suit unless he did, in fact, get the job and needed it for his career. Otherwise, casual clothes would do just fine.) If Wayne got the new job, he would be representing his new employer to the media, so they wanted to be sure he would make the right impression. They carefully looked over Wayne's clothes and coat.

Wayne *did* get the job, and the first thing he did upon learning the news was to rush out to the well-regarded Brooks Brothers store. The suits he chose would be tailored in time for his first day of work, two weeks away. He also bought two more suits at another store that caters to executives. To complete the picture, Wayne bought new ties, shirts, shoes, and a British raincoat that seemed to announce class and distinction.

Business Dress Do's

1. Whatever the dress code for your company, follow it. (In California, employees of some companies, such as independent film companies, rarely wear suits. Don't try that if you are a manager at a Boston bank.)

2. Within the dress code for your company, figure out the colors and styles that are most flattering to *you*. Paisley ties are appropriate for executives, but you may look better in a red and gray paisley rather than a blue and maroon one.

3. If you wear jewelry, it should be subtle and low key, not flamboyant, very large, or too noticeable. (For women, jewelry can still be part of the "look" of an outfit of a particular color without looking too much like the costume jewelry one might wear to a festive Saturday night party.)

4. Every part of your outfit—from your shoes to your tie or the barrette in your hair—should go together and be kept in tiptop shape: polished shoes, a pocketbook that does not look worn, fashionable shirts, well-pressed suits or dresses, ties without stains.

5. For men: Make sure your non-button-down shirt collars have stays in them.

6. For men: Make sure you take into account the standard dress code as it relates to the change in seasons—in general, in the East and Midwest, white and tan between Memorial Day and Labor Day only.

Business Dress Don'ts

1. For both sexes, white shoes are taboo before Memorial Day and after Labor Day.

2. Do not wait for someone else to point out that your shoes need to be polished.

3. Never wear the same suit or dress two days in a row.

4. Never wear white socks with a dark suit.

5. Never wear a tie with food stains unless it blends in with a dark paisley pattern.

6. Never wear riding boots to work (unless you are one of the top executives of the company with such a noteworthy job-performance record that no one would mind if you even brought the horse).

BEING ON TIME

Being on time, whether for a breakfast meeting or at your office to start the workday, reflects a positive attitude. Everyone knows how being late makes you and those you work with feel. There is a gnawing, churning sensation in your stomach, especially as you sit in your car or a bus or train, knowing you should be sitting at your desk. But you are trapped along the way—trapped because of your own poor planning that let you set out too late to begin with—and it gets later and later and later.

You want to be on time because it is the proper thing to do. *Being on time* is a value in our culture; there are norms (rules) about being on time, and to violate those norms inspires such social sanctions as reprimands, warnings that it might even lead to being fired, or finding yourself being questioned as executive material. The bottom line is that being late is just plain rude and inappropriate.

Unless you are the boss, being punctual is an essential etiquette rule. No one likes to be kept waiting. When you are late for work, everyone—not just your boss—but your co-workers and even your subordinates are offended. An occasional lapse in punctuality may be overlooked, but a trend in tardiness could and probably will eventually cost you, if not your job, a promotion. Being on time gives the impression that you are commited and dedicated to a staff, to a team, and to a company.

Woody Allen said that most of success comes from being there. I would add to this that in the business world, you should be there "on time" if you want to make a favorable impression.

Are you late because you want to get attention? You certainly do get attention—the negative kind. Are you late because you really do not want to go to your job? Until you find another job that you would really prefer to be doing, you had better get to your current job on time or you may not have one.

There are some executives who are aware that being late intimidates most people, and who will purposefully come late just to throw off whomever they are meeting, to give themselves a competitive edge. It is an unfair edge, however, and it is at someone else's expense. The late executive looks bad, whether or not he or she also looks more powerful.

Arrive at the time appropriate for your position at a particular company. Be aware of the norms about punctuality where you work. For example, I interviewed a top executive at one of the major New York advertising companies and she told me that the rule at her company is for the senior management to arrive early—around 6:30 A.M.—but to leave by 6 or 7 P.M. (This contrasts with lower level personnel who would arrive by 8 or 9 A.M. and leave earlier—if secretaries, by 5:30 P.M., and later, if midlevel management, by 7:30 or 8 P.M.)

Arrive at the appropriate time for the kind of industry you work in. Different industries have different rules about when it is acceptable to get to the office. Journalists, for example, are known to get in by 10 A.M. (and stay till 7 or 8 P.M.), and that is perfectly acceptable. Editors may get in by 9:30 A.M. But executives in a variety of departments in the financial services industry—from brokers to vice presidents in the communications area—may be expected to be in anywhere from 7:30 to 8:30 A.M.

Being on time is a value in our culture that assures predictability. "I hate waiting. It drives me beserk," says an insurance saleswoman who prides herself on being punctual. "I need a couple more days to rewrite this report," says a researcher at a think tank who is usually late, to the disapproval of his boss and co-workers.

At some companies, lateness is not tolerated by certain executives; they lock the door when a meeting is supposed to begin. Indeed, some companies consider punctuality synonymous with *executive*. There may be procedures for disciplining "front line" workers for lateness, such as the repair or clerical personnel at Dowty Aerospace Corporation in Sterling, Virginia, but executives are expected to be there consistently. "Most of our executives are in by 8 A.M. and don't leave much before 6 P.M.," says Carl Schupp, Director of Human Resources for Dowty. If repair personnel who overhaul aerospace landing gear, hydraulic units, and so forth, are late three times in a thirty-day period, a written warning is issued. If it happens again within another thirty-day period, that person has one day off without pay. If it continues so that there are four offenses—three times within a thirty-day period—it's a week off without pay.

Especially at the executive level, most companies, or bosses, are informal about the punctuality rules; that informality may be misconstrued as a seeming tolerance of lateness. "Sure, take a few more days on that report" or "We understand. Come in late, if you have to"—but that is only a surface acceptance. When it comes to lateness, like all other rules, it is important to watch someone's feet—not just hear the words. Those executives may say that occasional lateness is okay, but are they chastising those late workers by giving them harsh evaluations, declining promotions or raises, or badmouthing them to other workers? ("Here comes Bob. He's late *again!*")

UNDERSTANDING AND OVERCOMING LATENESS

If you have a problem with lateness, now is the time to confront it and overcome it if you want to improve your business manners. First, determine if you are late occasionally or persistently. Consider your average workday.

What time should you arrive at your office? _____

At what time did you arrive this morning? _____

Yesterday? _____

Do you have a pattern of lateness in the morning (whereby you were late more than twice in the last week)? _____

Now that you have determined how often you were late to work in the last week, try to figure out what caused it. Consider any of the following possibilities:

Possible Reasons for Lateness

Mechanical reasons:

    Alarm clock did not go off

    Alarm clock set for the wrong time

    Dawdling in the bathroom

    Spending too much time for breakfast

Transportation problems:

    Car broke down

    Poor driving conditions

    Trains delayed

    Backup at toll booth

    Other:_____

Psychological reasons:

Need to be yelled at

Need to be noticed

Angry at the boss

Afraid something is going to happen that day

Procrastinating because of a wish to avoid something about the job

Worrying about what is going on at home so reluctant to leave for work

Other: _____

Consider whether the reason you were late today, or this week, is likely to reoccur. If the cause of the lateness was a one-time occurrence, such as the car's breaking down, you will deal with your lateness in a different way than if it is due to a habit or routine that you may have to break, such as spending too much time over breakfast, which indicates a pattern of lateness that has to be corrected.

Knowing the pattern, or occasional circumstance, that causes lateness will give you valuable information to facilitate change. In this competitive business world, however, knowledge is fine but what really counts is actually *breaking* your lateness habit. Whatever it takes, you have to get to work on time consistently.

Another step in overcoming lateness, as I pointed out in my book, *Creative Time Management*, is to *plan better*. If you have to be somewhere at a certain time, make appointments with yourself to serve as time checks along the way. For example, "At six-thirty I have to be in the shower. At seven o'clock, I have to be out the door." Allow yourself *extra* time for last-minute emergencies, phone calls, or traffic jams. If you definitely have a chronic problem with getting to work on time, tell yourself you have to be in half an hour earlier, and stick to that earlier time, which, in your case, should get you there on time.

You also have to know what your company's etiquette is concerning *time off*. Some companies are very lax and will truly accept an occasional request for time off to hear your three-year-old sing in the nursery school holiday show, or for you to leave early to go to the dentist. Other companies expect you to be there the entire day, every day, unless you are legitimately sick, on vacation, have jury duty, or for similar acceptable reasons. What the standards are at your company is what matters; few universals apply. A computer analyst, for example, when she worked for a prestigious New York bank, came to work on a beautiful spring day and decided it was just too nice to stay inside. She left a note on her terminal, "Gone swimming. Be back in two hours," and found, from that point on, that her future at the company was in question. Not only was her imminent promotion suddenly denied, she was given the cold shoulder by her co-workers and boss. She was told that that kind of behavior was more suitable in the more casual work environment of Los Angeles or Malibu, California.

Within a year, the computer analyst decided maybe they were right —and she relocated to Los Angeles, where she has been happily employed as a systems analyst at the same insurance company for the last eight years. Although she still has rigid starting and finishing hours, her California company is much more tolerant when she takes time off "to go to the beach."

TABLE MANNERS

You should already know the basics about table manners from your own upbringing. "Wipe your mouth with a napkin." "Don't talk with a mouth full of food." "Don't begin eating till the host or hostess is seated and begins." "Bring your food up to your mouth, don't hunch over and shovel it in." Additional help or a refresher course about table manners may be necessary, however, if you feel yours are not up to par. Furthermore, some of the younger rising executives, raised by dual-career couples, may not have received the around-the-table training at home since often they ate at separate times. Image consultants and etiquette gurus do offer table manner seminars and courses for those who need basic training or a refresher course.

The obvious guidelines about table manners apply: use a napkin; put your fork down between bites; cut your food as you go along, rather than all at once as you do for an infant or child; and ask to have items passed that are too far away to reach.

In *Executive Etiquette*, Marjabelle Young Stewart (and Marian Faux) points out that there are two methods of eating: the American and the Continental. The American method of eating involves cutting a piece of food with the knife in the right hand, and the fork in the left hand, laying the knife down on the plate, then transferring the fork with the tines up to the right hand, and then bringing the food to your mouth. In the Continental method, your left hand brings the fork to your mouth with the prongs down. Stewart suggests that both methods are fine, but whatever method you use, you should be comfortable with it. If necessary, practice the method in your own home before you try it out in a public situation.

Try not to finish every last piece of food on your plate, and try to keep pace with the others with whom you are dining. Eating too slowly or too quickly draws attention to your eating habits, and you want your habits to be so impeccable that the focus is on the meeting part of the meal get-together, not the eating part. Rather than using your fingers to get at foods that are hard to pick up, use just your fork or a piece of bread as a "pusher."

To look in-the-know and sophisticated, avoid mistaking the busboy or maitre d' for the waiter.

Ask to be excused if you have to use the restroom or make a telephone call. Women should not powder their noses, look in a mirror, or put on lipstick at the table. Those actions should be reserved for the restroom.

Here are some additional suggestions by Elena Jankowic, founder and president of the Etiquette Institute, from her book *Behave Yourself!*:

A Review of Basic Table Manners

- Lay a napkin across your lap. Except when eating lobster, do not use it like a bib.

- Hold cutlery correctly and work from the outside in, with fork on the extreme left and the spoon or knife at the extreme right.

- To indicate you have finished eating, place your cutlery on your plate in the clock position of about ten to four.

- Pass the salt and pepper together.

- Take a piece of bread from the bread basket and put it on your separate bread plate. Eat only one piece before the meal; it is poor manners to eat all the bread and have to ask the waiter for more.

- Do not use toothpicks at the table. Excuse yourself, go to the restroom and, in privacy, take care of any pieces of food that are caught between your teeth.

- Do not dunk anything.

- Do not chew with your mouth open.

SPEECH

Proper speech refers to the tone, enunciation, pronunciation, loudness, and correctness of the words that you use. Speech is a key part of your image since, in person, it may be noticed simultaneously with the way you are dressed and, on the phone, it is the one way your image is conveyed. (Of course in rare cases an instant still photo image may be transmitted as you speak. For now, that is the exception rather than the standard for phone calls.)

Tape your voice and listen to it. Are you speaking clearly? Are there any unique ways of pronouncing or using words that are particular to your region that might be misunderstood or unclear to others? Do you speak too quickly, giving the impression that you are tense? Are you driven to tell an entire story without having an interactive conversation that allows the person you are talking to to make comments or even get some relief while listening to you? Is your voice so soft that words may be missed or someone has to constantly say, "I can't hear what you're saying. Could you speak up please?"

If you have voice mail or a phone machine at work, call your own number and listen critically to your own recorded message. How does your voice sound? How appropriate are the words you use? Are your words too familiar or too aloof? Is the tone of your voice too sexy for a work-related recording?

Your voice and the words you utter are another part of your professional image. Take the time to enhance your speech by practicing the pronunciation of the names of those you work with or the individuals or companies you do business with so you never embarass yourself. (No one likes his or her name mispronounced.)

One of the most important aspects of speech to keep in mind at the executive level is that foul language is not proper business etiquette. Even if your company president or your superior uses an occasional foul word, this is not justification for duplicating that speech pattern.

That foul language is heard even at the executive level in a variety of industries is a shocking truism. It is important that you take stock of your own behavior and guard against the use of expletives, especially when you are angry or frustrated. You never know what client, customer, or company executive is within earshot. For example, Janet Drake, Manager of Human Resources for Cogniseis Development, Inc., a software development company based in Houston, Texas, decided to sit in on her managers when they were interviewing possible job candidates just to see how they were representing themselves and their company. "One said a few profanities during the interview," Drake explains. "He said 'Something is a pain in the (rear),' but that is not the word he used. He could have chosen a better sentence [word] to relay it. I wish he hadn't done that because it makes a candidate think that that [using that kind of language] goes on in the company all the time."

At another software company, the executive staff is "pretty casual" and an occasional foul word is tolerated—but everyone recognizes that it is poor form in a business setting. The human resources administrator explains: "At a division meeting, for example, the division head was giving an address to his employees and he said, 'That's a real bitch to deal with.' There was a sprinkling of laughter around the room, laughing because we can all take it. There's nobody around this place that can't listen to that, but we do remember it's not appropriate to say *bitch* to people in a business meeting, but it [using foul language] does happen."

A personnel director at a manufacturing company notes that an occasional executive at her company will use foul language. "Foul language is not considered particularly inappropriate," she notes. "In my office, people will frequently use the expression 'f--- up' and they'll frequently say, 'Pardon my French.' The unspoken dynamic here is that if it's acknowledged [that it's inappropriate] it's okay."

It is not just foul language that should be banished from any business setting, off-color or improper words should not be spoken as well. How much negative attention someone gets by uttering such a word is typified by the fact that personnel directors, executives, or etiquette experts I interviewed could recall each and every instance of an improper word.

As Sharon Peake Williamson, Manager of Public Information for Mead Corporation, headquartered in Dayton, Ohio, points out, it is not just the swear words that anyone who wants to get to the top should avoid. Says Williamson: "It's a sign of something wrong if you have a lot of bad language. I've found that bad language usually correlates with stress. To me, bad is not just the swear words. It's sexist or racial language, or any manner of showing that you don't respect your employees or co-workers." Remember, your language reflects on your employers as well as on you.

Seattle-based etiquette expert Randi Freidig finds that *inappropriate conversation* is one of the biggest etiquette faux pas when it comes to speech. She tells this anecdote about what a young man said when there was a lull in the conversation among a group of men and women who were attending a conference: "He said, 'Excuse me. Can anyone tell me if any animals other than humans menstruate?' He probably grew up watching TV and saw people standing on the corner under an umbrella talking about their hemorrhoids.' "

ON THE PHONE: TELEPHONE ETIQUETTE

As companies become more cost-conscious about the expense of traveling, and individuals seek to maximize how many contacts they may make in a certain amount of time, the phone has become the favored way of connecting within and outside of companies. The telephone imposes certain demands on its users since such nonverbal cues, like the clothing someone is wearing, the way they move their eyes when a statement is made, or the office in which someone is sitting, are unavailable for scrutiny as a way of judging how the interaction is going. There are still, however, nonverbal cues that an astute telephone user can utilize, such as the timing of a pause, the length of a pause or silence, the increase or decrease of noises in the background, or the quality of the voice to indicate enthusiasm or agreement. Even how quickly someone answers a phone—on which ring the call is answered—can, rightly or wrongly, be taken as an indication of how busy the person being called is, how close the phone is to the person being called, or how anxious or eager the person being called is to pick up the phone.

It is important to remember that when you place a call, you are doing so because it is a convenient time for you. It may or may not be a good time for the person you are calling to speak to you. Do not take offense if someone asks you to call back later, or asks to return the call. You would probably not drop everything for a call if you were in the middle of something, and it is reasonable to expect the person you are calling should be granted the same freedom to say "No, now is not a good time to talk." When calling someone whose habits you are unfamiliar with, you may even want to begin the conversation by asking, "Is this a convenient time to talk?"

A telemarketing consultant finds that the biggest breaches of phone etiquette occur when you call a company and the person answering either does not identify the name of the company, does not give his or her name, or say's the name so quickly you cannot understand it anyway. "Another thing," she says, "is that they will rifle through the name and then say please hold, without asking whether or not you have the time to hold. Another annoyance is putting someone on hold without coming back and asking whether or not you can continue to hold. The biggest faux pas when trying to sell people on the phone is failing to know if that product is even feasible for that customer. Like someone calling you at home trying to sell you aluminum siding when you have a brick house." (That last faux pas would have been avoided if the caller had adhered to the fourth basic etiquette principle of being concerned with others, not just yourself.)

Here are other tips for improving your telephone etiquette:

1. If you are an unknown caller, it is perfectly appropriate for a secretary to ask you to identify yourself and to ask why you are calling. Give your name and a brief explanation.

2. It is rude and poor etiquette to pose as the personal friend of the person you are calling just to get your call through.

3. Career consultant Nella Barkley notes that the biggest breach of etiquette in business is *failing to return phone calls*. You should return phone calls as soon as possible but certainly within twenty-four hours.

4. If you are returning someone else's call to you, and he or she is not in or is unavailable, leave a message to say that you tried to return the call. You can still call back again, or leave a time and place where you can easily be reached. To avoid telephone tag, try to give a few times you will be available to take a return call.

5. If you need to have a long telephone conversation, such as an interview or a discussion of a report, try to set up a telephone appointment for your call so you know the person you are calling will have enough time to talk to you.

6. As more and more phone companies around the country offer caller-identification systems—whereby the number of the caller is flashed on a screen so you can decide by the number or other information about who is calling whether or not you want to answer the phone—discretion is necessary to avoid intimidating or embarrassing your caller. For example, if you know the name of your caller because you recognize the phone number, avoid saying his or her name until it is volunteered. It is jarring to the caller to have a feeling that "Big Brother" is watching him or her. Furthermore, the verdict is not in yet on whether these new calling systems are ethical or an invasion of privacy. Keep that in mind if you let it be known that you are engaged in prescreening your calls.

7. Do not chew or slurp loudly while you are on the phone. If you must sneeze or cough during a conversation, try to cover the mouthpiece of the phone so you will not be overheard. If it seems loud enough for the caller to hear, say "excuse me."

8. If you have call waiting—whereby when you are on the phone with someone you hear a beep and may put the first call on hold and talk to the second caller—try to finish up the first conversation before talking extensively to the second caller. If possible, just find out the name and phone number of the second caller. Say, "I'm on the other line. May I call you right back when I finish?" Except in absolutely dire emergencies, if you get off the first call because you prefer to speak to the second caller, you may offend your first caller who will see himself or herself as less important than the second call. However, if you have already finished your conversation with the first caller and were simply shuffling your feet on the phone

because you did not know how to terminate the conversation, saying that you have to take the second call *is* definitely a way out.

The rule, then, to be polite, is that your first call should only be terminated for the second call if you have already finished the conversation. If you are involved in a very intense conversation with the first caller you may, in fact, ignore the beeping that indicates a second call is trying to get through. In case you think the person you are already talking to will be confused by those beeps, simply say, "I have call waiting, but I'm not going to interrupt our call. Don't worry. They'll call back when they don't get an answer." In that way, you are taking control of your phone and not letting anyone, even if you have call waiting, interrupt a key conversation unless it is appropriate to do so.

9. As long as you are sure that your call has been computer generated, it is perfectly acceptable to hang up on such a caller. (I recently heard of an insurance salesman who programmed his computer to electronically call 2,000 persons over just one weekend. Even if he only sold one policy, it seemed cost-effective to cold-call strangers in such an impersonal way.)

10. If you have—or will have—extensive phone contact with a customer or client, try to meet face to face at least once. It will help to cement that relationship and to personalize your phone contact for a long time to come. You will get a lot of mileage in hours of future phone contact for even a fifteen minute to half an hour face-to-face meeting.

11. If you anticipate a long conversation, start off by asking, "Is this a convenient (or good) time for us to talk?"

12. With very busy people, set up a phone "date" and stick to it.

Polite Ways to End a Phone Conversation

It is a predictable situation that many of us find uncomfortable: telling someone that we have to get off the phone. The hardest type of caller to do this with is the person who simply talks far too long or goes off on unrelated tangents. We may not have a pressing appointment, and we may not have a call to return at that moment, but if we continue to stay on the phone we will never get any other work done and we just might miss an appointment later on. It is impolite to tell someone that he or she talks too much, is boring you, or is far afield from the original reason for your call. *Tact* is the most important ingredient in getting off the phone with a long-winded caller without offending him or her. In your tone of voice, convey a sincere interest in what is being said, but a matter-of-fact statement to the business truth we all live with: "I wish I could talk longer, but I have to get back to something I was in the midst of " or "Thanks for the call, but I have something pressing I must do now."

There are other situations that can be used to get off the phone without offending someone, but it is better if the situation actually exists so you do not have to live with the guilt of being a "white liar":

> "Excuse me, but my next appointment just arrived. I have to go now."
> "I don't mean to cut you off, but I have to leave for a meeting or I will be late."
> "I'm sorry but I have to catch a train."
> "It's been great talking to you, but I have to take another call. Can I get back to you a little later?"
> "I stepped out of a meeting to take your call. I'm sorry, but I have to get back to it now."
> "I'm in the middle of something, can I get back to you?"
> "It was so nice to hear from you, but I have to go now."

End a phone conversation as you would a memo—with some idea of what action is now expected. For example:

> "Let's talk again in a few days."
> "I'll call you next Monday with the answers you asked for."
> "Call me when you find out if you can make that meeting."
> "Let's talk again and see what we've both come up with."

Let's say you are talking to someone in September, someone you do not talk to very often. You should still resist the temptation to state overtly how long it may be till the time you speak again, like saying, "I guess we won't talk again till after the New Year." Even if it is true, it sounds too distant and impersonal. Instead, be upbeat and positive: "I hope to talk to you again" or "I look forward to talking to you again sometime."

When Someone's in Your Office: Calls to Take or Screen

If someone is meeting with you in your office, ask to have calls held. It is polite to put the person you are meeting with first, *not* the telephone interruptions. It also avoids having the person sitting in your office overhear private or confidential information. It makes the person you are visiting with and talking to feel important when you avoid countless interruptions. Furthermore, although having interruptions may make you look important and busy, it also makes you look rude.

When you are meeting with someone in person, let your secretary know what phone callers should be put through, and who should be aked to call back or be told that you will call them back. Make these rules clear or you could be very embarrassed. For example, an executive's wife called. When asked if she wanted to hold or if her husband could call her back, she said it was "important" and would hold. The secretary did not tell the wife that her husband was on a three-way phone interview call; the secretary interrupted the crucial call her boss was having by showing him a note that said, "Your wife is on the phone; she said it was an emergency." Not only did this interrupt the conference call, the executive was worried about the "emergency." If his wife had known her husband was on an important call, she most certainly would have said she could be called back. The executive also had to explain to his secretary that there is a difference between *important* and *emergency* so he could avoid future miscommunication.

Be careful about ignoring calls that "fall through the cracks." These are calls that somehow never get returned, or returned in a reasonable amount of time, because of various reasons, such as "telephone tag," which has you going back and forth for days or even weeks, and you finally get fed up leaving and taking messages without making contact. Perhaps someone calls at an inconvenient time and you say you'll get back to him or her, but you are already into something else by the next day, and you no longer have a pressing reason to return the call; it is not until a few more days go by that you realize you never called that person back. Perhaps calls are logged during your vacation and, once you return, you are so involved in the new day-to-day demands on you that those old calls never get returned. Maybe you leave a message to be called back and you act as if leaving that message is the same thing as making contact. Should you wait to be called back? Should you leave a few more messages? Should you continue to call until you make contact? Perhaps you call someone with a question but he or she is not in. You leave your name and number, but by the time your call is returned, you have already had your questions answered by someone else, who was in when you called. Now that person you no longer need has returned your call and left a message for you to call back.

Do you call, even though you no longer have a pressing need for their help? Do you chitchat, even confess you no longer need them, but you are returning their call anyway? Or do you try to follow through on your original reason for calling, even if it is somewhat outdated or unnecessary? Do you come up with a new reason for the call so your combined efforts are not wasted?

It is best to return all calls so those calls do not fall through the cracks, generating bad feelings or giving you a reputation for failing to return calls. You could explain that you were on a deadline and that you had to finish up the reason you called initially without their help. But you might also think of another way that their ideas or services would be useful without creating unnecessary work for yourself, even if all you do is business small talk. In that way, all the back-and-forth calling, and eventual conversation, would still be worthwhile for both of you in the larger scheme of things—strengthening interpersonal relationships.

The important point to remember in terms of manners is: return calls whether your needs are pressing or not. Be polite. Call back. (For more on follow-up, see Chapter 4.)

Now that we have discussed improving your attitude and image, table manners, speech, and phone etiquette, in the next chapter we will examine a timely concern in business protocol, namely, relationships at work, including male and female ones.

Chapter 3

Relationships at Work

Before looking at one of the most topical aspects of protocol at the office today, namely male and female relationships, let us look at more general information as it applies to a manager, whatever his or her gender.

WHAT MAKES A GOOD MANAGER?

Just what is a good manager? Here are some examples:

- Paul Critchlow, Senior Vice President for Communications at Merrill Lynch, wanted to reward his top managers for going out of their way to complete a special project which required two months of unpaid overtime and even some weekend hours. When the project was completed, Paul took his managers and their spouses out for an elegant, catered dinner in a private dining room. Paul also made a brief speech complimenting his staff and gave each of them a token of his appreciation in the form of a music cassette or compact disc of a popular new album.

41

- Once a month, Nancy Creshkoff, when she was project editor in the school division at Macmillan Publishing Company, had a staff lunch for her employees. Nancy also conducted a weekly class in grammar to help her employees improve their basic editing skills. Nancy was very punctual and always called her secretary to let her staff know her whereabouts if she was delayed or at a meeting away from the office. She rarely made personal calls during the workday and avoided passing along office gossip.

What is a good manager? As you will note from the examples above, a model manager is basically someone who follows all the rules of business etiquette cited so far in this book—being honest, reliable, responsive, competent, punctual, modest, and a team player. Someone who says "please," "thank you," and "I'm proud of you." Someone who is tactful and discrete when he or she has to criticize an employee, and will always do it in a kind and discrete way.

Letitia Baldrige lists in *Letitia Baldrige's Complete Guide to Executive Manners* some forty-four behavioral traits that define a good manager. For example, a good manager . . .

- Never expects others to follow rules he himself does not.

- Makes time *to listen to his subordinates* as well as give them orders.

- Keeps his promises, both large and small.

- Respects the ideas of others.

- Returns telephone calls within twenty-four hours, or has someone else return them for him.

- Answers important mail within four days and unimportant mail within two weeks.

- Does not pretend to be an expert on what he is not.

- Always returns borrowed property promptly and in good condition.

- Never repeats a rumor that would hurt someone's reputation.

- Knows how to dress on and off the job, and understands appropriate attire for business.

- Answers all invitations promptly, either by writing or calling.

- Is deferential in office situations when it is proper to be so.

- Knows how to introduce people properly and in a manner that makes them feel good.

- Knows how to compliment someone and how to graciously accept a compliment himself.

- Is punctual or, if delayed, always informs his host in advance that he will be late.

- Picks up the check in a bar or restaurant when it's his turn.

I have been blessed with having worked for several good managers over the years. Anyone who has worked for good managers knows how much they add to your day-to-day job experience. Conversely, anyone who has worked for an impolite and incompetent manager knows how much it takes away from the job, even a job you love. My very first boss, when I began working in publishing just out of graduate school in the early 1970s, was Nancy Creshkoff, an editor. Nancy was like a "good mother," not just a manager. Yet she walked that fine line between friendly and too familiar very well. You always felt Nancy was professional even in how much she cared about each and every one of her employees (about five of us).

For six months I had been planning a trip to Germany. It was part of the research I had to do for my first nonfiction book, a freelance project that included a study of Germany that had nothing to do with my regular editing job. I found out that in order to get a discount air fare to Germany, all I could afford on my $6,000 a year salary, I had to be away for three weeks. But I was only entitled to two weeks off.

I told Nancy about the air fare situation and was basically accepting the fact that I would not be able to go.

"Then I guess you'll just have to go for three weeks," Nancy said, matter of factly, with words I remember almost twenty years later.

I took the extra week off without pay, of course, but what was important was that I was able to pursue a project that was very important to me without jeopardizing my job, which I also valued.

The staff got together to have a going away lunch for me and I felt part of a team, a caring team.

Nancy was like an ideal parent in that she never played favorites with her employees; somehow, miraculously, she made us all feel competent, important, and irreplaceable. Yet she was able to teach and critique without embarrassing or debilitating someone. She put in for promotions or raises without being asked, and wrote recommendation letters whenever necessary. Since that was my first full-time experience in the working world, I was somewhat spoiled by Nancy's management style, and continued to expect no less an effort and role model with other managers I have had since then.

How do you stack up as a manager? Would you like a boss similar to the one you have become? If not, start changing into the good manager you want to be.

MALE AND FEMALE RELATIONSHIPS AT WORK

Whether you are a man or a woman, a secretary or a vice-president, the behavior of men and women at work has become one of the most pressing business etiquette issues facing us today. The key is to show good manners without being accused of being sexist. Look at the issue of a man opening a door for a woman. In my business etiquette survey, distributed and returned by 108 personnel administrators working at a variety of industries and companies throughout the United States, 77% wrote that it is considered etiquette at their company for a man to open the door for a woman; 57% said it was etiquette for a woman to open the door for a man. However, the age-old practice of a man standing up when a woman enters his office seems to be on the way out—a whopping 78% wrote that at their company, men do *not* stand up if a woman enters the office. It seems that as women are being treated more equally in the business world, and are being judged and promoted on their abilities rather than the fact they are women, some of the old-fashioned social graces are being left out of the corporate setting.

Having a door opened for a woman by a man may still be polite in almost all corporate or company settings, but having a man pick up a tab or lighting a woman's cigarette has become a less universal occurrence. In the first instance, the person of higher status or who initiated the meeting will most likely pick up the check, and in the second instance, our society increasingly condemns smoking so the subtle approval of it indicated by lighting a woman's cigarette is no longer necessary. By contrast, the etiquette today about smoking is that it is far more important that the woman who wants to light her cigarette ask the man in her company if he will be offended by her smoking than if she awaits his lit match. (This is a cultural issue, however. It has been pointed out that "European and Japanese businesspersons would find it rude to ask someone *not* to smoke.")

The vice president of an advertising company based in Wilton, Connecticut, wrote about male and female relationships in the office: "The most sensitive area in business is the female/male relationship when trying to establish relationships and networks on a business level. Both sexes are slowly evolving [changing] the normal social rules into a new set of business etiquette rules. Our generation is in transition so there are many miscommunications and wrongful interpretations as the opposite sex reacts in a more personal than business way. How many girls were raised not to rely on charm to get their way?"

What is emerging, rather than simply following certain rules because you are dealing with a man or a woman, is the prevailing attitude today that courtesy has nothing to do with sex. Even women will open the door for a man if he is carrying packages and it seems polite for her to do so.

In this, as in all other etiquette issues, *find out what is expected at your company and conform to those rules.* It is especially important that you notice what is done when the woman outranks the man—does a male secretary open the door for a female chief financial officer? (According to Miss Manners, the boss is the first to enter through a door.)

Preconceived Attitudes

Letitia Baldrige writes that a new double standard has emerged in the workplace. No longer do men automatically treat women with chivalry, doing some of the things that they may, alas, still do at home or in social situations, such as carrying her packages or walking curbside to protect her from any splashes. In *Letitia Baldrige's Complete Guide to Executive Manners,* she writes that ". . . people are supposed to treat each other equally and act according to rules of protocol, not of gender; and one sex is supposed to come to the aid of the other whenever either needs assistance." According to Baldrige, the "polished executive," whether a man or a woman:

- Moves quickly to open a door for anyone walking nearby who has his or her hands full.

- Picks up whatever someone else has dropped who cannot retrieve it as easily as he or she can.

- Stands to greet a visitor to the meeting or his or her office . . .

- Assists a colleague struggling to get in or out of his or her coat.

The equality to which Baldrige refers is, according to my findings, more theory than fact. It is my observation that despite the sexual discrimination laws that have been passed, and the sexual discrimination suits that have been won, there are still relatively few women in top management because men and women have not yet found ways to feel comfortable working together at high levels without compromising ingrained views of the "right" way to treat one another. A competent woman will get to the top because she does what a competent man does, namely she works hard and fits in with a particular company. If it is considered appropriate for a man to take off his hat in an elevator because a woman has entered, it will make working together more predictable and pleasant if he can do that whether a female secretary or a female chief financial officer has entered the elevator. To deny the differences in etiquette based on gender is to make the workplace more confusing for all employees to negotiate in and to muddle the main concern, getting the job done. If it is business etiquette for the senior person to pick up the check, it should be consistently true, whether the senior person is a man or a woman. If it is etiquette for the employee to open the door for the boss, it should be expected whatever the sex of the boss or the employee. Etiquette rules make the workplace, and male-female relationships at work, less discriminatory and more comprehensible if those rules are consistent and universally understood and applied.

"The one tip about working with a woman is you try not to let her sexuality influence the way you behave," said an executive who works near Wall Street. "You act the same as if she were one of the guys." However, in practice, he could recall an incident in which his boss asked him to give a report on what a colleague had said to a client. "I said I'd rather wait until the woman vice president left the room because the report contained some off-color words and I felt it was inappropriate. She didn't argue and after she gave her report, she left the room and I gave my report in private. Had it been another man, I probably would have gone ahead and said what I had to say. My report contained the *f* word and a graphic portrayal of how the colleague wanted to deal with a reporter."

Whether or not a man opens the door for a woman does not hold her back or advance her in a company, but if a female vice president leaves the room when a performance report is being given, she could be held back since she may be excluded from vital information for evaluating the staff.

Some reasons for such a small percentage of women in top management are beginning to emerge from recent research, such as a study conducted by psychologist Robin Inwald, Director of Hilson Research Inc., in New York. Dr. Inwald developed the Hilson Personnel Profile/Success Quotient (HPP/SQ) to measure five key areas related to success in the workplace. In comparing the results of 303 employed males to 152 employed females, males scored significantly higher on winner's image and competition; females on sensitivity to approval and on preparation. In short, although women may be better prepared with their work, men are more competitive. In another study of entry-level job applicants, of the 636 males and 295 females tested, men scored significantly higher on their social ability, winner's image, extroversion, drive, and competition.

According to Ann M. Morrison, Randall P. White, and Ellen Van Velsor and the Center for Creative Leadership in Greensboro, North Carolina, who reported their findings in a book excerpted in *Working Woman* magazine, these are the factors that 76 successful women managers and company leaders deem necessary for making it in a corporation: help from above, a superstar track record, a passion for success, superior people skills, career courage, and being tough, decisive, and demanding, and having an impressive image.

The work force is dramatically changing when it comes to the place women occupy and the rules relating to male-female relationships at work. In the past, women were either in low-level positions or, if in higher ones, they tended to be single and childless. Until recently, women were giving up personal goals in order to have even some of the high-level work-achievement pie. For example, in a 1983 study of 117 women executives polled by UCLA's Graduate School of Management and Korn/Ferry International, an executive search firm, 52% of the executive women had never married or were divorced or widowed, and 61% had no children. In a comparable study in 1979 of males, only 5% had never married or were divorced, and only 3% had no children. Similar figures held true for those in academia. Until recently, 90% of female college professors were single and childless; only 10% of male professors lacked a spouse or children.

As the recent statistics demonstrate, married women, even those with small children, are advancing to higher positions and maintaining those positions as they, like men, try to do it all. It is also not uncommon today to call the office of a middle-to-high-level woman and find a male secretary answering the phone. In certain industries such as publishing, the rule as recently as ten years ago was that men entered the profession through sales, a faster track, and women through secretarial work. Today men may enter more frequently as secretaries, as women begin to enter through sales.

As might be predicted, when women fail to advance as far or as fast as they would like at the office, they leave to form companies of their own. (According to the Small Business Administration, the number of businesses owned by women increased 33% between 1977 and 1980, compared to only an 11% increase by men.) Although this solution may work on a certain level for the women who choose it, it depletes companies of the talented women that they have trained. Furthermore, for all but a few of those women, their own companies may never advance beyond a certain economic level or management style and, indeed, if their own business fails they may return to a company disillusioned, and at an even lower level and with less ambition than when they left. If women who leave to form their own companies fail to overcome one reason they fail to advance as far as they could at the office—reluctance to delegate—their own businesses may not grow sufficiently either.

When a Man Works for a Female Boss

This is a relatively new situation that requires men, especially those raised before the feminist movement of the sixties and seventies, to take on a whole new set of attitudes and rules toward women bosses. In *The Complete Office Handbook*, office expert Mary A. DeVries offers these guidelines for men working for a female boss that may minimize, or eliminate, possible conflict or embarrassment. Here is an excerpted version of her suggestions:

- Avoid offers of help that have sexual connotations, such as "Since you're a woman, you'll be needing help from a man—feel free to call on me."

- Let your boss indicate whether your relationship will be formal or informal.

- Do not misinterpret her friendliness as a romantic overture.

- Allow your boss to set the time and pace for work-related duties.

- Treat her with the same respect you would grant a male executive.

When a Woman Works for a Female Boss

Ironically, this situation may also have problems that are part and parcel of the fact that the two women are *not* equals, but the subordinate, or the superior, may inappropriately cross the line of informality because they are the same sex. The secretary may feel comfortable "shooting the breeze" with or confiding in her female boss in a way she would never dare to behave if her boss were a man. As noted in the next chapter on executive communication, intimate details of one's personal life or problems are inappropriate to share in a company setting, especially with those who are either superior or subordinate to you. Do not let the sex of your boss or employee give you a false sense of comfort in deviating from that rule of business etiquette. At some point, the inappropriate confessions may hang over your head, sabotaging your advancement or making you feel unnecessarily uncomfortable in the presence of the one in whom you have confided.

The best way to avoid this situation is to *treat any executive according to the etiquette appropriate for someone at that level, rather than being concerned with his or her gender.* In other words, look at the rules for how a subordinate treats a superior or how two co-workers should treat each other, rather than how a woman should treat a woman or a man should treat a woman. Within those specifics, however, you will want to determine where you stand about such etiquette issues as having the door opened for a woman by a woman (or by a man).

Including Spouses or Mates at Company Functions

There was a time when the male-dominated executive level of a company had a specific female role for the wives of their executives, that of the "corporate wife." She was a woman, and often well educated, but one whose own career was cast aside soon after she married and began her family. After that, her job was to be at the beck and call of her executive husband, looking her best as she appeared at whatever company business dinner or function she was invited to. Some companies were even known to interview the wife of a potential executive, recognizing that his wife would be a factor in his success or failure at that corporation. Divorced or single male executives were discriminated against since their failure to conform to the status quo, or to have a suitable mate for company functions, made them less desirable executive material. At conferences, it became big business to offer "spouse programs" to spouses who dutifully dropped all their own personal or professional obligations to come along to whatever city or country their spouse had to be in for a conference of merely a few days' duration.

Times have changed, however, and the wives of executives may have their own careers that make them unavailable to be at their spouse's side for certain dinner or conference commitments. It may also be a man who has to interrupt his own business commitments to appear at the company function required by his executive wife.

In recognition of the busy, professional lives of their executives' wives or husbands, companies are more and more likely to minimize the number of spouse-invited events, or to plan an occasional spouse-invited event on a weekend when it is more likely both will be free. Companywide parties, such as at Christmastime, may purposely exclude spouses so they are spared from breaching etiquette by failing to show because of their own career concerns. Indeed, if a company function includes spouses, it is considered proper for the spouse to be present.

It should also be noted that if around fifty percent of married women, with or without children, are working, about half are not. You do not want to alienate this other half by considering them as second-class citizens. Indeed, when Smith College asked First Lady Barbara Bush to give the commencement address, a heated debate broke out with students and in the press as to whether a woman who has been the ultimate corporate spouse should be a role model for the graduating females. What is at issue here, and what you should remember when encountering a range of corporate spouses with or without other professional commitments, is that each corporate spouse has a right to choose how many personal or professional obligations he or she will handle. Every corporate spouse, whether it is a man taking care of twins so his reporter wife can work full-time, a former nurse taking care of her children for her financial analyst spouse, or a mediator who has a full-time babysitter and a high-powered career in addition to her wifely and motherly duties, deserves respect at company functions. Avoid asking corporate spouses, with or without children, who do not hold outside jobs of their own, "But what do you do?" as if having a career of one's own is the only acceptable role these days.

WHEN A BUSINESSWOMAN BECOMES PREGNANT

It is important to consider the etiquette issues involved when a woman at work becomes pregnant—whether this relates to a co-worker, employee, boss, or even your own situation.

If You Become Pregnant

The time and way in which you share with your employees, co-workers, or boss the news that you are pregnant should be handled with dignity and tact. Some women wait until they begin to "show" to make a public declaration of their pregnancy, which could be anywhere from two to six months into the pregnancy. (A few women may not even show right up to their delivery, but most women show by the fifth or sixth month.) Some women want to wait until at least after the first trimester (three months) has passed, since the majority of miscarriages occur during that time period.

Of course if you have a job that requires working conditions or tasks that might put the fetus at risk, you will probably want to tell your employer as soon as you know you are pregnant so you can be reassigned to other jobs. It is still being debated whether working at a video-display terminal is hazardous to the unborn fetus because of the display terminal itself. Some believe, however, that it is the failure to take work breaks every twenty minutes or so, and the stress and fatigue related to overwork at the computer or video-display terminal, that may be at issue.

If you have any doubts about the safety of the work you do, discuss it with your obstetrician. If he or she agrees you should be doing another kind of job during your pregnancy, talk to whoever you should about the situation—your boss or the human resources administrator—and find a solution that fosters the health of your baby.

Be aware that your company, no matter how long you have worked there and how friendly you are with the staff, will, by and large, view your pregnancy in terms of what it means to work schedules and staff assignments. Having a baby is the most wonderful and exciting event in the world to you and your husband, but to your company it is an event that may temporarily or for a prolonged time take you out of the workplace.

When you do decide to tell your boss you are pregnant, make sure you also let him or her know what your plans are for the rest of the pregnancy and after the baby is born. By telling your boss right then and there what you plan to do, you will show consideration for his or her needs. "I'm expecting a baby in May," you might say, quickly adding, "I plan to work right up until two weeks before my due date. Then I'd like to take a three-month maternity leave, returning full-time by August 20th." You might also consider helping your boss find a replacement during your absence, or some other way of easing the workload. "I will be glad to train a temporary if you bring someone in two weeks before I begin my maternity leave" or "I could start doing work from home two weeks after the baby is born."

If you are unsure about whether or not you will return part-time or full-time, you might want to keep the door open to that by saying, "At this time, my plans are. . . ." Soon after your maternity leave begins, you should be zeroing in on just how realistic your plans to return are in terms of when and on what type of schedule. If you want to discuss a part-time schedule with your boss, explain that you want to continue working for your boss, but you also need to be with your newborn a few days during the week, or a few hours each day, whatever part-time schedule that is best for your family and your employer. See if you might work out a flexible work schedule or a plan that might change as your child gets older. Always remember that you want to stress how much you want to keep working.

Throughout your pregnancy, your business dress should look *professional*. If you want to wear lacey maternity blouses or any overly "sweet" maternity clothes, save it for evenings or weekends. Fortunately there are now a number of maternity clothes stores that cater to working women. Suits, dresses, or jumpers are more appropriate for the pregnant working women than pants, blouses, and shorts. Your shoes, even if you wear low heels for comfort, should look professional; buy a size larger, if necessary, to accommodate your enlarged or swollen feet. Keep accessories as simple and elegant as you would with your regular business attire. Make sure your makeup and hair look attractive so you feel good about how you look as your figure changes. Watch what you eat so you do not add more pounds than necessary as you proceed to term. If you follow a sensible, healthy diet for a pregnant woman, it is more likely that you will be close to your pre-pregnancy weight soon after the baby is born.

If during your pregnancy or soon after the baby is born and while still on maternity leave, you decide you do not want to return to work, tell your company as soon as possible; write an appropriate resignation letter (see discussion of resignation letters in Chapter 4) stating how much you have enjoyed working there and how the only reason you are resigning is that you want to be a full-time mother. Keep the door open for returning part-time or full-time once you feel you can leave your child. "I would like to return to work at a later date if a position is then available," you might write in your resignation letter.

After the baby is born, call or have your husband call your boss, co-workers, and employees, as well as anyone else you have direct contact with on a daily basis, such as a secretary, to share the good news. Hospital stays have become so short following a normal delivery—just 2 or 3 days—so do not be disappointed if flowers or gifts from your employer or co-workers are not sent to the hospital; you might find them when you return home. But do not *expect* them. Although it is etiquette to do so, some companies do not send gifts or flowers as a policy; it is up to the individual workers who personally care about you to attend to such niceties. (Later on we will discuss the appropriate gift or card for a co-worker who has a baby.)

Call and find out if it is okay to come in with your baby while you are still on maternity leave. Remember that the maternity leave is a time for you to devote yourself to getting to know your baby and getting your strength back, but your co-workers are still working. They may try to be polite if you make an unannounced visit with your baby, and it may be unpleasant, awkward, and embarrassing if you come at an improper time and place. Some companies may tell you outright not to bring the baby because it would seem unprofessional. Although a TV series might show a lawyer bringing her baby to work, in reality it is hard to work with a newborn or infant around, as an executive who brought his three-month-old to work found out. Unable to work, he had to cancel all his appointments for a few hours so he could go home and take the child to a babysitter. Babies are adorable but they also make it hard for everyone to concentrate on their work. Babies not only make distracting sounds or annoying cries, workers may want to hold, rock, play with, or talk to the adorable baby.

Working with Someone Who Is Pregnant or Has Just Had a Baby

Having a pregnant employee around may sometimes be a strain on other workers. A pregnant woman may want to talk incessantly about her pregnancy—even in intimate detail—and you should indeed let her do so. But if this need for talk becomes excessive to the point of interfering with your or another's work, then you should very tactfully suggest to your co-worker or employee that right now is not a good time for conversation and perhaps suggest a time that would be better. Something like this: "Mary, I am so thrilled you're pregnant and that you want to share this exciting experience with me. But I have three more letters I want you to go over. Maybe then you could tell me some more about your Lamaze class last night." By the way, the previous remarks could apply to a man whose wife or loved one is pregnant and he is overinvolving you in the day-to-day details of the process.

In summary, it is polite to ask a pregnant woman at work how she is feeling from time to time throughout the pregnancy or to ask that question of a male employee about his pregnant wife's health.

FRIENDSHIP AT WORK

It is appropriate to cultivate friends at work, as long as those relationships do not distort your judgment when it comes to evaluating performance or carrying out day-to-day jobs. In the survey I conducted, 65% of the human resources administrators wrote that it was permissible to hire one's friend to work at that company; 35% wrote it was not. An example of how friendship may work for a company is borne out by the example of a president of a company in New York who decided, after about a year on the job, to resign and return to his Midwestern home town and a new job. He recommended his longstanding best friend, whom he had met when they both worked for the same company and who was then working at another company, to fill his job. His company did just that, thanking him for facilitating the introduction.

Everyone must be aware of the consequences of a somewhat different scenario: you recommend a friend for a job at your company, he or she is hired, and he or she does it badly. This person's performance *does* reflect on you at least to the extent that you may not be asked for another recommendation. You should also remember the maxim "Birds of a feather flock together." If you want to be seen in a favorable light, have well-regarded friends, especially if you recommend them for jobs at your company, or you befriend them at the same firm.

There are distinct rules of conduct when it comes to friends in the business world. I have observed these rules since I began my research into friendship in the early 1980s, including my dissertation, a scholarly book, and additional research and writings on friendship patterns in a variety of settings. In the business world, the unspoken rule, as screenwriter Carl Sautter, author of *How to Sell Your Screenplay: The Real Rules of Film and Television,* and others have pointed out to me in interviews, is that you *befriend at your level* or you may be seen as opportunistic. Writers should befriend writers, editors other editors, human resource managers others in that field, producers other producers, and so forth. In that way, you are equal and not seen as using each other for position or power. As Sautter says: "People try to become friends with people who are more powerful, thinking it will do them good. But ultimately, the people who do the most good are people just like them. When they get in, they'll help them. These writers are some of the best contacts I have. I ran around producer chasing, but none ever helped me. They thought I was irritating."

A friendship should be based on mutual interests and equality. It is for this reason that friendships often end—when levels become disparate because one person is promoted and the other is not, or one friend switches fields and the other does not so that there is not as much in common anymore. It is typical to hear the complaint, "We were the best of friends until I became a vice president and he stayed a manager," or similar power shifts.

In general, to play it safe, be friendly with those you work for, but reserve close friendship for those you used to work with or those outside your company. As Larry Stybel, co-director of executive outplacement firm Stybel, Peabody, and Associates, says: "I have very few friendships in business, but lots of chums. Chums are situational relationships. But if the situation changes, the relationship does not follow."

It is okay to be friends with those in the same field, but it is safer if they are at another firm. Some, however, find it even more comfortable to have friends who are completely outside their field, and therefore the possibility of leaking privileged information or jealousy is reduced, such as writers befriending insurance salespersons or teachers, and environmental consultants befriending lawyers or political advisors.

This advice, however, has to be tailored to the company culture you work in. Friendships within your particular company or industry may aid rather than hinder your advancement. Harvey Mackay, CEO of Mackay Envelope Corporation and author of the bestseller *Swim With the Sharks Without Being Eaten Alive*, writing in "Image: Cast a Tall Shadow" in *Success* magazine, suggests that you give your employees approval and spend time socially with them. "Make them your friends, one at a time. To a greater extent than you may realize, they're working for you and your approval, not a paycheck. Your success depends on their performance, so make yourself worth performing for."

There are also exceptions to the rule about keeping close friendship out of the workplace. In some rare instances, close friendship and work not only go together wonderfully, but the work and the relationship flourish because of that relationship. The risk—if the friendship fails, if it seems to compromise you because of "influence peddling," or if either one of you finds out intimate information that interferes with conducting business—has to be weighed against the benefits and your genuine instincts about a friend.

There are also rules to keep in mind if you have friends of the opposite sex where you work. Especially if one friend is married and the other is not, a platonic friendship may be misconstrued in the workplace—and be detrimental to one or more careers, not to mention possibly damaging to personal lives.

Here are tips to maintaining male-female business friendships in a proper way:

- If the friendship is primarily work-related, try to avoid calling your opposite-sex friend at home unless you have a specific work-related question, especially if he or she lives with a spouse or romantic partner.

- Remember not to give any other-than-friendly overtones or undertones to your friendship; dress appropriately at all times. For women, that means meeting your platonic friend in nonseductive clothing. For men, that means the same thing, down to having the right number of buttons buttoned on a shirt.

- Keep meetings to daytime hours, such as lunch get-togethers during the week rather than dinners or on weekends (unless you include your partners or spouses).

- Avoid talking to your platonic friend about problems you might be having with your romantic partner if you have any romantic feelings for him or her, since that might set the stage for a less platonic bond as you push out the "bad-mouthed" spouse or partner.

- Be clear in your own mind if this is a platonic or romantic relationship. If there is any implication of romance in the friendship, on either your part or your friend's, and you do not wish to cultivate those feelings, it will probably be necessary to break off the friendship. (If you wish the friendship to become romantic, that is another story. See the section that follows on company romance.)

- If either of you has a change in the romantic relationships in your life—you marry, he or she marries, you divorce, he or she gets engaged—be prepared that your platonic friendship will either have to be accepted by the new partner or be put on "hold" or ended. Respect the fact that your friendship may have a "honeymoon period" when your platonic relationship will be inactive as the new couple cements their romantic relationship. When appropriate, include your romantic partner in your plans with your platonic friend and be open and up front about your friendship so there is no innuendo about anything you have to hide. (If these changes make you realize you did, after all, have more than platonic feelings toward your friend, consider whether it is now appropriate to continue the relationship or if, for all concerned, you should bow out gracefully.)

COMPANY ROMANCE

Office romance is another key concern of anyone working in an office where there are men and women. A groundbreaking lawsuit was won a few years ago by an attorney with a Washington, D.C., government agency. The woman sued, and won, because she believed, as a woman uninvolved in an office affair, that the women who were having affairs with their supervisors were better able to get promotions and pay increases, advancing faster and farther than other women on staff. The U.S. District Court in Washington, D.C., decided in her favor; the attorney was granted numerous promotions and salary increases on a retroactive basis. Once again, however, this is a lawsuit that only reflects one instance of the variety of ways that sexual harassment and discrimination keep women back in the office.

However, having an affair at work can also end a woman's advancement at that company, as well as her job. Barbara, for example, is a thirty-five-year-old office manager in California earning $50,000 a year. She has held the job for almost four years; for the last year, she has been having an affair with the senior partner of the advertising firm. A divorced mother of two children, Barbara was attracted to her boss's incredible wealth, appearance, and power. Barbara also convinced herself that she would be the one to stop her boss, who was unhappily married and the father of three children, from his philandering.

For the last few months, Barbara has been emotionally upset as she realizes her affair has compromised her job and hurt her children, who have grown attached to their mother's boss-lover. As Barbara accepts the fact that he will not leave his wife, she begins to wonder what her options are. Fifty-thousand-dollar-a-year office manager jobs are hard to find, and she needs the income to support her children. But her mental health comes first, and Barbara tells her boss that the situation has become unbearable and she has to quit.

"Will you at least help me find your replacement?" he asks without emotion.

That was the ultimate insult to Barbara, who soon found out that her boss was already having an affair with someone else. After Barbara gave official notice, she cleaned out her desk and made sure she told at least one high-level executive about what his colleague had done. Within a few days, Barbara, devastated, was seeing a psychiatrist three times a week.

Fiction? A soap opera? No, fact. The year 1959? No, this happened during the last year. When it comes to male-female relationships at work, the old etiquette still applies: Do not have an affair with anyone above you. In fact, try not to have an affair with anyone within your department or company, unless one of you is prepared to find a new job, and certainly do not do it if your relationship would be compromising because one of you is married or otherwise engaged.

Some companies still have policies against hiring married couples. If employees date and begin living together or marry, one of the parties is asked to leave.

Other companies are very broad-minded about their employees' romantic involvements, especially if both persons are free and clear to enter into such a relationship. This is in recognition of the simple fact that after the college years the workplace, more than any other situation, is where single workers of all ages have the best opportunities to meet and get to know an eligible, potential mate.

In *Company Romance: How to Avoid It, Live Through It, or Make It Work for You*, veteran newspaper feature writer Leslie Aldridge Westoff begins with a fascinating reinterpretation of the political breakthrough situation of Walter Mondale and Geraldine Ferraro as the first male presidential and female vice presidential Democratic ticket. Westoff points out that this situation caused newspapers to write about a new "Etiquette Gap" and the behavior required of this unique pair. They were advised not to physically touch in public—and certainly not to hug or kiss—or their relationship might be misinterpreted as a sexual one. They were also advised to always have their spouses or someone else present so no one would think they spent too much time together without their spouses.

Westoff writes that love in the workplace, even love leading to marriage, is becoming more common, and companies are ill-advised to try to implement "no romance at work" policies that are unrealistic and go against nature's call.

I have observed that office romances become a problem when a romance creates a conflict of interest. For example, the married head of research for a nonprofit corporation has a girlfriend in another country whom he met through a work-related conference. He takes unnecessary trips abroad, and charges it to his employer, so he can rendezvous with his paramour. Or a newspaper editor gains the resentment of the reporters that he assigns stories to when he gives several plum assignments to his wife (whom he first met when they worked together on a freelance project). Or the company romance is between two married people who are violating not only a cardinal etiquette rule but one of the Ten Commandments: Thou shalt not covet they neighbor's wife. The manager of human resources at an insurance company in California told me that her company does not tolerate liaisons between married and unmarried workers. A married manager and a single female supervisor had an affair. "The male manager was terminated in that case," she said, quickly adding, "But we should have fired both of them."

Management professor Lisa A. Mainiero, who spent four years researching company romances for her book, *Office Romance: Love, Power & Sex in the Workplace,* said in a *New York Times* interview about her findings that whether or not an office romance jeopardizes someone's career depends on the corporate culture of that company. (It is interesting that Mainiero approaches this topic from a women-in-management perspective.) "In conservative cultures, I found that women in office romances do indeed have a stigma against them. . . . However, in more action-oriented cultures—for example, some of the companies I studied in Silicon Valley where everything is pretty free and easy—what I found was there were no stigmas attached to office romances."

The personnel director at a manufacturing company told me: "What is important here is that a person is using his or her time productively. If a man and a woman are seeing each other, and the man is in welding and the woman is in wax works, which is in a totally different part of the building, we would tell them to see each other on their break. We would tell them not to cruise. The expectation is that people will work."

Finally, the best advice about the etiquette of office romances is to be discrete, whether or not the romance is appropriate or inappropriate, as you would about any romantic liaison. The company is not the place to discuss your marital affairs; it is just as inappropriate to let the romantic affair you are having become the topic of conversation. Not only should you be discrete because it is inappropriate for you to involve the workplace with such intimate concerns, but you want to avoid becoming the topic of office gossip. The grapevine is ripe for office romance gossip and it can destroy a reputation or end a career. Sadly, at some conservative companies, the issue of whether or not the affair actually took place may be less important than the tainted image an executive has once the allegations are made, by the man or woman allegedly involved or by those reporting the gossip back to a superior.

Scrutinize your behavior with the opposite sex so that seemingly innocent gestures, like putting your hand on someone's shoulder or a quick hug, are not misconstrued as romantic ones. Experts suggest avoiding any touching of the opposite sex that a man or woman might misinterpret as sexual harassment, as well as any conversation that might make someone turn red from embarrassment. It is also best to keep meetings in public and within typical office hours. If you have to meet before or after typical work hours, career counselor Nella Barkley suggests that you take another colleague along. "Especially if you are going to have an all-night marathon," Barkley adds. If you have to have a dinner business meeting, Barkley emphasizes that you should not go home first and change your clothes. Have other people along, if possible, and "if you have a drink, keep it to one. You can be a little sociable. Warm banter between business colleagues is okay. But remember to get the job done and to end the evening before it is too late—preferably before 11 P.M." It may also be advisable to call someone of the opposite sex, regardless of their marital status, within working hours rather than in the evening or over the weekend.

In the next chapter, we will look at how to enhance your executive communication.

Chapter 4

Executive Communication

When Sid was starting out as a salesman of a wire service specializing in press releases, he tried to sell his product to Mercedes Benz. Everything was going along smoothly until Sid, using his normal sales pitch, referred to his product as the "Cadillac of the industry." Needless to say, that comment diminished Mercedes Benz' interest in his service.

After your appearance, when you address people in person, people will judge and form their opinions about you by what comes out of your mouth. When the first contact is by mail, they will judge you by how you communicate even before reacting to your appearance.

Your ability to communicate properly, courteously, and intelligently will probably be one of the most significant, if not *the* key element, in your chance to enter, thrive, and advance in the executive arena. Recognizing how pivotal communication skills are to success in the business world, more business schools are including in-person interviews to screen their applicants. This is in response to the complaint of a growing number of company employment directors that "some students can't communicate."

The wrong word at the wrong time has caused many qualified job applicants to be screened out from a coveted position, the rising executive from the next rung on the ladder, or if the communication is detrimental to the company's bottom line or image, from the job itself. Communication is so important that most large companies have entire divisions devoted to it to ensure that the correct message is disseminated; that the all-powerful word is used properly, effectively, and with care.

- After three interviews had to be rescheduled, Tom, a qualified job applicant, is taken off the list of candidates because he writes an angry letter complaining that his time is also valuable and he resents being treated in this manner.

- Once John got a new job, he wrote to all the business associates who had previously conveyed their shock that he had been fired and had offered their help to John in finding a new job, if he needed it. But John's "thank you's" were far less effective than they could have been—and even offended some—since his letter was a photocopied form letter.

- When Brenda, a junior executive, was asked to resign, some of the reasons included her occasional swearing and being verbally abusive to secretaries.

The actions of Tom, John, and Brenda are examples of poor business communication manners. At work, you have to conform to business etiquette in what you say whether it is in person, over the telephone, or in writing. (Phone etiquette was discussed in a previous chapter.) Even what you say over an intercom is up for scrutiny, since someone in your office or walking by it might be eavesdropping, or a caller might also hear the intercom if you forgot to put a caller on "hold" or "mute."

As an effective executive communicator, you also have to be concerned with rhetoric, or persuasive speaking, as well as elocution, the way you speak or utter words. Here are some guidelines for appropriate executive communication:

Tips for Effective Executive Communication

1. Avoid using slang or derogatory expressions.

2. Show an interest in what someone else is saying; be a good listener.

3. Use proper English as well as correct grammar in your oral and written communications.

4. Pronounce proper names, especially last names, correctly.

5. Keep all office secrets—professional or personal—to yourself.

6. Be careful about what information is overheard by co-workers or visitors when having meetings or conducting telephone business, especially if the conversations are of a personal nature.

IN PERSON
Names and Greetings

Unless you are intentionally trying to be vague or discrete, refer to individuals by their names, rather than as "she" or "he." *Remembering names* is a good way to get ahead at work. There is nothing as endearing as when someone you have met just once before somehow remembers your name.

Do you have trouble remembering names? One helpful tip is to get the business card of any new person you meet and make notes, right on the card, or attach the card to a larger index or address file card and make notations on that card. Include the date you met, any distinguishing physical characteristics that will help you to remember that person, such as height, hair color, build, and any other notable tidbits, such as town of birth, college attended, or hobbies. But keep in mind that others may have access to your card or address files, so be discrete in your descriptions and notations about clients or business associates.

Another way to remember names is to make a concrete association between the name or face of a new person and to write that association down, or memorize it. For example, someone by the name of Jim Peters may be tall and thin. The association that comes to mind might be the tall and thin Peter of Peter, Paul, and Mary, the singing group from the 1960s, so you remember the name *Jim Peters* forever more. Or for Lila Dempsey, who is quite active and energetic, you might remember her last name because she brings to mind the energetic fighter Jack Dempsey.

What should you do if you see someone you are supposed to know whose name you have forgotten? Try to avoid the impulse to blurt out, "Forgive me, but I don't remember your name" and instead take a moment or two to ask questions that might help you remember the name by associations. For example, you might say, "So nice to see you. What are you up to these days?" That question might lead to an answer that helps you put the person in the context in which you know each other and helps trigger your memory about how you know each other and what the name is. For example, you run into someone at a store near your company. She says hello to you by name, and you are at a loss as to what her name is, let alone how you know each other. Your question about what is new elicits this answer, "They are transferring me to a new library." Obvious follow-up question on your part: "Which one?" "The reference library in the second building," she answers. Bingo! She is the company librarian you have seen from time to time; her name begins to come back to you as well. "It is so nice to see you again, Jane. Good luck at the new location."

Find out the rules about names at your company *at each level* and follow those rules when addressing others or introducing yourself. It may be perfectly acceptable to say "I'm Bill," or it may be breach of that company's etiquette since only "I'm William O'Casey" will do.

When introducing yourself to someone outside your company, give your full name, not just your first name. Only use someone's nickname if he or she has given you permission to do so. For example, when you are first introduced, someone will say, "I'm Jonathan Franklin, but you can call me John." Otherwise, use a man or woman's complete name.

Charles Peebler, CEO of Bozell Inc., a major advertising company, tells the story of how at a meeting the inappropriate addressing of the chairman of the company by his first name by a junior advertising manager led to gasps around the room as well as a reprimand. Says Peebler: "He said, 'Well, Jim, this is the way we do this.' He also called me 'Chuck.' But even vice presidents call the chairman 'Mister.' " Peebler explains that it has to do with having a general awareness of what is "proper and sensitive to any situation," which includes being deferential to age as well as status. Says Peebler: "With many clients I am on a first-name basis. They call me Chuck, and I call them 'Sir.' "

When introducing people, introduce the lower-level person to the senior one. For example:

"Mr. Jones, I'd like to present Mr. Blank, Vice President of Marketing. Mr. Blank, this is Mr. John Jones, the president of our company."

Try to include descriptions of each person when you are making introductions. For example:

"Ms. Hastings, I'd like to introduce to you Sally Holmes, the winner of this year's executive communication competition. Sally, this is Ms. Alice Hastings, a published poet and the manager of our corporate communications writing division."

Making Conversation

Not only is it polite to include descriptions when you introduce people, it facilitates conversation since everyone starts off with at least one or more facts to begin an exchange. Using the previous example, a business conversation between Sally Holmes and Alice Hastings might go something like this:

"Alice, I think it's wonderful that you've had your poetry published. Have you found any other executives at Worthington Pen Company who are also poets?"

There are two parts of making conversation in a business setting that you should be concerned about: *speaking* and *listening.*

There is that old cliché that a good conversationalist is someone who lets other persons talk about themselves. That's a bit simplistic and a bit too one-sided, but it does make the point that you should not dominate a conversation. If you have to err on the side of one extreme or the other, err on the side of listening more and speaking less.

Talk about topics that are of mutual interest and appropriate in a work setting—business small talk—everything from general business trends to art, opera, music, movies, theater, sports, or best-selling books. Especially if you are conversing with someone outside your company with whom you hope to do business, stay away from controversial or emotion-charged topics, such as politics, religion, women's rights, as well as specific questions about someone's income or the cost of their house or rental. You do not want to seem nosey or to get into heated arguments that sway your potential client or customer away from working with you because of the ideas you hold that really have little to do with the business at hand. (The ideas may not even be cherished or important ones, but views you express that unwittingly enrage or push away your potential client. For example, you might get into a heated argument against vegetarianism only to discover the seemingly conservative businessman you are talking with, and hoping to do business with, had given up meat, fish, and chicken two years before. You really are not all that fired up against vegetarianism, but the damage has already been done.)

One way to head off such compromising conversations is to put your toe in the water about most matters by asking questions. For example, "Have you ever lived in the country?" is a good way of finding out just how much you might say for or against the country without striking a negative chord. If you had not asked the question, and you are making business small talk, you just might hit a raw nerve if you talk about how much you hate the country and how eager you are to find an apartment in the city, when the executive you are talking to detests the city and prefers the country and those who like to live in it.

Listen because it is polite and because you may learn a lot about the person who is speaking, whether a colleague, employer, or superior. You will probably learn more by listening than you will by speaking, but of course speak enough so it is a true conversation and not a monologue.

One way to make someone realize you are truly listening is to repeat back to the speaker an idea or statement he or she has just made, but in different words. For example:

"Then what you are saying is that there is a need for more movies about Wall Street if the public is to fully understand what brokers and analysts really do."

You might also nod your head or occasionally say "uh-uh" so your silence is not misinterpreted as indifference.

Executive communication should avoid volunteering, or asking, intimate personal details of a worker's life, such as marital woes or a parent's medical problems. Most of the time, those topics are too personal to ask or volunteer in an office or work setting. If you are the one being inappropriately asked such personal matters, politely decline to answer by saying, "I do not think that is an appropriate question." Remember: you are responsible only for your answers not for someone else's questions.

Avoid volunteering intimate inappropriate details about yourself in a work situation, because it can only come back to haunt you later. It is, quite simply, inappropriate executive work behavior. You may overhear someone commuting on a train bragging about her Friday night conquest the weekend before, and it may be interesting to eavesdrop on another's intimate conversation, but such conversations are offensive and a violation of etiquette in an office setting.

Be careful of the technique of someone telling you something inappropriate about himself or herself as a way to entice you to share something inappropriate about yourself. For example, a co-worker airs his dirty laundry with you, hoping, whether consciously or unconsciously, to elicit from you an airing of your own dirty laundry. *Do not fall for this tactic.* You may be trustworthy in keeping your co-worker's personal business to yourself, but he may go right to the boss with your intimate information, and you may be out on your ear before you even have time to straighten things out.

EFFECTIVE COMMUNICATION AT MEETINGS, CONFERENCES, AND SEMINARS

What procedures should others follow when wanting to meet with you in person at work? *Make your rules known about how co-workers and subordinates may contact you in person.* For example, you may find it useful to your job to have an open-door policy; or you may find it too intrusive, and guidelines need to be created. ("Call before you drop in on me, except in emergencies." "You can drop in on me the first half-hour in the morning and the first hour after lunch. At other times, call ahead and arrange a meeting.")

When it comes to superiors, anytime your boss wants to drop in is usually fine.

To make the most of any meeting, conference, or seminar, *have an agenda,* whether you are conducting the meeting or attending it. If writing materials are not provided, make sure you bring your own so you can take notes.

Arrive on time. Notice if there are any instructions on the chalkboard, or on large sheets of paper at the front of the room, advising you to do certain exercises or consider certain ideas while awaiting latecomers.

Begin the meeting on time (if you are running the meeting). Do not penalize those who are punctual by making them wait for those who are late.

Participate in a conference, meeting, or seminar when you have something useful to say, but not just to draw attention to yourself. Saying too much is as inappropriate as saying nothing.

Make your unspoken expectations concrete and known so you as well as those you are meeting with can fulfill those goals. If you fail to concretize your expectations, you may be unnecessarily disappointed that a meeting, conference, or seminar wasted your time. But by being specific about what you expect to get out of the encounter—for example, "I plan to learn what is so special about the new computer we are introducing next month" or "I plan to make one new professional contact with those in the East Coast office"—you can gauge whether or not you have in fact achieved something.

If your company is small and has few formal meetings, with most reports being oral, make a written record of what occurs. Kenneth A. Snella, Vice President of Berkshire Electric Cable, a manufacturer of low- and medium-voltage electrical wire and cable, explains why that is helpful: "Document everything that happens, even if it is verbal. Keep your own day-to-day diary, not so much for going back and hanging somebody, but just being able to put things in a proper perspective for recall six months down the road." Berkshire Electric Cable, a company of about 120 employees, has few formal meetings. "We're Tom Peters all the way," says Snella. "Impromptu meetings, resolve the problem, move along to something else."

FOLLOW-UP: IN PERSON, BY PHONE, BY LETTER

Following up is a key aspect of effective executive communication. Quite often, the initial communication, whether in person, by phone, or by letter, is very short and quick. It is the follow-up that may take minutes, hours, or days to accomplish. Examples? You ask someone to find out a certain statistic for you. Asking takes a minute. Finding out the information might take hours. Tracking down the person to whom you made the request and getting the information from that person may take one, two, or ten phone calls, letters, or visits to his or her office.

There might be lots of reasons that people fail to follow up, everything from being overworked and overextended with too many projects to attend to, to disorganization, to simply not having the answer and being reluctant to admit it. But you have to follow up if you want to be known for politeness and courteousness. As etiquette expert Barbara B. Chizmas tells her corporate clients: "I tell people, 'I'm in the little things mean a lot business.' "

Follow-up is a seeming "little thing" but it means a lot in terms of how effective an executive communicator you are.

"You can lose clients if you don't do your follow up," says executive recruiter Howard S. Freedman of Korn/Ferry International.

What form might that follow-up take? If you have been invited to a lunch or a more formal function, you should call (or send a note) to accept or decline the invitation. After job interviews, you might send a note to the interviewers, thanking them for their time, expressing your pleasure at meeting them, and emphasizing your interest in that particular job.

Follow-up allows the opportunity to reinforce a growing business relationship. It also allows another chance to make a pitch if a sale has not yet occurred. For example, in trying to get a company to take a product, a telephone follow-up might be used in this way:

> *Seller:* "Did you receive the material I sent you a few weeks ago?"
> *Potential Customer:* "Yes, but I just got back from a three-week trip and haven't had a chance to consider it."
> *Seller:* "Vacation or business?" (Trying to make business small talk.)
> *Potential Customer:* "Business. I literally just got back today."
> *Seller:* "I'm sure you must have a lot of work that piled up in your absence. Listen, I just wanted to make sure my packet got to you. Also, I just got some additional material. Would you like me to send it?"
> *Potential Customer:* "Sure, I'd love to see it. But I might not be able to get back to you for a few weeks."
> *Seller:* "Don't worry about it. I understand. I appreciate your interest."

Another very important reason for a follow-up is, quite simply, that your material may not have arrived, or your phone message may not have been received. Mail can be addressed to the wrong person or address. Packets can be switched so that persons receive the wrong material, or it never arrives at all. As farfetched as it sounds, it does happen that someone calls the wrong number and leaves a message on the wrong phone machine, and then awaits a return call that will never come since the right person never got the message. For inquiries with a low priority, a follow-up note or call after a reasonable amount of time—one to three weeks, depending on the situation and relationship you have—is not pushy, and assures that you have another chance to connect or reconnect. For matters or concerns of utmost priority, following up on the same day or next would be appropriate as long as there truly is a sound reason for a timely response.

Sometimes people may fail to follow up because they think they know what the other person is calling about, and they do not want to deal with that demand on them. Quite often, however, the reason is not the assumed one, and failing to return a phone call is simply seen as rude.

For example, an editor asks an author to agree to allow an article to be reprinted in an anthology without any additional recompensation. Initially the author says no. A few hours later, the author calls the editor and leaves a message that she has decided to allow the reprint and that the editor should return the call. The call is never returned. For months, the author was annoyed at being ignored by the editor and just as happy not to participate at all in the project. When, months later, she then talked to the editor on another matter, she was surprised to learn the editor had gotten her old message, agreed to reprint the material, and did not see any reason to return the call.

Here's another example. You are involved with someone on a certain project and you call on another matter. The person you call either ignores your call or has someone else call on his or her behalf, acting as if he or she already knows what you want. Example: Someone is trying to sell you something and you ignore one or two phone messages to return the call, only to discover he is calling to ask if you would like to have two free tickets to a basketball game that night because he is unable to attend.

As a telemarketing consultant says about those who fail to return calls: "Little do they realize they may be missing sales opportunities by not following up."

Another time following up fails to occur is if someone leaves too extensive a message on a phone machine. Since you do not want whatever is being offered on the machine, you figure failing to follow up is permissible, but it is not. Your "no" still has to be communicated.

But let's say someone has left a long invitation to a luncheon next week on your machine. The time, date, and purpose are all stated, and you realize you have a conflicting appointment that day so you cannot attend. In this case, failing to follow up, if you want to keep the goodwill of the caller, will be seen as rude and an example of poor communication.

If you do not want to burden someone you are calling with the need to follow up, tell a machine or a secretary just that: "I just called Mr. Davis to catch up on the meeting I missed last week. There's no need for him to call me back. I'll see him next week and we can discuss it then."

Upon whom the responsibility for following up falls depends on whether or not you solicited or initiated this offer or contact. If someone is contacting you for the first time, and you have not asked to be contacted, and if he or she needs you more than you need him or her, it is polite for the caller to call again until contact is made. The effort for a follow-up should be on his or her back.

In one instance, failure to follow up within the proper time frame resulted in a potential loss of $300,000. An agent at a reputable New York literary agency representing a screenwriter had an offer from a producer for a writer's script. After consulting the writer and negotiating a tentative deal with the producer, the agent then waited to get back to, or follow-up with, the producer because she did not want to, in her words, "appear too eager."

Ten days after the producer had made the offer, the agent called to say the writer had accepted the producer's offer. However, by then the producer had already purchased another screenplay and was working on the new project.

By failing to follow up quickly enough, the agent had lost a sale that could have netted her client $300,000. Not only did the agent lose the deal, she also lost the client, who immediately changed agencies.

IN WRITING

Your success as an executive will be enhanced if everything you write in a business setting adheres to the general etiquette principles of showing interest in others, using acceptable formats and language, and responding in a timely way.

Executives may be judged first by the kind of letters they write before they are evaluated by their speech or in-person skills, since often even getting the job begins with a letter of inquiry. Once an executive gets the job, positive evaluations as well as advancement may hinge on writing appropriate and effective letters.

Good business writing depends on four considerations: thought, readability, correctness, and appropriateness.

Thought is the content of your writing, or *what* you say in your letters, notes, or interoffice memos. You have to be clear about the ideas you wish to express, or you will not be able to communicate persuasively those thoughts or points to others.

Readability is the clarity of your writing. It is best accomplished by using short words, sentences, and paragraphs. A few well-chosen words will make a better impression than lots of empty phrases.

Correctness refers to the grammar and spelling that you use. There is no excuse for incorrect or awkward writing. When in doubt, consult grammar books, easy-to-read style books, such as Strunk and White's *The Elements of Style*, a dictionary, or have someone whose writing you admire read it over for you.

Appropriateness is the tone of your writing. The tone—your choice of words, how informal or formal a style you follow—should be tailored to the person to whom you are writing just as your clothing is tailored to the type of clients you are dealing with.

THE ART OF LETTER WRITING
Format

I know a woman in her late thirties who worked as a registered nurse, but found she needed to write formal business letters soon after she married an investment banker. She told me that she found a book on business letter writing and used the examples that were provided, simply substituting specific details for each of the letters she had to write. The technique worked and she recommends it to others. Here, then, are some sample business letter formats that you may reuse by substituting your own name, address, dates, and inside body of the letter.

Business letters are either blocked or indented. In the first example, the letter is *blocked*, meaning all written aspects of the letter (except of course the letterhead, which might be centered at the top of the letter or over to the right) are blocked to the left margin:

Example 1: Block Format

(Letterhead)
Company
Street
City, State   Zip code

March 6, 19__

Mr. Wayne Smith
Senior Vice President
Vita Associates, Inc.
21221 North Avenue
Denver, CO 07823

Dear Mr. Smith:

This is a block-style letter. You will note everything starts at the left margin, including the complimentary closing, such as *Cordially, Sincerely, Very truly yours,* cc (carbon copy), and enc. (enclosure).

Sincerely yours,

Your First and Last Name

cc: Wilma Peterson
enc.

The second format for a business letter is the indented style:

Example 2: Indented Format

(Letterhead and/or Return Address)
Company or Name
Street Address
City, State   Zip code

                                                    June 4, 19__

Ms. Cynthia Jones
41-58 212th Street
Flushing, NY 11364

Dear Ms. Jones:

   This is a modification of the block style. Although the inside address begins at the left margin, and the cc (carbon copy) and enc. (enclosure) notations are at the left, the rest of the letter has the first line of each new paragraph indented as well as my complimentary closing.

   The block format is more formal than this modified indented/

block format. Both, however, are correct. Which one you follow is a matter of individual taste or corporate style.

Sincerely yours,

Your Complete Name

enc.

Lengthy or formal business letters should always be neatly typed, on company letterhead, without any typing or spelling errors. If possible, personally sign your correspondence rather than have your secretary sign for you.

It is acceptable to send a short, handwritten note for more informal matters, such as indicating that a report or a reprint of a published article is attached, but only do this if your handwriting is *legible*. If not, type even the briefest note or letter.

Example of Handwritten Note

January 4, 1991

Dear Joe,

Here is a copy of that report I told you about. Let me know what you think of it.

Sincerely,
Bill

You may feel more comfortable typing even a short note, especially if you want to emphasize the business aspect of any encounter and you fear a handwritten note might be misconstrued as social. Here, for example, is a brief, typed note sent in advance of a meeting to assure that a forgetful employee is certain to attend. (The phone number is included to make it easier to call if the meeting has to be rescheduled.)

(On personal memo paper, 4½″ × 6½″)
Phone number

Date

Dear____,

Just a note to reconfirm our meeting at 4 P.M. on Thursday, October 9. I'm looking forward to it.

Sincerely,

Your name

Content

After you are clear about the proper format for your business letter, you may focus on the content. Effective business communications have to read well and say something tactfully and clearly as well as look right.
Here are some tips on writing effective business letters:

- For long or complicated letters, write a short outline—briefly summarize each key concept—of the main points you want to make. Shuffling the outline around so it is logical and clear is easier than reworking the letter as you go along.

- Attend to the *style* of your writing—be careful about the punctuation, grammar, tone, length, and organization of each letter you write.

- Correct spelling errors. If necessary, check questionable words by using the dictionary or one of the computerized portable dictionaries available for under $200. If you use a personal computer, run a spelling check program.

- Effective executive communications should be succinct, rather than wordy, with language that is descriptive, clear, and visual. *If you write dull letters you may be considered dull.*

- Use simple sentences to convey your ideas clearly.

- Keep your letters as short as possible. Although it may actually take you longer to write a short, succinct, well-thought-out letter than a longer, verbose, poorly planned one, it will take your reader less time to absorb a short letter, and that is the person you are aiming to impress. *When it comes to writing letters, less is more.*

- Follow the rules of clarity, or readability, as advanced by Rudolf Flesch in *How to Say What You Mean in Plain English*—namely, short words, short sentences, and short paragraphs.

Here are additional tips for producing excellent, appropriate business letters, excerpted from *The Complete Letter Writer*, compiled and edited by N. H. Mager and S. K. Mager:

- Write from the *you* rather than the *I* perspective. Instead of writing "I was happy to hear that my letter of January 5th provided sufficient information for the completion of the order for *us*" write "Thank *you* for *your* assurance that *you* have sufficient information for the completion of *your* order."

- Stress the positive and never start or finish a letter with anything negative.

- Write business letters that leave a nice impression.

- Use lively prose.

Make sure you provide whatever you promise in your cover letter, whether that is a resume, questionnaire, book, or samples. For example, if you say, "Attached is a questionnaire for you to fill out," make sure it is included. Not only does it make you look sloppy if it is missing, it requires the person who receives your letter to go to the trouble of calling you and getting the missing material. If the missing material is something that will actually benefit you more than the person to whom you have written, requiring the recipient to obtain the missing materials will backfire. If you write in your letter, "I am returning your material," make sure the material is indeed accompanying the letter. Otherwise, it is customary to write: "I am returning your material under separate cover."

Business letters should be just that, letters that relate to the business of the company you work for. If you want to write a letter complaining about the poor treatment your family received at a restaurant the weekend before, this should be done on personal stationery or on a blank sheet of paper with your home return address typed at the top. Not only is it poor manners to misuse the company letterhead for personal "business," it just might get you fired.

COVER LETTER WITH RESUME WHEN SEEKING A JOB

Remember that the main reason for a cover letter accompanying a resume is to bring yourself to the attention of the potential employer so he or she wants to meet with you. This letter is your way of getting your foot in the door. Considering the countless resumes that get circulated each year—directly to companies or through headhunters or employment agencies—writing a cover letter that stands out may mean the difference between a chance to sell yourself in person or your letter and resume's quick trip to the garbage can.

First of all, in order to show interest in the other person, a basic of business manners, make sure you are writing to a *specific person* whose name you spell correctly rather than to the "President" or the "Human Resources Manager." Furthermore, by addressing your letter by name to a certain individual you have the opportunity to show specific concern for a particular future employer or the company.

Second, and this fits in with having a specific name to write to, the job candidate should have some reason for writing to this potential employer rather than to someone else. If you receive a letter from someone you do not know, your initial response would most likely be, "Why me?" That question has to be answered right at the beginning. By writing to a specific individual, you have a better chance at satisfying that question in a way that flatters the reader and makes him or her want to read on.

Let us say you are looking for a job in advertising and are writing to the head of creative services at one of the major advertising firms. You begin your letter by noting, "Your commercial for ———— is considered one of the top twenty ads in the last five years. It is your professional excellence and well-earned status in the field as a creative innovator that motivates me to inquire if my talents and abilities would be an asset to your creative team . . . ."

Third, keep personal information to a minimum, as it relates to the job you are seeking. "I am an avid runner" might be included if one of the accounts at the advertising company you want to work for is Reebok or Nike. Spend most of the time in your cover letter pinpointing your unique abilities that qualify you for the job you seek. Again, try to toot your own horn through the words or awards of others so you seem more humble. For example, you might write: "In my last evaluation, my boss wrote that I 'display a keen awareness of what makes an advertising campaign assured of gaining the attention of the press and the public.' Perhaps you are familiar with my campaigns for Street's toothpaste, Venezuelan coffee, and Cartwright's baby shampoo?"

Fourth, the letter should be physically appealing. Use top-quality business stationery, engraved or plain with your complete address and phone number at the top. *Never send a photocopied "general" letter with your resume to a long list of potential employers.* If you do not take the time to personally write to each one they will probably respond in kind by ignoring your photocopied letter and resume.

Fifth, make sure the letter is grammatically correct. Says Kenneth A. Snella, Vice President of Berkshire Electric Cable Company in Leeds, Massachusetts: "If someone punctuates or spells incorrectly, or phrases a sentence incorrectly, I would view it negatively."

Is it ever appropriate to handwrite a cover letter accompanying a resume? Snella says it is sometimes effective because it makes your letter stand out, and you look less like a "professional job searcher." But, he points out, it's a gamble since being "informal and off the cuff" may not be viewed in a positive way by the person to whom you are writing.

Make sure your letters have wide enough margins and that your letter is only as long as it needs to be. Single-space your letter, unless it is extremely short.

Sixth, before you send out a cover letter with a resume or any business letter, ask yourself what the goal of that letter is and if the letter you have written accomplishes that goal. If you are unsure, try the letter out on a family member, friend, or co-worker. Never mail anything that does not present you in the best possible light.

Finally, the cover letter should not reveal so much as to leave little intrigue or interest in finding out more about you in a face-to-face meeting.

Example of Cover Letter Accompanying Resume

Return address
Phone number (Use home number unless you want calls at your current job)

Date

Inside address

Dear Mr. Walker:

Carla Smith, in your creative affairs department, told me you are looking for a new story editor. I am, therefore, pleased to enclose my resume for your perusal.

For the last four years, I have been responsible for reading thousands of solicited and unsolicited treatments and screenplays. I have personally been responsible for buying eight properties; three are already in post-production.

I look forward to meeting you, Mr. Walker.

Sincerely,

Your Name

enc.

RESIGNATION LETTER

Most companies require a formal resignation letter that will be put in your permanent employment file. This letter is not the place to air gripes and frustrations about your job or your boss. You should express sadness at having to leave your current job and state the positive things that you have accomplished while in employment there. The reason for taking a new job should be tied to something somewhat neutral, like a career change, an opportunity to develop different skills, or, if true, a relocation to another region or state. You also should avoid stating "personal reasons" as the reason for your resignation since that could be construed as some kind of marital discord or emotional problems that should not be part of your permanent record.

Keep your letter upbeat, positive, and sincere.

Example of Resignation Letter

Dear Jim:

It is with deep regret that I must submit this resignation and give you two weeks' notice of my termination of employment.

My decision for leaving involves a career change and has nothing to do with March Enterprises.

In fact, being here for the past two years has been wonderful. I have worked with a fine and professional group.

I'll especially miss working with you, Jim. You are one of the most exciting, talented, and challenging men I've ever met.

Writing this letter is hard enough, so I won't ramble on. Thank you for everything.

Yours sincerely,

Name
Title

REJECTION LETTER

Practically everyone has to write rejection letters or notes in the course of business, and those may be the hardest letters of all to write, or to receive. A rejection letter will be easier to write or receive, however, if you remember that you are rejecting a specific situation rather than the person. For example, if you have to reject someone formally for a job in your department, you should convey something positive and upbeat in your rejection letter so the rejected applicant feels there is an understandable reason— rather than a blanket "We don't want you"—that he or she is not getting the job. For example, it might be that out of a thousand applicants, this person was one of the ten top contenders, but a decision had to be made based on a background with similar work experience. You want that applicant to know he or she was an excellent candidate, and that if another job opens in the future, you would certainly like him or her to apply. Wish the applicant luck in his or her job-seeking efforts. (But do not say any of these nice things if you genuinely disliked someone. Sincerity has to come through, even in a rejection letter.)

It is impolite to delay writing a rejection letter simply because you find it an unpleasant task. Someone is patiently awaiting your answer and you have to be courteous enough to say no promptly. Rather than put off writing a rejection letter, do what some human resources managers have told me they do, namely, take care of the "no" aspect quickly, since it is unpleasant, but at least you get it over with.

The best test as to whether a rejection letter is appropriate and effective is if you read it and say to yourself, "I wouldn't mind receiving a rejection letter like that." I think you may agree that you would not mind receiving the following rejection letter, since it ends on such an upbeat and positive note that the specific rejection is almost secondary to the letter's overall enthusiasm and acceptance:

Example of Rejection Letter

Dear Ms. Kelly:

The entire staff enjoyed meeting you last week. We were impressed with all the research and experience you have in a variety of business settings.

It was a hard decision to choose one candidate from four such qualified finalists, but we chose someone whose word processing skills were just what we needed.

We all wish you the best of luck in all that you do.

Sincerely,

Name
Title

FOLLOW-UP LETTER

Again and again human resources managers and other executives complain that executives do not follow up as often or as promptly as they should. Follow-ups may be in person or on the phone, but can also be in writing. For example, a follow up could be a question of sending additional requested information, writing a letter of recommendation, attending a meeting, or taking care of certain matters related to a recent meeting, such as phone calling or letters. Another reason for following up is to let someone know you are still awaiting an answer to a letter, phone, or in-person inquiry that so far has been ignored.

Example 1: Follow-Up Letter

Dear Mike:

Just a brief note to let you know I am still awaiting word from you on the statistics that were missing in your recent report. The printer just called and said all changes must be submitted within two weeks (by March 25), or we will have to pay a stiff penalty fee.

Please call, fax, or send along those statistics as soon as possible.

Sincerely,

Name
Title

Example 2: Follow-Up Letter

Dear Clark:

Since I have not yet heard from you, I thought I would follow up on my letter of July 1 with this second inquiry about your company's plans for speakers during the next year. As you know, my clients are all outstanding business executives with excellent track records as executives, speakers, and innovators. We have videotapes available for practically all of our speakers, so please just let me know which ones you want to see and I will rush them to you. If there are topics you need experts on, let me know and I will supply at least two or three names from which you might select the right one for you.

Please contact me or I will call you in two weeks to see how we might work together for the best interests of our respective companies.

Sincerely,

Name
Title

REFERENCE OR
RECOMMENDATION LETTER

Placement attorney Jeffrey G. Allen has written an entire book on reference letters entitled *The Perfect Job Reference*. According to Allen, a "perfect" reference letter should be four paragraphs long with:

An *introductory paragraph* introducing you and succinctly mentioning how you know the person you are recommending

A *value paragraph* (the longest paragraph in the letter—no more than five to six sentences) written in a "sincere and persuasive" style, that details the applicant's background and pinpoints key abilities that will aid the company or the situation someone is seeking

An *action paragraph* (if using cover-letter style) asking the reader to read the enclosed resume and contact the applicant for an interview

A *closing paragraph* expressing appreciation.

If you are one of several persons asked to recommend someone for something specific, such as an award, fellowship, or job opening, your recommendation letter should be a self-contained paragraph that states all the key information necessary—about the person being recommended as well as the exact award, fellowship, or position that is being sought. Give examples and details that show why the person you are recommending is special and competent. Do not just write general platitudes; it is specific information that will be most useful to the recipient of the reference or recommendation letter. For example, write, "Ms. Jones has not had one sick day or one reprimand for lateness in four years" instead of "Ms. Jones is a reliable employee."

Example of Recommendation Letter

Dear Ms. Engel:

I have worked with _____ this past year as an acquisitions editor for _____ . I think _____ has done pivotal work in the areas that relate to women. Her books continue to reach a wide audience, and I hope she gets the opportunity for additional study and research in this area. I would highly recommend _____ as a candidate for an APF fellowship for 19 _____ . She has both impressive work and relationship abilities. I support her continued efforts to develop and publish her findings.

Sincerely,

Ann _____
Editor

THANK-YOU LETTER

You may write a thank-you note for anything, from a lunch or dinner to material someone has sent to you that helps you in a project you are researching. A thank-you note is a gesture of goodwill. It indicates you took the time and trouble to acknowledge someone else's time and trouble.

To be most effective, a thank-you note should be written soon after the event or the material is received. It should convey warmth and gratitude and be somewhat informal, even if typed and on business stationery. Try to keep thank-you letters short and to the point.

Example 1: Thank-You Letter

Dear Susan,

Thank you so much for the information that you sent along. I really appreciate the time and effort you are contributing to my job search. I will be going home to Washington, D.C., this weekend to rework my resume. The book you sent to me on writing effective letters has helped me to revamp my cover letter to be more "forceful and vivid."

Sincerely,

Name

Example 2: Thank-You Letter

Dear Katherine,

The labels just arrived by express mail.

As a way of saying "thank you" I'm enclosing an autographed copy of my most recent book, *Making Your Office Work for You,* which I also thought you might find of interest.

Sincerely,

Jan Yager

enc.

No matter how famous, infamous, or high up the ladder you are, it is proper to send thanks, preferably even in your own hand. If it is typed, you should certainly sign it yourself, as is the case in the example from former New York City Mayor, Edward I. Koch.

Ed Koch for Mayor

| 345 Park Avenue
(51st—52nd Sts., Level C)
New York, NY 10022

(212) 750 8900 | Campaign Co-Chairmen | Bess Myerson
Edward Costikyan
Hon. Herman Badillo
Hon. Charles Rangel | Campaign Manager   John LoCicero
Campaign Treasurer   Bernard Rome |

November 1, 1977

Ms. Janet Barkas
Cooper Station, New York 10003

Dear Janet:

    Thank you for your recent letter and enclosure. I look forward to your help on the campaign.

    All the best.

               Sincerely,

               Edward I. Koch

You may read more about thank-you notes in Chapter 10 on gifts and gift-giving.

THANK-YOU/RECOMMENDATION COMBINATION LETTER

You may also combine letters—writing a thank-you letter that might also serve as a recommendation letter; a resignation letter that is a thank-you letter; a follow-up letter that might also be a sales letter.

    On the opposite page is an example of an unsolicited thank-you letter that then became a recommendation letter sent by the person being thanked. It is enclosed in a packet distributed to prospective customers or clients, because it gives concrete evidence of the sender's abilities and may inspire confidence in prospective clients of the sender's skills.

Example 1: Thank-You/Recommendation Combination Letter

Kathye ____
Manager
____
City, State   Zip code

December 28, 1989
Ellen Gendel, Executive Associate
____
City, State   Zip code

Dear Ellen:

My husband and I would like to formally thank you for your help in finding and purchasing our new home in Chatham. We love the new house! Having just spent the holidays there, we feel like it has been "ours" for much longer than two weeks!

As you may know, my new position at ____ involves developing and implementing a Customer Satisfaction Program for ____ Group Department. As a result, I have read many books outlining what makes quality service and I have become very "tuned in" to customer/client expectations and how to meet those expectations.

Mike and I want you to know that you exceeded our expectations in every possible way! Not only did you quickly and adeptly recognize what type of home we were searching for, but also you were friendly, professional, and *always* available throughout the process.

I particularly appreciated your thoughtfulness while Mike was traveling. Also, I know you called us from home many times to let us know your plans . . . . I felt very comfortable and secure knowing you were there to assist us whenever we needed you.

For Mike and me, you will be the real estate agent against whom we measure all other real estate agents in the future. You provided our first impression of North Jersey . . . . You helped make a rather stressful time a very pleasant and positive experience. We sincerely hope that our acquaintance will not end here, and that we will see you in the future. Thanks again for everything!

Sincerely,

Kathye and Mike

cc: ____ , President

However, whether a recommendation letter is solicited or unsolicited, make sure you get verbal permission to use it. For example, if you want to use an unsolicited recommendation letter that a client has sent to you to build trust in potential clients, simply say to that client: "Mr. Smith, it was so kind of you to write that recommendation letter about me to my boss and to send me a copy. I was flattered by your appreciation. Would it be all right if I include a copy of that letter when I send out material to prospective customers? I would include it as is or, if you like, I can cross out any identifying details."

You will probably get an enthusiastic "yes," but in case your recommender turns you down, be polite and thank him or her for the letter anyway. In this way, you will avoid reversing the favorable impression a client or customer has about you by unwittingly offending him or her when a seemingly personal business letter turns up "in circulation." Undoubtedly at some point you will receive another unsolicited recommendation letter from someone else that you are free to circulate.

Similarly, if you write a recommendation letter but do not want it to be circulated, you might type at the top: *Confidential Correspondence; Not for Circulation.*

If you want to solicit a recommendation letter that you might circulate, you could ask a prior or current client or customer to write one. State in advance how you will make use of that letter. For example: "Mr. March, I am asking several of my clients if they would mind writing a short paragraph about our business relationship. I will be including these letters in a information packet about me that I am putting together to hand out to prospective clients. May I count on you?"

Example 2: Thank-You/Recommendation Combination Letter

Family Focus Inc.
Classes for Expectant and New Parents

April 12, 19__

Dear Jan,

Thank you ever so much for giving the ____ workshop on April 2. I think it went very well and that the women found it helpful. I especially appreciated your individualizing the class at the end, helping each person in the seminar define their priorities and find a solution that would work for them.

I look forward to your repeating the workshop in July.

Enclosed is your check.

Let's also talk further about the new workshop on ＿＿＿ I think it's going to be a hot topic!

All my best,

Diana Simkin, M.A., ACCE
Director

enc.

SALES LETTER

In *The Complete Letter Writer*, compiled and edited by N. H. and S. K. Mager, the authors suggest this traditional format for an effective sales letter:

1. Arouse interest.

2. Describe, explain, and convince.

3. Stimulate interest to the point of closing a sale.

To arouse interest, Mager and Mager suggest beginning your sales letter with these techniques:

- A striking statement

- An anecdote or joke

- A startling fact

- An analogy

- A startling offer

- A gift or free booklet—a 'bribe for listening'

Joe Girard, "the world's greatest salesman" and author of *How to Sell Anything to Anybody* (with Stanley H. Brown), emphasizes what a powerful tool sales letters may be—but you have to get them read. That means you "don't send them [prospective clients] things they can easily identify as advertising mail," writes Girard. Girard encourages getting sales letters, or printed literature with a short handwritten note attached, into the hands of former and prospective customers or clients. "And when you have somebody who remembers you and likes you because of what they get in the mail from you, you have made the best possible investment of your time and your money," Girard writes.

Bob Kalian, a direct-marketing copywriter/consultant, is an expert in writing sales letters. Kalian has these suggestions for writing effective sales letters:

> *Start off by visualizing one person, a real flesh-and-blood person, sitting there reading your letter. Remember you have at most five to ten seconds to grab his attention. Say something that will arouse his curiosity or that appeals to his needs. Do not—repeat, DO NOT—talk about how great your company or its products are. He does not care and will toss the letter instantly into the circular file. Instead, tell him how your product or service will benefit him—how it will make his life easier; how it will make him smarter, richer, whatever. Just be sure you are talking about his interests and not about you, your company, or your product or service.*
>
> *What most people forget is that the recipient of your letter does not want it. He didn't ask you for it and it is nothing but an annoyance. He is busy with a million more important things and wants to throw your letter out. And he will. Quickly. Unless you stop him. The only way of doing that is by appealing to his interests and doing it right up front.*
>
> *One very effective technique is to arouse curiosity. One of the most successful promotions run by* Psychology Today *magazine started off: "Do you close the bathroom door even when there's no one home?" It stops you and makes you think. You read on to see what's coming next.*
>
> *I often like to paint a picture. "Imagine yourself doing this . . . ." One extremely effective ad I wrote was for a book I had written called* A Few Thousand of the Best FREE Things in America. *The ad started off with, "Imagine yourself walking to your mailbox every day and finding it overflowing with valuable gifts of every type and description." The result was a successful promotion that sold close to 500,000 copies of that book and a companion book,* Free Things for Kids.

Another consideration when it comes to sales letters, except in unusual situations, is to avoid using photo memos or letterhead, or including materials, such as copies of press clippings, that have your photo on it.

Not only do you risk clouding your new or ongoing business relationship with a subjective favorable or unfavorable reaction to how you look, it gives an unprofessional image. Perhaps one reason is that it violates the etiquette philosophy of *reserve*—too much is exposed too soon. The person with whom you are communicating should be aware of your appearance at the appropriate time, namely, when meeting you face to face (not in a letter). Furthermore, you should be selling your services and abilities or your product, not your physical appearance. (Yet, when it is appropriate to show that physical appearance, a good one will put your services or products in even a better light.)

KEEPING-IN-TOUCH LETTER

Business often depends on maintaining relationships with clients or customers between sales or projects. Sometimes that might mean months or years would go by without any contact; for some business relationships, a once-a-year Christmas card is not enough to maintain contact. In those instances, a keeping-in-touch letter might be what you want to write. (You may want to follow up the keeping-in-touch letter with a phone call soon afterwards, or a few weeks or months later, since a letter alone may be less effective.)

Just remember this is a business keep-in-touch letter, so even though the tone should be warm, friendly, and upbeat, it should be as professional as possible. If personal news is shared—such as the birth of a child, moving to a new home, or a fascinating vacation you have just been on—do it succinctly and in a professional way, without going on and on with endless details.

Example of Keeping-in-Touch Letter

Dear Jan,

   Thanks for sending along a copy of your latest report. I enjoyed reading it and knowing what you are up to these days.

   I am pleased to enclose an article that recently appeared in the company newspaper. It highlights some of the trips I've taken over the last year.

   I look forward to seeing you again.

                                              Very truly yours,

                                              Name

DELINQUENT ACCOUNT LETTER

In various types of businesses it may be necessary to write a delinquent account letter, even if you are not in the credit or purchasing department. It is always nice to include a statement like "You may already have attended to this so please excuse this reminder" to let the person quickly take care of matters and save face. Even though you are in the right in feeling annoyed, angry, or disappointed that your account is still outstanding, keep the tone of your letter positive and unhostile. The reason for the delinquent account may be due to extenuating circumstances or a simple oversight; you may want to do business with this person again.

Often delinquent account letters in large companies are handled with photocopied form letters. But if you have a personal relationship with someone, you may even want to intervene and write a personal note instead.

Example of Delinquent Account Letter

Dear Bill,

I hope this letter finds all is well with you.

Bill, I am sorry to point out that we have not yet received payment for the shipment that our warehouse sent to you over three months ago. In case you have already taken care of this, please disregard this reminder and accept my apologies for making another inquiry.

We appreciate your business and look forward to doing business with you again in the future.

To facilitate your payment, a preaddressed envelope is attached.

Very truly yours,

Name

UPCOMING EVENT NOTIFICATION LETTER

If you are sponsoring an event and receive verbal in-person or telephone RSVPs, you might want to send a reminder letter to those you most want to attend. Mail the letter so it will arrive a few days before the event. This is a courtesy, since so many businesspersons are inundated with requests that your event, even if responded to verbally and marked down on a busy calendar, may be forgotten by the time the event occurs.

Example of Upcoming Event Notification Letter

Dear ____,

I was so pleased when my secretary told me you called last week to say you would attend my division's presentation.

I look forward to seeing you there and to discussing it with you afterwards, if you have a few spare moments.

See you at the State Street Restaurant, Wednesday, July 27, at 2 P.M.

Sincerely,

Name

INTEROFFICE MEMOS
Format

Date all your memos and indicate how many persons will be seeing the same memo.

Use company or personal memo paper; some sort of imprinted name should be at the top. It may be inappropriate to use "cute" memo paper in business, unless it is part of your company logo, whether it is a bird perched on a tree with a slogan underneath it, or a picture of an executive seated behind a messy desk. *Keep the emphasis on the contents of the memo rather than on the memo paper.*

If these memos are truly interoffice and not for outside persons, thinner paper of a variety of colors is acceptable. But some interoffice memos are sent outside the office. In that case, use good quality paper; it reflects better on you and your company. One style that is simple but effective is a strip of imprinted heavy card stock paper, about three inches wide and six inches long.

Content

The general rule for interoffice memos is: Put praise in writing; reprimand face to face.

Keep your memos short, no longer than a page, and end a memo with a request for some kind of action. This helps cut down on communication lags.

Even though this is an interoffice memo, all the rules for effective writing presented in the previous section on writing appropriate business letters should be followed—you should be as concerned about the impression you make on the co-workers, subordinates, and superiors who receive your interoffice memos as you are on those outside the company who receive your more formal business letters. (Always be aware, as well, that interoffice memos can get in the hands of "outsiders," as evidenced by the interoffice memo that a network TV show anchor wrote complaining to management about some of his co-workers, and that somehow landed in the hands of the media and found its way to newspapers around the country. You will note he violated the first rule about interoffice memos: reprimand in person; praise in writing.)

Reputations and business relationships have been ruined by mistakenly getting an interoffice memo to someone outside the office, or enclosing a business letter intended for one person to another one, even if those situations were not newsworthy enough to get on the headlines of major newspapers. One writer had to fire her agent because the agent presented herself as being on the writer's side, but by unwittingly enclosing a cover letter to the publisher the agent was trying to sell to, the agent showed she was taking the publisher's side rather than standing up for her client.

You should also realize that even though the etiquette is that *you* control anything that you write, some breach that rule and use what they have gotten from you in whatever way they want. Often it is too much bother to make an issue of it, but it is an annoyance. Therefore, follow the rule: do not write anything to anyone—whether it is a business letter, interoffice memo, or even a notation on a Christmas card—that you could not live with seeing in print.

It is not always possible to follow the rule of never putting anything negative in writing, however, especially if your boss has asked you to critique someone or something in a memo. Before you put it in writing, however, try to talk to your boss face to face or over the phone about his questions; that might suffice and a written critique would then be unnecessary.

Memo Announcing Meeting

Date

All senior supervisors are expected to attend an 8 A.M. breakfast this Thursday when the new product line will be introduced. Call my office if you cannot attend.

Progress Memo

Date

Here are the projects under consideration this month, with comments about their status and what negotiations have been accomplished so far with each one. We will meet Monday to discuss this list.

cc: Brian Smith
 Brenda Wiggins
 Melvin Sharp
 Doloras Owings

Memo Accompanying Report

Date

To: Roger
From: Paul

Here is the monthly report. Let's talk about it over lunch tomorrow.

WRITING TOOLS

Caring about your professional image necessitates being concerned with the form and content of your business letters or interoffice memos, as well as with the utensils you use for writing. Obviously your memo will have the same words, whether you use a good-quality typewriter ribbon or an old one, but by using the former you are saying that as a businessperson you are concerned with image and details; using the latter implies that you are too busy to care about such specifics as readability and clarity. But the appearance of what you write is an important detail, since it is also harder to read lightly typed material.

If you use a computer that is compatible with a letter-quality or laser printer, use one of these instead of a dot-matrix printer, which is good for a first draft or for your own use but not for showing to others. Once again, it is harder to read. (Some newer model dot-matrix printers, however, approach letter quality and will suffice if that is the best you can manage.)

What kind of pen do you write with? An inexpensive one or one of good quality? Do you use a Mont Blanc? Schaeffer? Parker? Bic? A ballpoint, fountain pen, or cartridge pen? There are some who believe that a fountain pen is actually easier to write with. Do you use pencils that are imprinted with a sales pitch for your company or someone else's? Are your pencils sharpened or dull? Do you use a high-speed electric sharpener, a slower battery-operated one, or do you have someone sharpen pencils for you?

Take stock of your writing equipment and make sure it is of the best quality and also reflects the business image you want to project.

The next chapter will look at how the appearance of your office will help you rise faster and further in the business world.

Chapter 5

How Your Office Should Look

Just as how you talk and look should be appropriate for a rising executive, how your office appears is also part of business etiquette. Consider for a moment just how much most offices reflect a company's image, as does the tie of the CEO, the suit of the human resources administrator, or the dress of the communications director. A financial services corporation closely identified with a conservative image—taste, decorum, tradition—has offices that are quiet, covered with thick carpet, and plush with appropriate furniture reflecting the status and level of each company employee. Even the accessories on the desk match the corporate image.

By contrast, another office in a small advertising company is zany in its colorful posters, breezy, loud style, laid-back manner, and uncarpeted, noisy corridors.

Remember that your office is up for scrutiny as well as the manners you exhibit in that office, such as whether or not you stand to greet guests, how you talk to your secretary or co-workers—do you use an intercom, walk over to them, or shout? (Ninety-six percent of the personnel administrators I surveyed wrote that offering a chair to a visitor is considered etiquette at their company.)

The office is a reflection of who we are as a worker, and even as an industry.

Many in business will try hard to get clients, customers, or potential clients and customers to come to them; as with the business lunch, getting someone to come to your turf is often indicative of who has the greater power.

So you want the turf you get those persons on to be impressive; to be a place that will advance your business career, not curtail it. That means your office should be appropriate for your company, for your position in your company, and for your industry.

Let us look at the office of an accountant who has her own two-person company—herself plus a full-time secretary. The offfice is a one-bedroom apartment she uses as a business office; her home is two blocks away and completely separate from the accounting office. What is appropriate about this office? One of the best and most considerate aspects of this office is that the accountant provides chairs with armrests for her clients to sit in, rather than sofas. The chairs are positioned in an L-shape so that those who want to sit next to each other may, and those who prefer to sit farther away have that option as well. There is a problem with sofas in a business office where many clients or customers unknown to each other may have to congregate for anywhere from a few moments to an hour or more. Sofas open up the possibility of being too close to each other and even forcing physical contact among strangers, which is inappropriate in most settings. In some situations it is not only poor etiquette, it is a health hazard, if you consider physician's offices that only have sofa seating available so that you go in, healthy, for a check-up, only to find yourself sitting for up to an hour on a sofa next to a very sick person who is coughing and sneezing all over you.

The accountant's office shows goodwill in that there is a coffeemaker available for clients as well as for the accountant and her staff, and the refrigerator is stocked with cold drinks if anyone requests one. There is a range of magazines near the chairs for clients to review. The bathroom has soap in a dispenser, a far more sanitary and pleasing way to get soap than a communal cake of soap. There are also paper towels rather than a communal cloth towel.

The accountant lets her clients know her rules: "No smoking, please," reads a sign on the front desk. But she keeps her blinds down so that natural light is blocked from the room, making it a less cheerful place to be, and the plants, lacking the necessary sunshine, are a detriment to the office since they are all dry and dying. Without the softness that curtains might provide, the opportunity to make clients feel at home is lost, even though the magazines and beverages somewhat offset the more "office" appearance. Similarly, the harsh fluorescent lighting could be toned down and the overflowing wastepaper basket should be emptied for a more proper look.

A phone, placed near the chairs clients use, is available to them for making local calls, a courtesy that endears the accountant to her clients who often have to call this one or that one to say they are running late or to ask a question. The cost of the phone is absorbed as another business cost.

Ten Key Office Etiquette Tips

1. A messy desk is insulting, so be neat at all times. Never have personal work or grooming items around.

2. Do not eat lunch at your desk, if possible. If you have to, make sure no clients or customers are around watching you and that you clean up afterwards, especially the crumbs.

3. If you drink coffee or other beverages at your desk, use a ceramic cup or a plastic glass, rather than cardboard or styrofoam "take-out" cups.

4. Look at your office in a new way and ask yourself, "Would I want to visit someone who worked in this office, and if I did, what would it tell me about that person?"

5. Consider your office, whatever its size, as your home away from home, and judge every aspect of it in terms of its appropriateness—as you would your own home furnishings and ambiance.

6. Make sure every accessory in your office is purposefully chosen to enhance your image. Don't pick things just by a whim or because you want to get rid of knickknacks or art work in your home.

7. Be certain you keep your office neat and attractive, as you would your business clothes.

8. If you need lots of papers when you work, consider having a front office, which is always kept neat and where you see visitors, and a back office, where you do your actual work. If your office is a small space, or only a desk, consider having a "dump drawer" where you can quickly put your clutter if someone visits you, or using a screen to conceal clutter not meant for anyone else to see.

9. Keep confidential phone numbers or papers away from the roaming eyes of either other employees or visitors.

10. Avoid using a speakerphone if you can help it. The sound quality of most speakerphones is not flattering to either party; you tend to

shout into a speakerphone, which is intrusive to those working around you, and those within earshot of the speakerphone can overhear what your caller is saying, which is a violation of privacy. Furthermore, a speakerphone may make those around you, or calling you, think that you are lazy because you do not want to pick up the receiver. (If the receiver hurts your shoulder or neck, consider getting a good headset that works like a regular phone except that the pressure is off your shoulder because the mouthpiece is small and lightweight, but extremely sensitive and clear.) If you do have to use a speakerphone, explain to the other person just why you are using it.

Compare how appropriate or inappropriate the following two offices seem to be. Steelcase, Inc., a leading manufacturer of office furniture as well as a researcher of office trends and systems, provided these photos of how adding so-called open-office systems of panels, partitions, and elevated filing systems (see the second photo) gives a sleaker and neater look, as well as more privacy to employees, in the same amount of space. Photos supplied courtesy of Steelcase, Inc., Grand Rapids, Michigan.

CREATING AN APPROPRIATE OFFICE

Whether you own the company or you just work there, here are some points to consider for creating an appropriate office:

- Cost
- Time required to implement changes
- Who will be in charge?
- Reasons for maintaining the status quo
- Lighting
- Color
- Furniture

- Wall hangings

- Holiday decorations

- Controlling clutter

- Privacy

At first glance, you may think you have little or no control over the above considerations in creating an effective office image, especially in terms of lighting, color, and furniture. You will, however, have some control depending on the kind of company you work for and your position in it. If you are a top executive at a major corporation, you may be asked how you want your office painted, decorated, and furnished. If you are the owner of a small business, you will probably grant yourself the same power. If you are a middle manager at a corporation, you may have little direct control over those issues, but you might be able to exercise some influence by working with the facility or human resources managers who are open to your suggestions about how you (and your office) will function better. The best way to get help in changing your office is to stress that its current condition is causing you to be less productive than you might be. As Dorothy Paleologos, Director, People/Technology Services for Aetna Life Insurance Company, points out, companies care about how well your office works for you. Says Paleologos: "We look at how well the office supports the work you're trying to do. Is it enabling you to do your work effectively, or is it creating obstacles that make it inefficient or cause muscle stress and strain when you try to do your job?"

Management will probably be open to your suggestions and concerns about your office if you can show it will help your work. There are also office-related issues discussed below that practically every worker *does* control, namely wall hangings, holiday decorations, clutter, and even privacy.

Cost

Someone has to absorb the cost of improving your office image. But you need not spend a lot of money to enhance your office image. You may decide on a reasonable budget for any changes so you will not have to raise your prices, or you may decide the only way to absorb the cost of new lighting, accessories, or furniture is to raise prices. Without obligating yourself, you may want to involve a designer or architect to find out what price range you are talking about for the kinds of changes sought.

Time to Implement Changes

Some cosmetic changes, such as painting the walls, may take only a week or two to implement; others, such as building extensive built-in units or rewiring, may take weeks or months. In all cases, disruption in the workplace should be anticipated. Even a small paint job may require placing books and files in temporary storage and covering computer equipment to prevent damages, thus stopping employees from doing some of their usual work. If you or your employees are involved in a project that requires intense concentration or creativity, you may want to reserve *any* changes in the office until after the project is completed (or find another office to work in while changes take place).

Who Will Be in Charge?

Are you going to handle the office changes or delegate them to your office manager, or will you hire someone outside the company, such as an interior designer, architect, or space planner?

If you hire someone, he or she may be able to provide you with all the information you need. Otherwise, you may want to find experts in a variety of fields, such as facility managers or office organizers, to consult with or employ for your office overhaul.

Reasons for Maintaining Status Quo

A psychologist has a very messy yet comfortable office with old furniture that looks as though it might fall apart. You might think his office could use a complete overhaul, but it works for him and for his patients.

Or consider the dentist whose practice was going along fine for some thirty years—the same basic chairs, furniture, and accessories that he had started out with were still there. But he decided to overhaul the waiting room by exchanging the painted green walls for high-gloss effect wallpaper in primary-color stripes. Old secondhand furniture was replaced by new, Scandinavian design in bright reds and blues. The patients, rather than being impressed and excited, were fearful that this dramatic change meant price increases were soon to occur as well. Some clients, like those dental patients, prefer an office to remain the same. As a psychologist I interviewed once explained to me, she tries to keep everything in her office the same from session to session; it is comforting to patients who feel there is already too much unpredictable change in their lives.

Lighting

Keep in mind that the type of lighting used in your office will differ if you have a video display terminal, and if you have some natural light or are in a completely sealed-off room. Artificial lighting should be bright enough for your needs, but not so bright that there is a glare on the paper or on a computer screen, or that you or visitors get headaches. Similarly, natural light should be muted if at certain times of the day it produces glare or too much heat.

Color

Most companies will not ask you what color you would like for the walls of your office. But in case they do, or if you work for yourself, here are some things about color to keep in mind: light-colored walls make a place seem bigger; dark walls make walls contract; turquoise and purple are considered inappropriate colors in a business setting; pastels may work in the West Coast but not in the Midwest. An accent wall of blue, for example, may enliven a bland room without overpowering it, as might happen with an all-blue room. Soft colors, such as beige or light gray, may be more pleasant to work in than bright white.

Furniture

Your company may provide you with the furniture appropriate to your level and title, so this may not be too much of a concern for you, or it might allow you to choose among several types of desks or chairs at your level. Comfort is a key concern when it comes to office furniture, but you also want it to be tasteful, attractive, and reflective of the office image you want to project.

Wall Hangings

Twenty-eight percent of those I surveyed on business etiquette wrote that their company dictates what may be hung on walls. Make sure you know if your company also scrutinizes what can be displayed.

Find out if your company provides a book of art prints that it owns from which you can choose what to place on your walls. When selecting the prints, consider the image you want to convey—a Monet print of water lilies will make a different statement than a Picasso line drawing of a mother and child.

If your company does not provide a selection of prints, and instead allows you to bring in art that you buy, consider the color scheme of your office as well as the overall decor of the company. Do you work at a conservative bank? a relaxed and ultramodern advertising company? a design-conscious consulting firm? Depending on your answers, think about the type of art that would complement your concerns. The bright colors of a Matisse or the modern lines of a Klee might be more suitable for a publishing company than a financial institution. In conservative offices, a still life or such old favorites depicting a more ordered society of bygone days, such as Rembrandt or Sargeant, may be better. Avoid prints that have nudity or scenes that might be considered offensive. You could also pick modern painters whose work is concerned mainly with color and design, thereby avoiding associations with the subject matter that might occur with more representational art.

In some companies, your wall hangings may have to please the head of your company as well as your immediate boss. For instance, I was told about the president of one of the major television networks who had a painting removed from an executive's wall because it did not fit in with the president's taste.

Holiday Decorations

Keep in mind the comfort of your co-workers, clients, or customers when you decorate your office whether for a religious holiday such as Christmas, or a nonsectarian one such as Thanksgiving. Those who work in offices with an international clientele should be sensitive to the fact that their clients or customers may not be comfortable with all the pumpkins, pilgrims, and Indians that are representative of the American holiday of Thanksgiving. When in doubt, keep the holiday decorating in your individual office to a minimum; allow the office building or the floor to create the holiday mood.

Controlling Clutter

Clutter is one of the worst offenders of sensibilities in an office. Not only can it hinder work efficiency, or your corporate image, it can be stressful to the person who has accumulated all this clutter and does not know what to do with it. It can also make visitors or co-workers feel as if the clutterer is out of control. Clutter is improper in a business setting because one of the basics of correct business etiquette is that you appear to be *in control.* Just how important it is to have a clutter-free office is demonstrated by the fact that 22% of those personnel administrators I surveyed wrote that their company had rules against clutter in the office.

If you cannot get rid of clutter on your own—some people simply accumulate things and even get so emotionally attached to paper and possessions that getting rid of clutter is like giving away part of themselves—hire someone to do it for you. (See the listing for members of NAPO, the National Association of Professional Organizers, provided in the appendix.) Or you might ask someone who works for you or is in your company to be your clutter "buddy." It may not be his or her job to actually go through the clutter and store it, donate it, shred it, or discard it, but he or she can supervise or just be there for moral support as you complete the necessary but painful task. Do it after hours, if you have to, and put on some pleasant background music to make the chore more palatable. Recently a government administrator called me to say she was overwhelmed by the boxes of files that had accumulated, some dating back twenty years that she knew she would never use again, and she was at a loss over what to do. I suggested she find someone to go through the boxes with her. She found someone who worked in her building, gave her a small hourly fee, and together over a few hours after work they were able to sort through and toss out three huge cartons of stuff.

Privacy

In order to carry out the etiquette maxim—*be discrete*—you need an office that offers privacy. Some companies are recognizing that their workers need a lot of privacy to perform their jobs well, and they are getting away from the more open offices of the last few decades—with low panels, systems furniture, or workstations separating workers, if anything, rather than the traditional office with its walls—by replacing the low panels with floor-to-ceiling ones. As Dorothy Paleologos of Aetna points out: "Floor-to-ceiling offices with glass are used for selected functions in our company. These offices offer both visual and acoustical privacy while at the same time instill a feeling of openness to the occupant as well as the people outside of the office."

If you still work in a more open office or a fishbowl, affording little privacy, be especially careful about what might be overheard during your telephone conversations or meetings with others. If you must reprimand an employee, do it out of earshot. If you must do it in person, take that worker to a private conference room area or an empty office that does have a door. In that way, by modifying your behavior, you do have control over even how private your office is whether or not you have walls or share an office with four other people.

ETIQUETTE ISSUES IF YOU WORK FROM HOME

You may have an outside office at a company or in an office building and you just work at home on an occasional basis, or you may be one of the estimated eight million Americans who work completely from home. You might also be part of one of the work-at-home programs offered by more than thirty-five companies where you are basically a salaried employee but happen to work at home. Whether your working-at-home situation is part-time or full-time, you have to consider business etiquette in terms of how you conduct your business as well as how your office appears.

The primary etiquette concern of anyone who works from home is that he or she is preceived as a professional businessperson. The business has to come first; the fact that it is home-based is secondary. That means, if possible, have a separate business telephone and do not allow your spouse or children to answer it when you are busy; if necessary, have an answering service or a telephone answering machine pick up your calls and take messages.

You should also try to block out any non-office sound when you are talking on the phone. Failing to do so creates an unprofessional image. An entrepreneurial woman, realizing how important it is to convey the office aspect of a home-based office, created a cassette tape of typing and other office sounds so callers could hear those sounds in the background rather than screaming children or a blaring television.

Visitors to a home-based office have to be handled with special discretion. If you work alone at home, consider meeting with clients or customers of the opposite sex in a less compromising situation, such as the corner coffee shop, a nearby office you can rent by the hour, or going to your client or customer's office. If you work alone and decide to have customers or clients visiting you, especially of the opposite sex, ask a friend or associate to sit in your home office and work there for a while when you meet with your client or customer, or pay an assistant to be there so the situation seems more appropriate.

If you feel comfortable having visitors of the opposite sex in your home office, carefully plan your home office situation so you can receive visitors in the most appropriate setting possible. For example, you may actually have your office in the corner of your bedroom, but you see visitors in your living room, which looks very much like the reception area to the executive offices of a large corporation. If you have a large entrance or hallway, you might consider setting up a bench or one or two chairs there for meeting with visitors; this will eliminate the necessity of even inviting them into the living area of your home or apartment.

Consider carefully all of the stationery requirements of a business professional with the idea that when working from home, your letterhead, business cards, and memo pads should look as formal or professional as if you work in an outside office. Through your behavior, image, and business accessories, such as your stationery, attaché case, or the dress or suit in which you meet your clients or customers, you will look every bit the part of the appropriate executive. Avoid greeting even messengers in a bathrobe or cut-off jeans if you want to feel like the business professional that you are. Or, if necessary, have two distinct standards—one for when you are alone and working on a report or making telephone calls, and the second when you are having visitors or going out to meetings. In the first instance, a t-shirt may be just fine; in the second instance, only the most appropriate business attire will do.

Remember that those you are doing business for or with—the client, customer, partners, or co-workers—do not care where you work, as long as your work is good. You are in competition with those who work in outside offices and who have access to the latest equipment or personnel. So if you do not have the budget or the space for a photocopy machine or a fax (facsimile), make sure you have a good working relationship with a photocopy store and someone nearby who receives fax copy, such as the paid mailbox stores that have sprung up throughout the United States, especially in major metropolitan areas, that will allow you to receive or send fax transmissions for a small per-fax-copy fee.

Remember that because you have a home-based career, you need to make as much use of outside environments and situations as anyone else, for your professional growth as well as your psychological well-being. The necessary relationship building that is behind every successful business career needs face-to-face contact outside the home office to develop and grow. To avoid never venturing outside your home office, except for an occasional professional or business meeting, consider some of the outside-the-home office options available to you. You may go to the local or college library to read as a change of scenery, or to escape family distractions. You may rent office space by the hour or the month in most communities. Some professional associations or alumni clubs have offices that members may use for interviewing or networking at no cost except annual membership dues. You might also consider working an exchange with someone else who works at home—there might be fewer distractions, and it may be more appropriate to meet with strangers at each other's homes than working in your own. If you do not want to advertise that you work from home, consider getting a post office box, or using one of the paid mailing services. For a monthly fee, you use their street address for your mailing address.

In the next chapter we will examine the basics of etiquette around the world in such countries as England, France, Italy, and Japan.

Chapter 6

International Etiquette

Understanding the basic business manners in other countries is a major concern for executives who travel abroad. It is also useful to know foreign business etiquette if you are doing business in the United States with someone visiting from a foreign land or conducting international business by phone.

In some cases, you need not leave this country to need to know about the etiquette of a foreign land: hundreds of Japanese companies have set up offices in this country in just the last ten years, for example. Other countries, such as England, own and operate major American companies as well.

Although the world does seem to be shrinking in some ways, the necessity of respecting and observing the business manners of another nation is as important as ever. In fact, it is more important since readily available information about foreign business etiquette means there is less of an excuse for ignorance. Just by reading this chapter, you may avoid the most common faux pas committed by businesspersons.

This chapter is based on my firsthand experiences in conducting business in such countries as France, The Netherlands, India, England, Nepal, Italy, Scotland, Ireland, Canada, Germany, and Austria, additional interviews with men and women from those countries or who worked there for a period of time, including international protocol authority Dorothea Johnson. Two popular books on the subject that I consulted are *Do's and Taboos Around the World*, edited by Roger E. Axtell and compiled by the Parker Pen Company, and the chapter on international protocol in *Behave Yourself!* by Elena Jankowic and Sandra Bernstein.

You need to know enough about the etiquette in a particular country so you do not unwittingly offend its customs. Behavior also affects the business you may do. For example, a Florida-based company that administers addiction-recovery programs for those with drug, alcohol, and food addiction problems would never think of offering a food-addiction program in their hospital in Ireland. The Irish just do not see food problems as an addiction in the same way they view alcohol or drug abuse, explains the company's personnel director.

Behavior also affects whether or not an individual will be allowed to continue doing business in another country. Expert Dorothea Johnson tells the story of an American executive who was sent by his company to work in an office they were opening up in China. "He was given three hours to leave the country," says Johnson. "It seems he had pinched a waitress you know where, and the Chinese simply don't tolerate that kind of thing," Johnson continued.

Before addressing the etiquette of individual countries, here are some general international etiquette tips. According to Roger E. Axtell, editor of *Do's and Taboos Around the World*, the four basic areas you have to get right are:

- How to say people's names
- Eating
- Dress
- Language

You may know all the rules for the typical American business situation, but for each of these concerns and for each country you are doing business with, whether it is China, Japan, England, or Israel, you should learn what is proper.

Most countries are more formal than the United States. When in doubt, use someone's full name rather than just their first name. In some countries, it is considered polite to eat the food of the country you are visiting ("When in Rome . . . "). If you are having a meal at an ethnic restaurant in the United States with someone from another country, it is also polite to eat the traditional foods on the menu (rather than a burger and fries).

If you are conducting business in a country where English is not the first language, and you are unable to speak in the native tongue, consider having a translator along at your business meetings. That way, if your foreign business associates wish to speak in their native tongue they may; you are not forcing them to speak English just for you.

When traveling, unless you can wear native dress, such as a sari, with incredible flare and comfort, dress in a business suit or dress and, if it is appropriate and unoffensive, wear the local dress for fancy or ceremonial occasions.

International expert Dorothea Johnson, who has been training diplomatic attachés for decades, points out that the biggest fault she sees with Americans in doing business with other cultures is their *hastiness*. Says Johnson: "We operate under the theory that time is money. Do you know what the Japanese say about us? They say that we practice 'ready, *fire*, aim.' We fire before we aim. Americans do not take the time to prepare. But if you know the rules, you can play the game better." One of the ways that the hastiness of Americans backfires when doing business with other cultures, Johnson continues, is in how quickly they want to jump right in and get the business out of the way. But people of other cultures spend more time first building a relationship with each other; the business deals evolve out of that trust.

AUSTRALIA

According to Neil Allison, Australian Airlines Sales Manager for the Eastern United States and Canada, business dress is basically the same in Australia as it is here—suits and ties for men, suits or dresses for women.

In warmer climates, such as in Cairns, a more informal attire, such as safari suit or dress shorts without a jacket or tie, is permissible.

Allison notes that everyone in Australia speaks English. You would introduce yourself by providing your full name and then firmly shaking hands.

Business meals are eaten at restaurants, rather than private homes. Says Allison: "Exchanging gifts is not the norm. However, for international business meetings, it would be appropriate to give a small present that represents the area that you are from, perhaps a tie, baseball cap, or pin."

Australians are "informal and friendly," Allison claims, and the most common faux pas an American makes when doing business with an Australian is "perhaps not listening enough." "Don't be frightened to admit when you don't know something. Australians will not hold it against you. In fact, the reaction would most likely be one of increased trust for not bluffing your way through."

CANADA

There are two official languages in Canada, English and French, although English is spoken almost everywhere except Quebec and in some parts of New Brunswick and Nova Scotia. (When you call the Canadian Consulate in New York, the operator answers, "Canadian Consulate, *bonjour.*")

Canada is a more formal country than the United States. *Conservative* is one way to typify how the Canadians conduct themselves in business. Businesspersons are less inclined to get on a first-name basis than are Americans.

Business dress is similar to that in the United States, with men wearing suits and ties and women wearing business dresses (more often than suits). But businessmen may dress in a more European way in a Canadian city, such as Toronto, which has more to do with fashion.

It is customary to shake hands in business. Business entertaining is more likely to be done at a restaurant than in someone's home. Any kind of food would be appropriate except for official Canadian functions, when something distinctively Canadian might be served, such as sockeye salmon from the west, Arctic char (type of trout), or Nova Scotia salmon. British Columbia produces cider, and Ontario and British Columbia are developing their own wines.

The worst faux pas an American doing business with a Canadian might commit is to say to a Canadian, "You and I, we Americans . . . ." Canadians are touchy about being taken as Americans. Just because Canadians speak English does not mean they see themselves as American, and it is presumptuous to think they should. In fact, if Canadians feel any ties, they would be sentimental ones—to England.

Business hours are about the same in major Canadian cities as in the United States, with most nonretail businesses closed on Saturdays and Sundays.

There are women in business in Canada, but overall women are seen in a more traditional light than in the United States.

CENTRAL AND SOUTH AMERICA

Although specific customs may vary in Venezuela or Argentina, Axtell points out certain generalizations for all these countries that you should keep in mind when you are doing business. For example, those in Central and South America have a different idea of what is appropriate "personal space" or distance from another person. They will tend to stand closer to you when you speak, and that is perfectly correct. (If you pull or step back, it may be seen as impolite.)

As in Japan, business cards should be printed in both English and the local language.

It is acceptable to be thirty minutes late.

Lunch is the main meal of the day throughout Latin America, often followed by a siesta (nap).

Gift-giving is customary; perfume for women and men's accessories for men are appropriate gifts.

Sociable is one way to describe those of Central and South America. It is not uncommon for a business meal to last hours.

PEOPLE'S REPUBLIC OF CHINA

Trudi Gallagher, a real estate sales associate with Houlihan Lawrence, Inc., in Armonk, New York, spent a year in China with her husband, who was sent there by American Express. Says Gallagher, "*Patience* is the number one thing for the Orient (China, the Philippines, Hong Kong)." Gallagher suggests sitting back and watching Asians, rather than taking the initiative, until you know their rules.

In China, business entertaining is done banquet style, big affairs, with two to four tables of eight to ten persons at each table. The host is in complete control of what occurs. No one starts to drink or eat till he does, and no one leaves until the host gives the signal. Gallagher explains that the project her husband came to China to accomplish reached an impasse. Rather than be upset or discouraged, the Chinese businessmen explained what happened philosophically. They said, "We loved your husband. He is a teacher to us. China isn't ready. It wasn't your fault. It wasn't our fault."

Very few women in China are in business, except for such small operations on their own like a grocery store or selling factory-overrun clothing.

According to *Mastering Business Etiquette and Protocol* by Marilyn Pincus, there is some business-related gift-giving in the People's Republic of China. But any gift-giving should occur *after* all business transactions have been completed. One gift to avoid is a clock, since the word for clock in Chinese resembles the word for funeral. "Small mementos are appreciated" and ". . . Offer a good reason for presenting the gift. The recipient can use it to justify accepting it," writes Pincus.

ENGLAND

"First and foremost is the British attention to detail," says Linda Phillips, co-director with her husband Wayne of the Executive Etiquette Company in Taunton, Massachusetts. The Phillipses lived in England and were privately tutored on the business manners of the British.

Formal is the rule in England. Says Phillips:

> *Even in correspondence, take the more formal approach. You would never, never address someone by their first name, unless they give you permission to do so. The American style is more casual. We tend to call people by their first name. That would be unconscionable in England.*
>
> *The idea of titles is important but you never give yourself an honorific [title]. You will hear an American doctor say, "I am Doctor Smith," but in England he would say, "I am John Smith," and someone else calls him "Doctor Smith."*
>
> *The British are very formal in introductions. Whose name is said first in an introduction is very important. The Japanese bow. The British look for whose name is said first. You're introducing someone to another person. For example, in a business situation, the client would have priority in an introduction because the client is the most important person. Let's say the client's name is John Smith. "Mr. Smith, may I present Mr. Robert Brown, the president of our company." In this instance, the client's name is first because the client is the more important of the two. If introducing a colleague to a superior, the superior's name is first.*

Business dress in England is formal too, with women wearing business suits or dresses and men wearing a suit and a tie. Hats are removed after entering a building.

Axtell points out in *Do's and Taboos Around the World* that it would be poor manners to talk with a British person about business after the business day. To the British, "shoptalk" should conclude with the end of the workday, even if you have drinks or dinner with a business associate. Phillips explains further: "Never discuss business until after food is ordered unless a client has brought it up first. This is a courtesy to the staff [waiter]."

Phillips also points out that you have to use "silent service" to let the waiter know you are through with your meal, which is indicated by the way you place your utensils. If you are still eating, but are resting, cross

your fork over your knife. "That cross says, 'Don't remove my plate.' " If you
have finished, place your knife and fork in a parallel position. "Let's
pretend that your plate is like the face of a clock," says Phillips. "The tong
of the fork and the blade of the knife would be pointing to somewhere
between eleven o'clock on the face of the clock and the tips of the handles
would be around five o'clock in a parallel position. The fork tines are
down."

A lot of business in England is conducted over tea. Linda Phillips shares
the intricacies of the tea ritual so you will handle yourself in the proper
way:

> It is always afternoon tea, never high tea. In fact, high tea is
> considered slang. It is really a poor man's supper. It comes
> from the contraction of "isn't it high time we had something
> to eat." But in the United States you often see in hotels a
> listing of high tea and of course the British would laugh at
> that. It's really afternoon tea. You never hear them say "high
> tea." That's a common American faux pas.
>
> The tea is very important to the British, and it comes in
> courses. You're first presented with a choice of tea. Your
> waiter or waitress would identify which types they are serving.
> You would choose the type you like and it is brought to the
> table. It is loose tea and it would be accompanied by another
> pot, which would contain hot water.
>
> When it's brought to your table, you allow it to steep or
> brew or mash for a few minutes. Then you would pour. Of
> course, if you were taking someone to tea and you were the
> host executive, you would say, "May I pour?" and you would
> offer them the tea first. You would put the strainer on their
> cup so it would collect any loose leaves, technically called
> bastard leaves. You'd pour that into the cup and you would
> pour the tea into the cup. Then you would take the strainer
> and rest it on a bowl of its own. That bowl is called the slop
> bowl. You take those bastard leaves, emptying into the slop
> bowl, and resting the strainer on that bowl. If the tea is too
> strong, add a little hot water.
>
> You either drink the tea black or with milk and one lump
> or two of sugar, never with cream.
>
> Sandwiches, such as watercress or cucumber, would
> accompany the tea. You eat with your fingers because they
> are finger sandwiches.
>
> After the tea and sandwiches, you have the scone. A scone

*is a small sweet-tasting bread with raisins. You bring a little
bit of butter and jam to your side plate. You cut the scone in
half and you only butter or jam the portion you're going to
bite. You don't butter the entire scone. The real test is how
you eat a scone. You spread the jam and butter as you eat it,
bite by bite.*

*You may end the ritual of tea with a little bit of Sherry, and
with a little bit of luck, you'll be celebrating a new account.*

FRANCE

Cautious is the word to describe the French in business according to
Howard Seligmann, an investment attaché, who lived in France for six
years and is married to a French woman. Says Seligmann: "There is a
protocol in France. There is not as much correctness as [with] the British
but the French are cautious."

Conducting business over meals is common in France. A business
lunch may last from an hour and a half to two hours. A business dinner,
including entertainment, could last the evening.

Introductions have to be made by someone known to the person you
are doing business with—through an attorney, a banker, or a friend. "But
once the introduction is made and legitimacy is proven, the door is open,
of course," says Seligmann.

There are fewer women business executives in France than in the
United States.

Even though most Frenchmen speak English, many will not admit it so
it is probably best to bring along "someone of respectability," says Seligmann, "who can speak the language—an acquaintance, another business
associate."

Business entertaining is done at elegant restaurants more often than at
someone's home.

GERMANY

Barbara Chizmas, head of Chizmas Business Etiquette International,
based in Redlands, California, lived in what was formerly West Germany
for three years, working primarily with German executives. There is
greater *formality* in Germany than in the United States. Chizmas talks
about German formality as well as other aspects of German business
manners, such as introductions, seating, dress, and conversation:

Introductions are the same as in the United States—you say the higher-ranking person's name first. If it is a very formal presentation, use the word "presents." "Herr Schmidt, may I present Frau or Mrs. so-and-so." If less formal, say, "Herr Schmidt, I'd like you to meet Frau so-and-so." You present the less important person to the more important one.

Dining etiquette is distinguished by the Germans eating continental style—holding the fork in the left hand continually and the knife in the right hand. You never put the wrists below the table. In America you have the left hand in the lap when you're not using your knife. Anytime you eat European style, you have both wrists on the table.

The biggest difference in the way Germans conduct business is the degree of formality. They are very reserved and very formal. In fact, people often perceive them as unfriendly. Where we [Americans] strive for instant rapport, they look upon it almost as a negative. They make appointments very far in advance. To do anything on the spur of the moment, such as making an impromptu presentation, is not appreciated. They would consider that a lack of planning. For example, I would talk about the vacations I was planning three or four weeks in advance. They plan their vacations six months to a year or more in advance.

There is also a strong emphasis on punctuality.

Dress is conservative. Men don't have to wear dark suits to the extent that they do in other countries, but pants are still taboo for women.

The whole culture is geared to women staying home. All the stores close by 5:30 P.M. and they're closed Saturday at noon. Once a month, there is absolute bedlam when they have "long Saturday" with stores open until two.

Lunch is the big meal of the day. School children, and even many people who work, come home for lunch for about an hour to an hour and a half every day.

Lunch is the main meal for business meetings.

Ask permission to take notes at a meeting.

Don't ask where they were during the war and don't even ask if they're married or not, or if they have children.

When you're speaking with a German or shaking hands, never leave either hand in your pocket. That is considered very disrespectful.

Use a translator if you're conducting business and you are not fluent in German.

INDIA

Food customs are very important. Most Hindus are vegetarians and consider the cow a sacred animal, so try to avoid eating meat in the presence of a Hindu. Muslims will not eat pork or drink alcoholic beverages.

Do not be offended if you observe cow manure drying on the tops of walls throughout Indian cities and towns. It is used for fuel.

Once again, try to observe the customs of those you are doing business with, although western-type meals are available in all major Indian cities such as Delhi, Bombay, or Madras.

There are dozens of religious groups in India, in addition to the Hindus and the Muslims, such as the Sikhs, who identify themselves by the turbans they wear and do eat meat, and the Jains, who practice non-violence and do not eat meat, honey, or root vegetables (such as potatoes, radishes, turnips, or garlic), and do not engage in certain professions such as agriculture or trade.

Almost everyone you will do business with in India will speak English. Greetings are the same—"Hello" or "Good morning." A more formal greeting is to join palms of both hands together, but shaking hands is perfectly acceptable.

Wear business clothes that are acceptable there. It is unnecessary for women to wear saris when they do business in India. If they do wish to wear a sari, they should be sure to wrap it in the traditional way and to wear one only to a party, not for any official purposes. Instead, women should wear a suit with a regular knee-length skirt, or a pantsuit. Pantsuits are even worn by Indian women—in two styles, depending on whether the top is loose-fitting or more tailored to the body.

When I was doing research in India and stayed with a family in Bombay, the emphasis was on the honor I bestowed on the family for staying with them. When I left after a few days, the family gave me gifts—a beautiful sari, food, and some trinkets—to thank me for being their guest.

Be careful not to overtip in front of residents. They will explain to you that this may spoil the rickshaw drivers or other service workers who will expect more from them.

Remember there is a very strict caste system in India. Be aware of the caste of the businesspeople you are dealing with and any restrictions they may have—such as not being able to mingle with lower castes—so you will not ask them to do things against their principles.

Do's and Taboos Around the World suggests two things: punctuality and using your right hand to accept or pass food. It also suggests avoiding conversations about personal matters, India's poverty, military expenditures, or the large amount of foreign aid. Men are cautioned not to speak to a woman walking alone in public, or to touch a woman.

ISRAEL

Straightforward is the word Howard Seligmann, Investor Attaché for the Israeli government, uses to describe Israelis. "Sometimes Americans will be surprised by the straightforwardness or straightforward attitude that Israelis have as opposed to trying to hide something."

Seligmann, who lived in Israel for a year and has been there many times, explains some of the common business practices:

> *Israel is very cosmopolitan. You greet someone with either a "Shalom" or "Hello." Virtually everyone speaks English as well as second or third languages, especially in the business environment.*
>
> *When you introduce someone, you would say, "This is Howard Seligmann." After one or two meetings, we might even call each other by our first names. Even at the first meeting, someone might say, "Why don't you call me Howie."*
>
> *Giveret is a terminology [word] which, in Hebrew, since the beginning of time has meant Ms.*
>
> *Many times a restaurant will serve both Middle Eastern food like falafel or humus as well as Western food. Nobody will be looking to put you under pressure [to eat Middle Eastern food].*
>
> *[Business over meals?] It's a way of doing things. It is a way of working. It is acceptable as well as having a meeting and inviting someone for dinner afterwards. It is not impolite to discuss business at dinner. Discussing family is a nice thing. But in the rest of the Middle East, it is an insult to mention one's family [in a business meeting].*
>
> *If you are coming from America, a gift is unnecessary [for a business dinner]. But a small book for someone's child would be appreciated, or flowers for someone's wife.*
>
> *Israelis are serious but physically [their physical appearance is] very casual. You have a business executive who might not be wearing a tie. They'll wear a jacket and have their shirt opened up, or [wear] a dress shirt and not a tie.*

There are more women in the business world in Israel than in most other countries. After all, women serve in the army and one of Israel's great leaders was Golda Meir. (One out of three doctors and dentists is a woman, notes Seligmann.)

ITALY

Having a certain *reserve* is how an Italian trade analyst describes Italian businesspersons, that is, they are quite formal.

In business, you introduce yourself by saying your last name only, such as "Smith," and then shake hands. Even women shake hands. The custom of kissing a woman's hand is more likely in a social situation than in a business one.

Italian businesspersons are more conservative than American ones and they dress more formally.

Do not assume that all Italians speak English when you are doing business. When in doubt, bring a translator along.

Business entertaining is done at restaurants, not in the home. In Rome, businesspersons take a long midday break and work until 7 P.M. In Milan, business hours are more comparable to American ones—9 A.M. to 5 P.M.

Gift-giving varies, though it is customary to give something nominal as a Christmas gift, such as a bottle of cognac or something like that.

What is the worst faux pas an American could make? Said an Italian businessman: "The biggest failing of Americans until recently is to think that all Italians come from Sicily, or speak with a Sicilian accent, simply because the majority of Italian Americans come from Sicily or Southern Italy. Italy is a vary varied country, where there are all types of physical types—short, tall, fair, dark, redhaired. Not really one prototype Italian. Likewise, there are different colloquialisms and different dialects and accents and different customs."

JAPAN

According to Diana Rowland, author of *Japanese Business Etiquette*, the exchanging of business cards is extremely important when starting to do business with the Japanese. Rowland, who heads San Diego-based Rowland and Associates, a company that trains people who want to do business with Pacific countries (Japan, China, Singapore, Hong Kong, the Philippines, Australia, and New Zealand), explains why:

> *Business cards are extremely important because the Japanese are very hierarchical. Two people need to determine right away what their relative status is. The most common way of doing that is by exchanging business cards.*

They will first of all look at [the card to see] the company you work for and its relative status to theirs. If one comes from a very large prestigious company and the other comes from a smaller firm, then the person from the larger firm is going to have a higher position than the one from the smaller firm. [They look for] your position within the company. The title has to be very clear, which is not easy because we don't have the same exact positions in America as Japanese companies, but you need to get as close as you can. For example, we might have hundreds of vice-presidents at an American company, but the Japanese usually have only one.

Business cards are a representation of the person so you need to treat them with care. Don't carry them in your wallet stuck in your rear pocket. Have a card holder and carry it in a front pocket or inside a coat pocket. Women may carry it in a holder in their pocketbook.

Always treat their card with respect. Don't clean your fingernails with it or pick your teeth with it. I've seen Americans do this.

Giving or receiving anything with two hands elevates the other person. This can be important when meeting someone of a much higher status. If the person is of a lower status than you, you could be sending the wrong message. But it's always better to err on the side of being polite in Japan.

If the person is of a lower status than you, give it with one hand, and receive their card with one hand. But it's still nice to hold their card with two hands, or hold it with your right hand and touch it with your left hand as you carefully read it. If you don't pause to read it, it implies that the person you received it from is not important. Make remarks about it. "Oh, you're the section chief of the products department," or something like that.

Put Japanese on the reverse side [of the business card], but be sure it's a good translation. I know of somebody from a telecommunications research company that had his cards translated for free . . . when he got to Japan, everybody he gave it to laughed. He was head of the light guides department, which had to do with fiber optics, and it was translated as "Chief Lighthouse Keeper."

According to *Do's and Taboos Around the World*, shoes should be removed before entering a Japanese home. The first greeting is not a handshake but a "long and low bow."

Use a complete name—never just your first—in introductions. "To say 'Mister (last name),' simply say the last name and add the word *san*," writes Axtell.

It is best to avoid talking about World War II.

Punctuality is important.

It is perfectly acceptable to talk about business after the workday. In fact, the Japanese carry their business meetings into the evening hours at the geisha houses, private clubs, bars, and nightclubs that they frequent.

How would Japanese business etiquette expert Rowland characterize the Japanese? "Extremely formal," Rowland says. "They place a high value on protocol."

What is the major faux pas to avoid when conducting business with the Japanese? "Certainly pushing to get right into business" explains Rowland. "It's a long-term prospect in Japan. The thought is that once you decide to do business with somebody, it's like deciding to get married. Very rarely is it a single transaction. A lot of time has to be spent investigating a person or the corporation ahead of time and deciding if this is a person they feel good about working with the rest of their lives." Another major mistake Americans might make, according to Rowland, is to be informal in a formal situation. Work is a formal situation. "Telling jokes or touching people, things like that, are simply not done during work hours," says Rowland.

THE MIDDLE EAST (Algeria, Egypt, Jordan, Saudi Arabia, Iran, Iraq, Libya)

According to *Do's and Taboos Around the World,* here are some overall suggestions if you visit Middle Eastern countries (see separate entry for Israel)*: All business activities cease five times a day for Islamic prayers. Although visitors need not kneel to or face Mecca, you should respect your host's right to do so. During Ramadan, the ninth month of the Islamic calendar, work ceases after noon. Thursday or Friday is the Muslim day of rest and worship.

Outside the home, handshakes are common. However, your host may greet you in his home with a kiss on both cheeks, which you should duplicate. Like Japan, business cards should be printed in English on one side and a translation into the local language on the back of the card.

---

* Because of its invasion of Kuwait, a boycott on doing business with Iraq was imposed in the summer of August 1990. Check to see if that, or any other, restriction still applies on visiting or doing business with Iraq.

Avoid talking about religion or politics. You should be on time, but your host may be late.

Use only your right hand to eat. There is a prohibition against pigs, pork meat, or alcoholic drinks.

SOVIET UNION (U.S.S.R.)

Jankowic and Bernstein point out in *Behave Yourself!* how important it is for people doing business in the Soviet Union to remember the unique political system in that country. However, as the Soviet Union revises its economic policies and attempts to conduct more business with the rest of the world, some etiquette and protocol issues will undoubtedly change.

Business hours are 9 A.M. to 6 P.M., with an hour at noon for lunch. Dress is conservative—dark suit, white shirt, tie.

Jankowic and Bernstein point out that all business meetings have to be made far ahead and confirmed in writing with official approval.

What faux pas should you avoid? Calling the country Russia, rather than the Soviet Union, and calling an associate a "comrade," a term reserved for only Communist Party members.

John Wagner, Director of Mission Support for FMCS, the Federal Mediation and Conciliation Service, spent two weeks in the Soviet Union doing business for FMCS and the Academy of Sciences. Wagner did not find the Soviets to be always punctual, but they were genuinely concerned if someone was late. Explains Wagner:

> *I was doing a number of presentations and training*
> *for a whole host of audiences. I made myself on time.*
> *I didn't always get to speak on time. There were so*
> *many contingencies that were always coming up. I*
> *don't think they were particularly offended that a*
> *program didn't start at nine o'clock. I think they*
> *might worry if they don't know where you are—about*
> *your well-being as an individual—rather than starting*
> *on time. They would worry about what happened to*
> *you. "Let's make sure we know where he is."*

Since credit cards may not be accepted in a restaurant, bring cash. Tipping is discouraged "but it never hurts to leave a small amount of money on the table," writes Jankowic. Wagner comments that you may also tip with goods. A pack of cigarettes is welcome or a small gift of your country, like a memento of Washington, D.C., or a United States flag. Says Wagner: "They're very much into enamel pins, such as a pin of your profession, or flags, especially if it shows the Soviet and American flags together."

SWITZERLAND

According to real estate sales associate Trudi Gallagher, who was born and raised in Switzerland, the Swiss are basically very frugal people who spend their money only on things of good quality. Says Gallagher:

> *The standard of living is extremely high. The Swiss are very private people and it will take a long time for a foreigner to be invited into a home. There is one similarity the Swiss and the Germans share in that they have the polite (Mr./Mrs.) or the familiar (first name) forms of address. If you meet someone and call them Mr. and Mrs., you probably will call them that forever.*
>
> *The Swiss entertain in restaurants and hotels. It takes quite a while for them to get to know you, and to invite you to their home. They are very private people and are closed-mouthed.*
>
> *The Swiss adapt easily and are very inquisitive. Four languages are spoken within the country. Everybody will try to speak English when you visit Switzerland. Tourism is one of their main industries so they want to accommodate foreigners.*
>
> *The biggest faux pas is comparing them to the Germans. Or breaking your word. When the Swiss give their word, they mean it. They are also very punctual and very correct. Down to making sure the i is dotted.*

In the next chapter we will look at how to behave at a business breakfast, lunch, or dinner.

Chapter 7

The Business Breakfast, Lunch, or Dinner

Combining business with eating may be one of the most effective ways for a rising executive to move up even faster—as long as he or she shines in those situations. But business breakfasts, lunches, and dinners all have their advantages, disadvantages, and distinct rules. Some overall standards and tips apply, such as basic table manners, but there are other guidelines you should know about that will increase the likelihood that these eating events will thrust you forward on your professional ascent.

The business breakfast, for example, may be the best meeting time for business executives who work straight through lunch, whose lunch calendars are booked weeks in advance, or who need to get together to prepare for an event happening later that day. But the business lunch may be the least compromising food-related circumstance for a male-female business interaction to occur. The business lunch is far less ambiguous than the business breakfast, which could raise questions of where the pair spent the night before, or the business dinner, which could evoke gossip about where the pair will go at the end of the evening.

The business lunch is a marvelous opportunity to get better acquainted with those you work with and for, whether that means your clients, co-workers, superiors, or subordinates. For example, a consulting firm with 3,000 employees that is based in Illinois has a policy of its unit managers and groups going out for lunch or dinner instead of giving Christmas gifts, with guidelines in terms of reasonable expenditure and time away from the office.

Since success in practically every business these days rests on *relationship-building*, the informality of and added time available for a business lunch, versus a rushed meeting in the office or a faceless telephone conversation, may enhance your career.

There are, however, drawbacks to a business lunch if you fall into the trap of any of the following practices:

1. Showing such poor table manners that your prestige is lessened.

2. Blurting out too many inappropriate personal things about yourself so that your professional image is compromised.

3. Having so many alcoholic drinks that you are viewed as having a drinking problem; or if you become tipsy, offensive, or just plain drunk, and end up insulting other guests or even jeopardizing your career by arriving back at the office in bad shape.

Otherwise, the business lunch is a fun and productive opportunity to do business, get you midday nourishment, and feel connected to those you work with and for. One benefit of the business lunch over the business breakfast is that you may be more awake and relaxed at noon or 1 P.M. versus 7 or 8 A.M. Also, having a business lunch on your calendar, you may be in especially top form that morning, accomplishing so much at work that you exude confidence and self-esteem at your business lunch meeting. You might also have been using some of that time between arriving at work and meeting for lunch to make last-minute preparations for your business lunch, so that you can accomplish more than if you just rolled out of bed and into a business breakfast meeting. You might find the morning hours more convenient for a 7 to 8 A.M. game of tennis, with the benefits of before-work exercise as well as a definite starting and ending time that a business breakfast lacks.

Lois Wyse, co-founder and president of Wyse Advertising, says in her chapter on "The Power Lunch: Getting What You Want on the Table," in her book, *Company Manners*, that the power lunch is so important that the editor of *Good Housekeeping* magazine gave up hosting a noontime radio show because, " 'The job of an editor is to have lunch.' "

Wyse personally feels it is important to get out of the office at lunchtime, whether or not you have a power lunch planned, even if all you do is go to a museum or take a walk. She finds she needs to personally connect to the world during the lunch period. "It's depressing to stay in the office and have yogurt at your desk on a regular basis," writes Wyse.

Another advantage of the business lunch is that people who are otherwise not accessible to you—because family or even recreational commitments eliminate any time for getting together except during office hours—can be yours if you make that phone call and invite them to lunch. You may have to compromise about *where* to have lunch—if you are going to get more out of the lunch or if you initiated it, you may want to volunteer to go to your invitee's neck of the woods than have him or her travel all the way to where you work—but at least you get to connect and keep that all-important business-related relationship going.

A key business-lunch-related idea to remember is that you should not throw around the phrase "Let's do lunch" to a business colleague unless you mean it. The business lunch is serious business to anyone in the work world; only suggest it if you mean it. If you mean it, set up a specific time and date. If you only mean you would like someday to do lunch, state that as well, "When we get over this pretax deadline crush, let's find time to do lunch," a harried but sincere accountant might say.

If you invite someone to a business lunch and you go to a restaurant, food selection is up to the two of you. If you invite several persons to the executive dining room, you may want to plan the menu with the help of the chef so that your lunch seems more formal and prearranged. It also takes on a more cohesive feeling when all four participants eat the same foods, a course at a time.

Some companies today even employ a chef, and keep a small corporate dining area (that may double as a conference room when the meal is finished) in recognition of how important the business lunch, as well as serving good food, has become to the business community. If you are hosting the lunch, the menu you select, as well as the quality of the food you provide, just like the suit or dress you wear and the way you speak or write, are part of your company or business image. Take the time to plan a menu that is imaginative but not so extreme, like tongue as an appetizer, that few want to partake of your selections. Those in the business community, however, look forward to diversity at the business lunch as one of the perks of working.

Many of the concerns regarding the business dinner are the same as for lunch, namely the type of invitation you will extend—verbal or written; where the meal will occur—a company or public facility versus a private home; and the food and refreshments that will be served. (As an invited guest, your main concern is making sure you RSVP.) Other than the business dinner, business entertaining is discussed in the next chapter, Written Invitations and Executive Entertaining.

There are some differences between the business dinner and the business breakfast or lunch. First of all, it tends to be more formal than the business breakfast or lunch. This formality extends to the way invitations are made—usually in writing rather than by phone—as well as to the kind of dress expected. Whereas the attire worn to work that day is perfectly acceptable for the business lunch, the business dinner may require a change of clothes, especially for women, to something of a dressier nature.

Another consideration for someone hosting a business dinner which is not usually a concern for a business lunch is transportation. If possible, it is polite to provide transportation for your guests, especially transportation home for those guests who did not drive private cars to the dinner. Another concern is entertainment or music, which is more likely to be provided at a business dinner than at a business lunch. That entertainment might include a guitarist, a chamber ensemble, recorded background music, or even a standup comedian employed just for this occasion.

The business dinner also requires a decision about whether the dinner will occur on a weekday night or a Saturday night. Although most business lunches will occur during the Monday through Friday workweek, it is possible to have a business dinner on a Saturday night, especially if the dinner includes guests from a variety of companies who work in different parts of a city and have conflicting hours. For those types of dinner guests, getting to a dinner on a weekday night might be more of a hardship than giving up part of their leisure time on a weekend.

Finally, the business dinner requires a decision about whether or not spouses or romantic partners are included, rarely a consideration for the business breakfast or lunch.

Business dinners allow for more creativity in terms of place and menu. Rather than just your typical company dining room or restaurant catering to the business trade, you have a range of interesting places and experiences to choose from—from chartering a boat or yacht to take your guests down the river while they dine, to renting an elegant dining room that has the feel of a dinner party at a private home but is really part of a tastefully renovated townhouse whose owner is a gourmet chef and whose dinner guests are all private corporate dinner parties. (See the appendix for some sample business dinner menus.)

When you mix business with salad at lunch or with an appetizer at dinner, remember that the business comes first. Even if you or your business-lunch colleagues slip in some appropriate but personal information, such as the college or graduate school you attended, or family-related tidbits that somehow tangentially apply to the topics at hand, the primary focus should be business. Let's say you are a consultant and are meeting with a potential client. You might spend most of the lunch just chatting about work-related issues, but not quite zoning in on "closing the sale," so to speak; focusing on the business aspect of the lunch should occur by the time you finish the entree and before dessert and coffee, if not before. If you are the one with the stronger business agenda, it is important that you keep in control throughout the lunch and get the business part of it accomplished. It is frustrating to have a pleasant business lunch, to feel connected to your colleague, boss, or potential client, to even feel positive enough about the connection to pick up the rather large tab, only to realize an hour or so after the meal ends that you failed to do the business that was the initial reason for setting up the meeting.

Having a business lunch that is pleasant, nonpressured, yet true to its business motives might at first be difficult to pull off effectively, but with practice, it is possible.

By the way, be careful not to boast too much at a business lunch about how busy you are, or that potential client or employer might say, "I guess you are too busy to do a job for us," a point of view you have unwittingly created that may be hard to undo.

Consider your goals when you decide if you will ask someone to, or accept an invitation for, a business breakfast, lunch, or dinner. Could your business be conducted better in the office than in a food-related setting? Is the more casual atmosphere of a lunch in your best interest? If persons from a variety of firms or locations are involved, perhaps a business dinner is better since it allows more flexibility about arrival and departure times as well as the location of the dinner?

"Be up front about why you are taking someone to lunch," says business etiquette expert Randi Freidig. Since any kind of meeting that revolves around a meal may take from one to three hours of someone's time, make sure it is warranted. Continues Freidig: "Maybe it is something that could have been sent to them in the mail or you could have referred them to the right person. Everybody's trying to balance their lives, so be very respectful of people's time. Maybe you could do something over the phone. But sometimes people like to get away from the phone, and a meal is a fairly uninterrupted time to do so."

WHO?

The first "who" to consider is with whom it is productive and appropriate for you to have a breakfast, lunch, or dinner meeting. The first scenario is where you know the person you are having breakfast with, either because you work together or have had dealings before, and breakfast is simply the most convenient time for both of you to have your meeting. Or you might have lunch with a co-worker as a way to combine eating with discussions about a project you are working on together.

In the second scenario, the breakfast meeting is your first meeting with each other, possibly following up several phone calls or letters. In that case, your ability to quickly and accurately size up the person you are meeting with will help you to know how to handle yourself during the breakfast meeting as well as in the relationship that may ensue. A meal is more open-ended than a meeting at an office. Should you open yourself up to that situation with a person or persons unknown to you? (See Chapter 9 for a discussion of the "types" you might first encounter at a breakfast or other meeting.)

The "who" of these business-related meals is important, especially if you initiate the meetings, because usually the one who initiates the meeting picks up the tab. Except for extenuating circumstances where the meeting is considered of mutual benefit and the more senior person picks up the tab, be prepared to pay for the meal if you do the inviting; otherwise, avoid a meal situation.

WHERE?

Once you decide that a breakfast, lunch, or dinner meeting is appropriate, where to have it is a matter of what type of eating facility fits your needs. Just some of the numerous options are the coffee shop near your office, the executive dining room, the breakfast room of a hotel, an elegant restaurant, a restaurant near a tourist attraction, the hotel suite of a visiting business executive (only if this is not compromising; and it may be better to have other colleagues along), or someone's home or apartment.

The choice of location should be a matter of courtesy and consideration. Do you wish to impress the other person, or does he or she wish to impress and please you? It shows consideration if you travel to a restaurant that is close to someone else, so keep that in mind when the place you meet is chosen. But you should also consider such etiquette issues as whether the person you are having breakfast with has a physical problem that might make it more reasonable for you to go to him or her; for example, if someone is in a wheelchair, is in the later months of pregnancy, or has a foot in a cast.

Another concern is who will get more out of this meeting. Is it in your best interest to ingratiate yourself with the person you are meeting with by going closer to his or her neck of the woods? If you do want to be the one to pick the place, it is more likely to happen if you are armed with a list of three possible restaurants and their addresses.

Try to pick restaurants that reflect the business level of the people you are meeting. In major cities, the dining room of a nice hotel can often be an elegant and quiet place to have a meeting, especially since most of the hotel's clientele (and staff) are geared to breakfast business meetings. But it can also be expensive, so be prepared with a credit card, ample cash, or the expectation that someone else will pick up the tab. If the person you are having breakfast with is staying at that hotel, it is probably better to suggest meeting at another hotel dining room, or he or she might think you are manipulating payment of the bill onto his or her room charges.

If a man and woman are having a breakfast meeting, make sure it is at a public restaurant, or if someone insists it will be easier to talk in a hotel suite with room service sending up breakfast, make sure there will be enough persons along to ensure a professional meeting without any possibility of hanky-panky or of rumors flying. If necessary, bring along your secretary or a co-worker to neutralize a situation that could be potentially anxiety-provoking or even damaging.

WHEN?

For some, the earlier the better when it comes to having a breakfast meeting—6 or even 7 A.M. is more convenient than 8 or 8:30 because it means they might get into work too late. Be careful you do not compromise yourself by agreeing to the earlier hours. This could happen not just by being seen coming out of a restaurant with someone at 7 A.M. but by being too tired at that time in the morning to function, let alone conduct a meeting and have a meal. If the time someone picks for a breakfast meeting is just unworkable for you, try to arrange a meeting in his or her office at a later time, or even a lunch date.

If a business lunch is more convenient for you or for those you care to dine with, be prepared to allocate at least two or more hours for your meeting and meal (depending on how far you have to travel and the kind of restaurant chosen), or it will seem too rushed.

A business dinner, depending on its starting time, may last anywhere from two to four hours. If the business dinner is truly combined with work, it may last until 11 o'clock at night. If possible, be considerate of the social and family obligations of those you are dining with when you consider what kind of meeting—breakfast, lunch, or dinner—would facilitate your professional goals. For example, a working mother who has to scramble to find evening childcare and deal with the stress of not putting her two toddlers to bed that night might find it more considerate if a meeting could be conducted over lunch rather than an evening dinner meeting.

ACCEPTING OR CANCELING

Any meeting arrangement implies a promise to another person that you will appear at the agreed-upon time and place. For breakfast, lunch, or dinner meetings, there may be other people involved for whom your presence is considered essential, whether that means other participants in your meeting or even the restaurant that has reserved space for you and your meeting party. Furthermore, the persons with whom you have agreed to meet have blocked out time in their busy calendars to be able to have this meeting with you. Once you accept an invitation for a meeting—or your invitation is accepted—you and the other participants are obligated to follow through on that business function. Terms that should be agreed upon include the who, where, and when of the meeting. If someone tries to change them, you can reconsider the meeting, if necessary. For example, if you are under the impression you will be having a private breakfast meeting and your invited guest calls to tell you he plans to bring along his secretary and a manager visiting from another city, you can decide if this breakfast meeting is in your best interests and if you have to follow through on it. It might be better to reschedule for a more convenient time when it can be just the two of you.

If you have to cancel, do it as soon as you realize you have a conflict that prevents you from keeping your appointment. A reason for your decline is unnecessary, but if you want to provide a reason, make it believable and sincere without being so detailed as to be inappropriate. Try to be tactful when providing reasons for canceling so that the person you are canceling with does not feel less important than your new commitment. Attaching the reason to obligations rather than to individuals may prove helpful. For example, "I am closing on a new co-op apartment and I have to meet with my broker at the time we were planning to have breakfast," instead of "I have to meet with my broker." Or "I need to work through dinner to get this report to the printer by our deadline" instead of simply saying "I cannot get away for dinner tonight."

To offset the disappointment of canceling, try to reschedule immediately for another time and date. Reassure the other party or parties involved that you do not foresee anything interfering with your next meeting. Apologize profusely for canceling, since you do not want to get a reputation for being unreliable.

SEATING

When you enter a restaurant, first check your overcoat and briefcase. (Of course, keep with you any materials you may want to present during your meeting.) By checking your coat, you avoid the problems that may occur if you place it on the back of your chair and someone walks by and accidentally knocks it down. If there is no place to check your coat, see if there are coat hooks or a self-service coat rack somewhere in the restaurant. Certainly if there is no one responsible for these self-service situations, take any valuables, including an expensive coat, along with you to your seat.

If you or those you are meeting made a reservation, it is polite to wait until your entire party arrives to be seated. This is because waiters do not make any money if you are sitting at a table awaiting other guests. They could lose one or two seatings of tips that way. (If you frequent a restaurant often, as a courtesy you may be allowed to be seated in advance.)

Always wait until a table is completely cleared and reset before you sit down. The host will lead the way for a woman, who will then have her seat pulled out for her.

As Marjabelle Young Steward and Marian Faux point out in *Executive Etiquette*, if you have to spread out papers at a meeting with just one other person, you still might want a table for four, rather than for two, and then you might have good reasons for wanting the other person to sit at your right rather than across from you, or vice versa.

At a business dinner, it is customary to separate spouses in the seating arrangement—whether by putting other people between them at one table or by seating them at separate tables if there are two or more tables. This allows married couples to converse easily with others. Unless there is a very good reason to take objection to this practice, try to comply.

Here is a seating arrangement that William Thourlby in *Passport to*

Popular Seating Arrangement at Home or in a Restaurant [Reprinted with permission from *Passport to Power* by William Thourlby (New York: Forbes/Wittenburg & Brown, 1990).]

	Guest	Co-Host	Guest	
Male Honored Guest				Female Honored Guest
	Guest	Host	Guest	

Power indicates is a popular one when entertaining at home or at a restaurant. Writes Thourlby: "The host and co-host (or couple) take their places on opposite sides of the table, indicating that honored guests are to be seated at the ends of the table, usually with the woman guest to the right of the woman host."

TABLE MANNERS

Table manners were discussed in Chapter 2 in the section on image. In this chapter, I want to emphasize that at any type of business meeting involving food, whether it is a breakfast, lunch, or dinner, your table manners are easily scrutinized. Try not to exacerbate the situation by eating foods that are uncomfortable for you. As etiquette expert Randi Freidig notes: "Remember you are there for business first, not to eat. Don't order things you love to eat but are real difficult and messy things, like French dipped sandwiches and French onion soup. For me, since I was brought up by Norwegians on meat, potatoes, and gravy, I have a hard time with fettucini. I have to concentrate a lot on getting the fettucini from the plate to my mouth."

Stick with familiar foods and eat slowly since that is polite; it also indicates you are confident, reserved, and in control of yourself and your food.

Smoking is tolerated but less acceptable in the United States, although some diners may still want to smoke at the table. Smoking should not be done at the table. A smoker should ask to be excused at an opportune time, and smoking should be done at designated smoking areas in a restaurant or outside the hall of an apartment or in the outside open air. Depending on how much you want to ingratiate yourself with the smoker, particularly foreigners for whom smoking is still more acceptable, you may decide to allow him or her to smoke at your table. The smoker should always ask, "Do you mind if I smoke?" to the host or hostess, although it would be even nicer to make sure everyone at the table is in agreement. If the smoker does not ask if anyone minds, and you or another guest does mind, try to voice your objections in a neutral way, placing the blame on a medical problem rather than the smoker's offensive habit. For example, say, "I'm sorry but I'm allergic to smoke. Would you mind smoking on the terrace?" If the smoker is the guest of honor, you may decide to let him or her smoke without such comments or restrictions.

As mentioned before, the meal is the excuse behind the business that is to be conducted, so try to stick to business. If you do talk about something else, make it interesting conversation rather than personal matters.

WHO PICKS UP THE TAB?

Etiquette dictates that whoever initiated the meeting, or whoever is in a senior capacity, should pick up the tab. However, there are exceptions. For example, if one person is on a business account and the meeting is business-related, and the other person is a freelancer or self-employed, the salaried person who can charge it as a business expense may want to pick up the check even if the other person initiated the meeting. You might also suggest going Dutch if there could be any possibility of misconstruing the situation as an attempt to win someone's favor when neutrality is essential. (This is true of many persons in the media, such as journalists or television reporters, for whom accepting even a business breakfast could be misinterpreted as attempting to influence someone and might be looked upon unfavorably by employers.)

When it comes to lunch in a corporate dining room or lunch in a restaurant with one person as the host or hostess, it should be clear from the format of the business lunch that the host is taking care of all costs (except possibly tips for the coat checker or the bathroom attendant, if an outside facility provides such services).

HOW ABOUT A THANK YOU?

Although the formal, written thank-you note may be more commonly associated with more elaborate executive entertaining, saying at least "thank you" after the event is important for the business breakfast, lunch, or dinner as well. Claudia Kahn, who is head of corporate public relations for Merrill Lynch, says that a failure to send thank-you notes is one of the most overlooked aspects of business etiquette. Says Kahn: "We go out of our way to encourage sending thank-you notes," especially whenever an executive is invited to a business dinner. Kahn thinks it is important to send thanks, yet people tend to forget, or fail to make it a priority, so they make time to do it. Therefore it may be nice to telephone a thanks, but a written one is more proper.

In the next chapter we will look at written invitations and executive entertaining.

Chapter 8

Written Invitations and Executive Entertaining

Sometimes it will be more advantageous to your career to have your executive entertaining outside of the business breakfast, lunch, or dinner meeting. Whether you initiate and host the event, or simply attend it, executive entertaining demands the same planning and attention to image and appearance that you are giving to every other aspect of your career. What are some of the do's and don'ts of executive entertaining? Will a holiday party further your career? If so, should you be the one to host such a party or simply to attend it? If you do host a party, should the guest list represent employees at all levels in your department, or just those at your level? These are some of the questions to consider about executive entertaining that we will answer in this chapter.

Executive entertaining should be considered carefully from a male-female standpoint as well. Having a business party at a restaurant or club may be less compromising than if it is in a home or apartment, especially if spouses are omitted from the guest list.

In her chapter, "The Art of Business Entertaining" from etiquette expert Letitia Baldrige's corporate Bible, *Letitia Baldrige's Complete Guide to Executive Manners,* the following four criteria are suggested for how we do our business entertaining:

- Time available

- Resources available

- Cost of what you wish to do

- Importance to your business objectives of the person you are entertaining

All four guidelines need to be considered whether you decide to organize or host a business lunch, dinner, or other type of business entertaining. The resources available could be the on-site facilities at your company, such as the executive dining room, employee cafeteria, or a conference room; or outside facilities, such as a coffee shop, restaurant, college or graduate school alumni club, athletic or social club, or a private home or apartment, yours or someone else's. *Time* considerations might influence whether you entertain in the nearby executive dining room or in a faraway restaurant. Will you entertain on a weekday or over a holiday weekend? Will you allot two hours or from 8 P.M. on?

Cost relates not just to *where* you entertain and *what* is served, but to every detail about your business entertaining, such as *invitations*, support personnel, such as waiters or waitresses (tipping or employing, if in a non-restaurant setting), possibly a bartender, coat checker, additional maid or clean-up services, and transportation costs if you plan to provide such a service for some or all of your guests. *Food* and *beverages* are significant cost factors, whether included in the prix fixe at a restaurant or computed by adding up the costs of catering or purchasing refreshments.

INVITATIONS

Invitations are another necessary aspect of business entertaining, whether that means a simple phone call to a business associate with the offer "Let's meet for lunch," or a more formal invitation elegantly written by a professional calligrapher and customized for each of the twenty guests at a business dinner party. (See sample that follows.) In all but the most formal dinners or parties, verbal invitations over the phone are acceptable.

If invitations are to be printed (or handwritten by a professional calligrapher), you must allow at least three weeks for just that task. Allow three weeks for giving the text to the printer, having it typeset, and checking over the proof before the invitations are actually printed. Add another three to four weeks for addressing and mailing the invitations, especially if you have upwards of a hundred to address.

> *Dear Fred and Jan,*
>
> *Toni and Bill*
>   *cordially invite you to be*
>   *our dinner guests at the*
>   *Country Club*
>   *New Jersey*
> *on Friday, December 15, 1989*
>
> *Cocktails will be served at 7:00 pm*
>   *and Dinner at 8:00 pm*
>
> *Happy Holiday*
>
> *RSVP*

Whenever written invitations are involved, allow at least two (preferably three) months from the time you decide on the dinner or party until the time you print, mail, and receive replies on your invitations. If you do your inviting by phone, a minimum of two weeks' advance notice is acceptable; however, during certain times of the year when there is a proliferation of competing business entertaining events, such as the period of Thanksgiving through the New Year, or around Memorial Day or July 4th, when company picnics and family outings are common, an extra week or two may ensure that your invitation gets priority treatment and scheduling, compared to others that arrive afterwards.

Although Letitia Baldrige finds engraved invitations with blank spaces to be filled in by hand in black ink to be acceptable and economical for business entertaining, I personally dislike the look of such an invitation. I find it far more elegant—and not that much more time-consuming—to write each entire invitation by hand or have the handwritten master copy offset at a photocopy shop (rather than printed in more costly raised lettering). Here is a completely handwritten invitation:

Mr. Harry Smith
requests the pleasure of your company
at 7 P.M.
on Tuesday, June 1st
at Brian's Restaurant
One Main Street
R.S.U.P.

Or you may use a simple store-bought preprinted invitation with an elegant cover, such as the one on the opposite page that has "You Are Invited" printed in gold script on the cover of the invitation. This type of invitation requires that you write in all the specific information.

Following are some examples of classic formal invitations. The first one is for a book publication party hosted by a publisher. Two hundred fifty of these invitations, printed with black, raised ink on white card stock, were hand-addressed and mailed out three weeks before the date of the party.

Only fifty copies of the second invitation (see page 142) were printed and mailed out. To save money, the printing is not raised thermograph but flat. Because it was a business party in a private home, a formal invitation seemed more appropriate than an informal one, or even a phone call, since it tried to emphasize the business, rather than social, nature of the entertaining.

All written invitations require a return address clearly printed or written on the envelope. Nana Greller, who worked with Letitia Baldrige, points out that the post office will not return undeliverable invitations unless the return address is on the upper left-hand corner of the front of the envelope. This is in direct opposition to the more conventional style of placing the return address on the back flap of the envelope. This preferred style is decidedly less elegant than the back-flap style, but you have to weigh that fact against the importance of getting back invitations that cannot be forwarded or delivered. (See sample on page 142.)

You Are Invited

For <u>Private Reception</u>
Date <u>December 30th</u>
Time <u>6-8 PM</u>
Place <u>main Street Plaza Gallery</u>
<u>Des Moines, Iowa</u>
R.S.V.P.

Doubleday cordially invites you to
celebrate the forthcoming publication of
MAKING YOUR OFFICE WORK FOR YOU by Jan Yager, Ph.D.
and to meet the author
on Tuesday, July 25th, from 5:30 - 7:30 P.M. at the
Decorative Arts Center (4th floor)
New York, New York

R.S.V.P.

Jan and Fred Yager
cordially invite you to a
Holiday Open House
Tuesday, December 20th, 1988
from 6-9 P.M. at their home
New York City

R.S.V.P.

Preferred Placement for Return Address on Invitation Envelope

---

RSVPs

Unless you accept instantly an invitation extended in person or over the phone, all business lunches, dinners, parties, or other events that you are invited to require a proper RSVP (response). Business dinners and executive entertaining, the more formal types of business entertaining, require the most care about providing an RSVP. Unless the person inviting you is a personal friend who might be offended if your secretary called on your behalf, the person doing the RSVP is not as important as having it done. If there is a time specified on your invitation—"RSVP by December 4," comply with that date. If no date is specified, respond with a definite yes or no immediately. If you are undecided, take into account the type of affair you have been invited to in terms of how long you may wait until you give a definite yes or no. If food needs to be ordered, or the number of yes or no guests changes the set-up of the affair—such as needing one table for dinner versus two or three—give as much notice as possible, preferably at least a week.

Whether your invitations are printed or written in preprinted commercial or company invitations, allow enough time for your guests to respond to it. There is nothing more embarrassing (and frustrating to the guest) than to receive an invitation on November 25 for a function on November 26th that says "Please RSVP by November 22." You can blame the post office if you want to, but you have to allow enough time for creating, addressing, and mailing invitations since ultimately you and your staff are the ones to fault in these situations. (By the way, the inviter of the above example did confess that she did not even mail out some of her invitations until *after* November 22, a week later than she was supposed to.)

If you decide to RSVP in writing, and a preprinted acknowledgment card is not provided, send a short handwritten note, centering each line, like the sample that follows:

> Mr. John Jones
> accepts with pleasure
> the kind invitation of
> Mrs. Cynthia Graham
> for Friday, the fifteenth of December

If you must decline an invitation, do so by phone or in writing, following the format of the handwritten, centered acceptance note, with these sample words:

> Mr. John Jones
> regretfully declines
> the kind invitation of
> Mrs. Cynthia Graham
> for Friday, the fifteenth of December

You need not give a reason for declining.

The most important thing to remember is that all business invitations require some kind of RSVP. An invitation has been extended to you and you either have to accept or decline. Ignoring the invitation is the height of poor etiquette. It can undo months or years of good business rapport with someone you never would intentionally miff or offend in other ways. Also note that if at the last minute a yes becomes a no, or vice versa, call and tell your host or hostess. Do not just show up unexpectedly, or fail to appear, if your plans have changed.

EXECUTIVE ENTERTAINING

There are numerous possible occasions for executive entertaining beyond the business breakfast, lunch, or dinner, including:

- Celebration of an individual's promotion, award, or some other kind of professional achievement
- Celebration of the completion of a project or of a particularly hard job done by a group or even the entire company
- Departmental or companywide annual events such as the company picnic or holiday party
- A quick way for a new department or company head to meet and socialize with his or her new staff
- A celebration of an individual's achievement, such as the opening of an art show or the publication of a book; or a time of year, such as the beginning of the new fall season or the new year

Proper seating can make or break any event, especially if you entertain a small group for dinner. Merrill Lynch executive Claudia Kahn notes that seating is one of the hardest aspects of event planning. "Make sure you haven't seated someone next to somebody they dislike or have problems with," says Kahn. She adds that not only should everyone be seated comfortably, but if flowers are on the table, you should be careful that no one's view is obstructed by them.

If your business entertaining takes place at a restaurant or corporate dining room where you have little choice over the type of table your guests will be seated at—square, rectangular, oblong, round—at least consider preselecting the seating arrangement and concretize it by arranging elegant place cards at each place setting. In that way, you are taking control of the seating; you will have the best chance of making the seating work better for your needs as well as facilitating the enjoyment of your guests.

Do not overstay your welcome. Etiquette experts suggest leaving no later than one hour after coffee is served.

With the emphasis today on interpersonal relationships and not just technical skills, it is becoming more of an issue of why are you doing so little business entertaining rather than finding a reason for what entertaining you do do. Of course business entertaining takes time, money, and creativity to make it memorable and an asset to your executive image. The investment, however, is worth it if you function well in large groups. If you do not—and many people freeze up at parties whether for business or social reasons—you may be better off doing your executive entertaining in business breakfast, lunch, or small dinner settings.

Even in small settings, however, you have to be careful about your behavior. As Judi Kaufman, a Beverly Hills-based home economist/ etiquette expert, notes: "There's no question that how you come across at the table can affect the future of your career. I remember the executive here who ordered halibut, medium rare." Other etiquette mistakes in business meal settings? "A lot of talking with their mouths full," says Kaufman, "and looking totally perplexed when the table is set with formal service, or arguing with the waiter when the service is bad, especially the host himself. We recommend [that you] quietly excuse yourself and do it in private."

One of the skills that top executives seem to share—from a company CEO to the President of the United States—is the ability to "work a room." However, according to Paul Critchlow, Senior Vice President for Communications at Merrill Lynch, many rising executives lack that skill. "It always surprises me how many executives do not properly know how to mix, or work a room," said Critchlow. "The first thing they do is find someone they know, take them into a corner and talk shop.

"The more successful corporate executives, such as the two top executives at Merrill Lynch, Bill Schreyer and Dan Tully, are very good at this," he added. "When they walk into a room, they never stay with one person too long. By the time they're done, they've connected in a small way with everyone in that room. They make everyone feel important."

According to Critchlow, the key to working a room is not being shy.

"People, by and large, like to talk about themselves," he explained. "Ask questions. 'What's your name? What do you do? Where do you live?' It really does open people up very quickly. Be careful not to get into a position where you're just talking about yourself, unless that's your assigned job."

If large parties are uncomfortable for you, there is help available for those with social phobia, as it is called. One such program is a twelve-week course of cognitive behavior therapy led by Dr. Richard G. Heimberg, director of the social phobia treatment program at the State University of New York at Albany's Center for Stress and Anxiety Disorders, as reported by Dava Sobel in "Social Phobia" in *The New York Times Magazine*. If you consider yourself shy, you are not alone. A survey of 10,000 Americans conducted by Stanford University social scientists found that 40% listed shyness as one of their personality traits.

But if parties do not overwhelm you and you know how to "work a room," executive entertaining on a grand scale may be perfect for you. If you plan to be the host or hostess, once again you have to pick the appropriate place for your soiree—outside or at home. If at home, you may have to rent extra chairs, serving utensils and trays, cutlery, and dishes, as well as a place to put the coats, if the event takes place during the cold or rainy seasons. You will probably want to have food available in buffet style, unless you have tables and chairs for a sit-down party of twenty or more.

If your executive or holiday event is held at home, you should have the essential equipment for a home bar, unless you plan to serve only wine or all nonalcoholic beverages. See the appendix for a list of items to include in a home or office bar. Sample menus for business or holiday parties are also included in the appendix.

The business holiday party may be a joyful, useful executive event, or it can be the downfall of someone's career if he or she behaves badly. Some companies, recognizing the stress that is caused by the company holiday party, have abolished it. In the mid-1980s, BBDO, the advertising agency, eliminated its companywide Christmas party. Former chairman and CEO of BBDO Worldwide Inc., Norman W. Campbell, explains: "I think from a lot of years of Christmas parties that it was an event people were not as comfortable with as they might have been." No one at BBDO complained that the company was giving its 4,000 plus employees off from Christmas Eve until the day after New Year's as an extra vacation week instead of having a Christmas party. Campbell continues: "One particular issue of increasing concern by companies over the years is their liability in the event of alcohol-related accidents."

However, other companies find that a Christmas party helps to reduce stress. Lee Hecht Harrison Inc., a national outplacement consulting firm headquartered in Manhattan, gives a Christmas party for all its clients who are looking for new jobs. Says co-chairman Dr. Robert M. Hecht: "The party is a way of celebrating that there is a support system there, a sense of cohesiveness, even though they no longer have an office or any of the benchmarks related to a job. Since our clients also get to meet our entire staff and each other, the party also serves a networking function."

Are families included in most company holiday parties? A survey of 1,104 companies conducted by ADIA, a nationwide employment agency, found that 64% invited spouses and guests to holiday Christmas parties to increase the participation of families, notes Marcia Pear, a former associate director of ADIA's communications, who now has her own company. I once attended a Christmas party hosted in a loft by Barnes and Noble for all its employees and their spouses and children. It was an impressive occasion with lots of food, music, and decorations, a yearly event that employees and their families eagerly anticipated from year to year.

Indeed, for independent or freelance workers, such as writers, consultants, public relations advisers, anyone who is primarily a solo practitioner, or salespersons who need to reconnect to the home-office staff, holiday parties sponsored by the home office or professional associations that they belong to, or parties that they give themselves for colleagues, associates, or clients, may offset some of the social and professional isolation less familiar to those who work in more typical nine to five (or eight to six) corporate settings.

But remember that your behavior, whatever type of entertainment setting is chosen—breakfast, lunch, dinner, party, holiday bash—is always under scrutiny. Good manners and etiquette apply *especially* in these seemingly unofficial settings. Ironically, it may be even more important to scrutinize your every word, as well as what you wear and how much you drink or eat, in these pseudosocial situations, where you might be tempted to let down your guard, than even in the obviously business face-to-face meeting with your boss in his office. Business entertaining may stimulate the interpersonal relationships that help business to grow, but it is still primarily a business, not a social interaction.

One dubious custom associated with executive entertaining should be mentioned in a book on business etiquette—the corporate "roast." This is the custom of roasting, or saying lots of nasty things as an "inside" joke about someone in their presence in the guise of humor. Roasts occur all the time as a party-like event that celebrates someone in business, such as an employee who is nearing retirement; some in the entertainment industry receive national publicity in this way. You, however, should be careful about being one of the roasters. Although everyone may laugh at the time, the long-term wounds created by biting comments about a co-worker, superior, or subordinate may taint your image long after the roast, the reason for the negative comments, has been forgotten. Rarely is anything positive gained from criticism and biting put-downs, no matter how much it seems to be sanctioned by the custom of a roast. If you can get out of speaking at a roast, do it. Pass the buck to someone else in a positive way: "I think someone who has worked with so-and-so longer might be in a better position to roast him" or "I heard you already have eight people to do the roast; one more might take too much time." Assure the person asking you that you will attend the roast, enjoying the occasion, and thank him or her for asking you to attend. But avoid insulting someone else, especially publicly, and be discrete about laughing at other people's criticisms when you attend the roast as a guest not as an active roaster or participant.

In the next chapter we will look at the types of individuals that you might encounter in a work-related situation, and the best ways to deal with them.

Chapter 9

Types You May Encounter in Work-Related Situations

It is useful to know what "type" of person you are meeting or working with to avoid making any faux pas. By accurately and quickly sizing up someone you meet, you may avoid unwittingly offending someone. If you believe someone is not trustworthy, you could avoid making any compromising revelations about yourself or your company.

Increased social mobility means that mixing is more and more important. Making the most of a business breakfast, whether it is with someone you have just met or a co-worker, is one way to network and get further up the ladder. Networking is, after all, a skill that may be learned, and with that skill business success often is facilitated.

You will encounter many different types of people at breakfast, lunch, or dinner meetings, at your company, or in working with clients or customers, but chances are they will fall into one of the following categories.

THE COURTSHIP TYPE

The courtship type needs to be courted before making any decisions. If you are dealing with this type, you should not, under any circumstances, pressure them into a "yes" or "no" on a particular subject at your first meeting. With courtship types you are better off having several meetings, with some time between each one, than trying to get an answer right away. For this type, the wooing and the process of getting this person to say "yes" is as important as the final decision. Courtship types will prefer working with you, rather than others, if you indulge their indecisiveness by giving them even more items to choose from, whether that is pictures of possible houses to buy, several projects that might be worked on, or ways of completing a certain task.

THE NEED-FOR-CLOSURE TYPE

In contrast to the Courtship type, the Need-for-Closure type must come to closure by the end of your meeting. To deal with that type, make *something* concrete happen, such as "I'll call you on Monday" or "I'll send you a copy of that article I told you about," especially if *you* want to avoid a "yes" or a "no." Since there is this need for closure, you have to be careful that this type does not provoke a "yes" or "no" just to finalize the matter. Acknowledge this person's needs, "I know you want to finish up this project," but introduce your different approach by saying "but let's keep the door open another few weeks." Allay his or her fears by emphasizing that closure is not too far off: "Don't worry. I'm confident we'll nail down this new campaign by the middle of next month."

THE SPY

Someone who pumps you for information, under the guise of being interested in you, but does not give any information back, is a spy. Or if they give information back, it may be false or inconsequential. Spies may also be in the position to use the facts and opinions you have given them against you, within your own company or at a competing one. Be wary of someone who asks you excessive questions. If you do not see a mutually beneficial reason for revealing so much information, switch to another topic.

THE MENTOR

In contrast to the spy, mentors are those who genuinely care about others succeeding, sometimes even at their own expense. Recognizing and be-friending a mentor in a business setting can help you since he or she will introduce you to others who can also help you along. How do you recognize a mentor? If this person begins sentences with "I can teach you" or "I can show you"; or they open up their network to you by saying something like "Let me introduce you to . . . ."

THE BRAGGART

You have to listen patiently to every personal and professional achievement that the braggart has accomplished. Try to avoid drawing attention to your own triumphs; braggarts are insecure and want the platform all to themselves. It is best to let braggarts get their fill of bragging; then go on to the business at hand. Without being too obvious, give praise throughout the meal to boost the much-too-low ego of the braggart. For example, compliment their choice of restaurant (if they selected it), how they handled the waiter, or ask for any recommendations for dishes they have tried on the menu.

THE TELL-ALL

The tell-all type needs to relate every minuscule detail of what went on right before your meeting. For example, at a morning meeting, a single man or woman who had a date that was particularly pleasant or traumatic the night before might want to share the experience with you. You might just as well sit back and enjoy the tale that the tell-all shares. Be supportive, empathetic, and nonjudgmental, but also be cautious since the tell-all just may repeat to others anything personal or professional that *you* relate.

THE MANIPULATOR

Watch out for this type since everything, from what is said to who picks up the check, can be manipulated by this type, who needs to control the situation. They are really insecure people who are unable to trust their instincts as situations unfold, so they try to manipulate every sentence, every situation. Stay calm and pleasant since you understand the manipulator's game.

THE WORKAHOLIC

Workaholics are missionary in their commitment to their job, so you may have to hear about how hard they work, and what sacrifices they make for that job. Be sympathetic and congratulate them on their dedication. Avoid analyzing the psychological components of such a lopsided existence, since work is the defense that those who are frightened of relationships and free time hide behind. Workaholics will probably remind you throughout your meeting that they really do not have time for a leisurely talk—they should already be at work—so accept whatever time they can give you as the best they can offer. Workaholics have more of a need to tell you about their work rather than to hear about your own, so be a patient listener.

THE HIDDEN AGENDIST

This type gets you to a meeting on one pretext; it is only by being astute and a good listener that you learn, sometime during your meeting, that there was a completely different motive for the encounter. For example, a co-worker might ask you to lunch on the pretext of discussing a report you are working on together. It is only halfway through the meal that you realize the hidden agendist wants to find out if you would give this person a recommendation if he or she were to give your name as a reference to a headhunter he or she is seeing. It is important when meeting with a hidden agendist to switch gears easily from the presumed to the actual reason for the meeting, and to be cautious for the remainder of the meeting since the motive for the meeting might even switch again.

THE LAY PSYCHOLOGIST

This type has a need to analyze everything you say or do. Do not take it personally. However, this person does need affirmation, so humor the lay psychologist by saying something like, "How astute of you" or "That's quite an insight; you could have been a psychologist."

THE OFFICIAL HOST

This is the person who actually called the meeting. When more than two are meeting, however, you can lose sight of this distinction as others may take over this role. Official hosts, however, may be insulted if their official host capacity is questioned or overthrown. Who is seen in this light may also determine who picks up the tab or brings the meeting to an end.

THE UNOFFICIAL HOST

This is the person who takes on the role of host, even though it is really someone else who set up the meeting and is responsible for the check.

The unofficial host is a strong personality type that rarely feels comfortable in the subordinate role. If you are dealing with this type, it is best to share the decisions at the meeting, such as where people will sit, who picks up the check (if meeting at a restaurant), and when the meeting is over, rather than make the unofficial host uncomfortable and anxious.

THE NERVOUS WRECK

Avoid laughing when nervous wrecks knock over water glasses, mistake the half-and-half for milk that someone can drink, or get their sleeves in the coffee. Nervous wrecks cannot help it, and the meal setting only exacerbates their nervousness. These types are best seen outside of a food context, such as at a meeting in their office where they are most comfortable. But sometimes breakfast, lunch, or dinner meetings with them are necessary and then it is best to be tolerant and compassionate about their nervous habits and accidents.

THE SUCCESS-STORY TYPE

There are types who have achieved something that the other person (or persons) at a meeting has not yet done and feel the need to share that story with the others, whether they want to hear it or not. Success-story types have a need to share and educate, and you just might as well sit back and listen and possibly even learn something, because they need to tell it to you anyway. It could be a happily married woman telling a recent divorce how to meet someone and get married again. It could be a vice president telling a new manager how he made it to the top. Since you understand that success-story types have a need to share their tales with anyone, do not take it personally as a put-down of your own achievements. They mean well.

THE "LIFE IS A STRUGGLE" COMPLAINER

No matter how well things go for the complaining types, they dwell on the problems and setbacks they or others have faced. Being overly positive with them can just infuriate them, so listen patiently and agree that life can be a struggle without being condescending or becoming as depressed as they seem to be. Avoid bringing up all the joys in life as a counterpoint since this only fuels their angst.

THE PARENT

This type is so enthralled with every stage a child is going through that he or she cannot resist providing every fact, even if it means detailing every struggle with the introduction of solid foods or toilet-training successes and failures. The best way to deal with this type is to listen intently—do not look bored or you might seem offensive—and say something like, "Isn't that cute" or "Isn't that very advanced for that age?"

THE "ON-THE-MAKE" TYPE

Be cautious with this type and avoid saying anything that could be misconstrued as giving credence to their fantasies. Dress appropriately, avoiding anything even somewhat risqué. Similarly, avoid using any sexual double-entrendres, sexual phrases or expressions, or alluding to anything personal that could be taken as approval, on your part, of this person's behavior. This person arrives at the meeting turned on; it is your job to avoid fueling that aspect of your meeting's agenda. Neutralize the situation and stick to business.

In the next chapter we will explore a key etiquette concern—business gift-giving and receiving.

Chapter 10

Business Gift-Giving and Receiving

There is probably no other area fraught with so much confusion and unfair bad-mouthing as the business practice of gift-giving. Yet, when the motives are clearly the fostering of goodwill and relationship-building, rather than a manipulation of influence through material goods or favors, business gift-giving and receiving may enhance business and a positive business climate.

In Japan, business gift-giving has been an established institution since feudal times, notes Yumiko Ono in the *Wall Street Journal*. Called *oseibo*, it occurs during the first two weeks of December. Today, the Japanese spend over $10.5 billion each year on *oseibo*, giving such traditional gifts as seaweed, cooking oil, or instant coffee to bosses and others that they wish to impress.

Except during the holiday season, Americans do not have a set time, or type of present, that is appropriate in fostering goodwill in business. In the United States, any legitimate reason to give a gift is an excellent opportunity to cement a business relationship or to make known your positive feelings about an employee, client, or customer.

Some companies, however, because of the nature of their business or their own corporate culture, have strict policies against certain types of

155

gift-giving, such as from a client or any other company that does business with the company. These policies help to prevent a conflict of interest that might compromise the integrity of the company and its employees. The employee handbook of a major financial services institution states its policies on gifts and gratuities in this way:

> *Employees (including members of their immediate families) may not, directly or indirectly, take, accept, or receive bonuses, fees, commissions, gifts, gratuities, excessive entertainment, or any other similar form of consideration, of other than nominal value, from any person, firm, corporation, or association with which [name of institution] does or seeks to do business. Conversely, it is generally against corporate policy to give gifts or gratuities absent special approval by the General Counsel or his designee.*

When conflict of interest is not an issue, business gift-giving usually involves small gifts—everything from pens, pencils, baskets of fruit, chocolates, figurines, silver letter openers, tickets to a sports event, a book, a picture frame, a piece of clothing for a newborn baby, flowers or plants, or donations to charities in the name of the honored person, to providing a service, such as advice, tutoring, or training.

One way to control the possibility of abusing the positive business spirit of gift-giving and receiving is to keep the cost of gifts relatively small, below $50, and preferably between $10 and $25—except for very special occasions or gifts bestowed by the highest levels of a company. Indeed, U.S. government allots a maximum of $25 for a business expense for a business gift, and the President of the United States is restricted from accepting any gifts that cost more than $100.

No one is going to be manipulated into making a major business decision that goes against his or her ethics or the needs of his or her company because he or she receives a $10 basket of soaps or a $25 pen. What will be exchanged, however, is a concrete extension of the goodwill and favorable spirit shared by those who work for the same company or by certain business executives who want to convey their caring for certain clients or customers.

Letitia Baldrige suggests these additional cost guidelines for business gift-giving:

- Spending $10–$25 by junior executives or middle managers to their clients

- Spending $25–$50 by middle-to-upper managers

- Spending $50–$100 by senior executives for their top customers or close business friends

- $100 or more should be spent only on very important or rare occasions

Based on my survey of human resources managers at companies throughout the country, the most typical cost recommended for a holiday gift for an employee is in the $11 to $25 range. The question was: "How much money does your company recommend spending on a Christmas gift for an employee?" Here are the answers:

$11–$25	27%
$10 or less	21%
$26–$50	4%
Not applicable	11%
No recommendation	10%
Other	8%
None	8%
Decided by employees	4%
Not allowed	2%

Another requisite to gift-giving beyond the cost of the gift is that there be an appropriate and immediate occasion for the gift, whether that includes congratulating someone on the birth of a baby or thanking someone for inviting you to the phenomenal business Christmas party that he or she hosted. There should be a legitimate and obvious reason for the gift as well as a definite positive feeling between you and the gift-giver or receiver so that neither one will remark, "I can't believe so-and-so sent something to me." Letitia Baldrige wisely points out that you should *not* send a gift to someone with whom you are negotiating a deal; it could be seen as trying to influence the outcome of the deal.

Similarly, you should be sensitive to what is going on in your life and how your actions might be preceived by those to whom you give a gift. Look at the executive who suddenly realizes he failed to get another executive a baby gift when his second daughter was born ten months before. He now wants to get the executive a baby gift because they have become closer business colleagues in the months since his baby was born, and he feels guilty that he never gave his colleague a baby gift. Since the etiquette is that you have a year from the wedding to give someone a wedding gift, he wondered if the same rule applied to his situation. (If baby gifts are not given immediately, it loses its impact as a baby gift. Even if you technically have a year to give a wedding gift, waiting longer than a month also loses its effect.)

But, it turned out, the etiquette of giving a baby gift ten months late was not even the issue. This executive's wife was expecting their second child within a month. The couple decided that it would look as if they were setting it up so the other executive would feel obligated to get them a baby gift if they suddenly gave his child one. (If the gift had been given at the appropriate time, that is, immediately, this issue would not have come up.) Instead, the couple decided to let it go and if the executive got their baby a gift they would then get his child a gift out of reciprocity.

Incidentally, if for any reason you feel it is inappropriate to accept a gift—your company forbids it, you think the gift is too personal or too expensive for a business situation, or you fear a gift might compromise you in any way—return it as soon as possible, including a brief note that might say, "Thank you for your recent gift, but I am unable to accept it." Keep a copy of your note for your files and make sure you return the gift in a way that you receive a written record of its return, which you also should save in case you need that documentation in the future.

Reciprocity is an important aspect of gift-giving. The fact that most people feel obliged to return a gift of equal value is a rule of human nature that you can use to your advantage in the business world. That is why gift-giving—like Christmas cards (discussed in the next chapter) or executive entertaining (discussed in a previous chapter)—is usually a question of keeping the scales balanced since you get what you give. If you receive a gift from a client and fail to send the client one in return, the relationship will be off balance. For that reason, it is important to be sensitive to how you handle the gifts others give you, as well as the ones that you give.

REASONS FOR GIFT-GIVING

In general, the reasons for giving a gift in business are to advance goodwill or to advertise and promote a product or a service. Gift-giving is one way of demonstrating that you practice one of the basic etiquette principles advanced in the first chapter of this book, namely, showing an interest in others. By giving a gift to denote a special occasion or event, you are taking the time and trouble to show an interest in someone else's life. Your thoughtfulness is probably more memorable to the recipient of your gift than its monetary value (especially if you follow the $50-and-under rule).

In all situations considered appropriate by the company and society, such as a married executive having a baby, find out if the company policy is to send a card, a gift, or even have a shower for a female. If the situation is viewed somewhat more ambivalently, such as a single woman having a baby, it is proper to recognize the joyfulness of the event, but greater discretion may be more appropriate in such situations. Similarly, if someone you work with is getting married, how grandiose a celebratory display you should engage in may be tied to the circumstances. For example, more discretion should be used if one of the two parties has just gotten out of a difficult divorce and there are children involved than if the pair is unattached and in their thirties.

What is important is that you acknowledge all these events in some way appropriate to your relationship and the circumstances. Even if you just send a card to someone who is sick, you are doing something to indicate your concern about those you work for or with. The boss of a forty-year-old woman who works both as a secretary and a production assistant on shoots for the production company of which he is part owner, gives her a lavish reception when she marries, and that is appropriate. The editor at a newspaper gives his secretary a $50 gift certificate as a present when she marries, also an appropriate gesture.

Within the general motivations of advancing goodwill or advertising for gift-giving, here is an extensive list of more specific reasons for sending a gift to those you work with, clients, customers, or service providers (those who deliver your mail, dry cleaners, hairdressers, waitresses or waiters who frequently service you, accountants, florists, physicians, dentists, etc.):

Congratulations

- Birth of a baby
- Wedding
- Promotion
- Earning an award
- Write-up in the newspaper or magazine
- Appearance on television
- New job or the opening of a new store
- Graduation

- Notable achievement of any kind, such as acquiring the hundredth client, achieving x amount in commissions, selling x number of books, selling the first painting, etc.

Good Luck

- Retirement
- Special birthday (21st, 30th, 40th, 50th, 60th, 75th)
- Special wedding anniversary (every five years up to the 30th, then the 40th, 50th, and 60th)
- Special work-related anniversary
- Relocating to another division, town, or city
- Switching careers
- Buying a new house

Thank You

- For an extraordinary job done during a difficult time (usually recognized by a boss of his employees)
- For a rush job (of a service provider, such as a printer)
- For doing someone a big favor that is completely optional
- For showing you around when you were in another city
- For hosting you at a special business breakfast, lunch, dinner, or other event

Apologies

- For a misunderstanding
- For offending someone
- For forgetting or failing to attend an important event such as a store or gallery opening or a holiday party

Expression of Caring or Sympathy

- For death in the family
- For illness

- For bad career or financial setback such as losing a job, declaring bankruptcy

- For upcoming surgery or recovering from hospitalization

THE WHEN AND HOW OF GIFT-GIVING

We have already established that the closer the gift-giving is to the time of the event that the gift acknowledges, the better. Of course there is common sense involved here. A birthday present that arrives a month late looks a lot sillier, and loses almost all of its impact, compared to a present for a promotion that arrives a month after the event.

You may need a master list that is revised on a yearly basis to help you to keep track of birthdays, anniversaries, and holiday gift-giving that reoccurs from year to year. (A way of keeping track of gifts you receive and give is provided at the end of this chapter.) This master list could be arranged on a month-by-month basis with a code for each type of gift; for instance, just the name and date for a birthday, an asterisk (*) before the date for an anniversary, such as the first day working at the company, and two asterisks (**) or an H before a date for someone who should receive a holiday gift. Here is a sample list:

Master List of Birthdays, Anniversaries, and Holiday Gift-Giving

January

    5—Marilyn Williams (secretary)

February

    *12/87—Marilyn Williams (anniversary of first day on the job)

March

    15—Brian Jones (boss)

December

    H—Marilyn Williams

    H—Wayne Little (receptionist)

    H—Tom Wyatt (colleague who provides advice and help throughout the year)

Giving a gift in person need not be a steadfast rule. First of all, a lot of gift-giving is done for long-distance relationships; indeed the gift is a way of cementing a relationship that is harder to maintain than the one you have with a nearby co-worker with whom you have lunch once a week. In those long-distance situations, giving a gift in person is impractical. Also your motives may be questioned if you try to get an appointment with a busy executive so you can give him or her a gift. The gift may then look like an excuse for getting your foot in the door, and the emphasis will shift away from the real reason for the gift.

Remember, with gifts, as with the questions people ask you, you are only responsible for being appropriate as to the *why, what,* and *how* of your gift, not for the response of the recipient. People react in all sorts of ways to receiving a gift and it could have little to do with you or your gift; it could have everything to do with their own unconscious views of themselves that makes it comfortable or uncomfortable to receive gifts from others (or their company may prohibit gift receiving). Someone with low self-esteem may actually feel uncomfortable and angry because you have given him or her a gift. If a nice, appropriate gift seems to elicit anger rather than gratitude, try not to take that reaction personally; it is a reflection of the temperament and psyche of the receiver rather than a reaction to your appropriate and thoughtful gift. (If, however, you know someone has a reputation for disliking gifts, avoid stepping into such gift-giving situations that will backfire and consider an alternative, such as a card or providing a service.)

Any gift should be wrapped nicely, even if it is an inexpensive item, like a small box of chocolates. Think of the wrapping of the gift as the first impression your gift creates—just as the clothing you wear and the office you work in are other first impressions you make in the business world. Keep a supply of all-occasion wrapping paper in your office or at home— red polka dot or multicolored striped paper is suitable—as well as a package of assorted bows for that extra touch.

How a gift is presented can endear you to someone as much as the gift itself. You have to be creative and show you really know the person to whom you are giving the gift if it is to have its full impact. For example, a vice-president of communications went to Scotland for a week with his wife to celebrate their thirtieth wedding anniversary. Upon arriving at their hotel in Edinburgh, they found in their room a bottle of champagne elegantly displayed in a basket with a card from both the chairman and president of the company congratulating them and wishing them a wonderful trip. It was the perfect gift, and having it waiting for them in their hotel was the perfect way to present it. It would have been far less effective if someone had given the executive a bottle of champagne on his last day at work before his trip began.

Another important issue to keep in mind is that except for rare exceptions, such as congratulating someone on a marriage or a birth, gifts should be exchanged with employees or clients, customers, or service providers but *not* upward to bosses. The implications of giving a gift to a boss are obvious; however, if a boss and an assistant have a tradition of exchanging Christmas presents, that precedent should be respected. In those exceptional situations, the employee should be careful that the gift is within the appropriate price range and that it comes from the heart, reflecting a truly exemplary working relationship. When all those guidelines are followed, a boss may point with pride for years to a gift from an employee. A top executive at an advertising company in New York, for example, keeps the sterling silver miniature basket that her secretary gave to her one Christmas on her desk, using it as an unusual business card holder. Another executive brings home with joy the eight enormous balloons that his secretaries surprised him with for his birthday.

Whatever gift you give, try not to be overly commercial. In other words, especially if you are in a product business, if you give a sample product, or engrave a gift with your company's name or logo, make it discrete and secondary to the gift itself. An attractive calendar with your company's name, address, phone number, and slogan imprinted discretely in the corner will impress the gift recipient more than if the calendar looks like a self-serving advertisement that someone would be less likely to use or display.

Practically every gift can be inscribed or engraved but, once again, consider if that will further the reason you are sending the gift. It might be as useful to enclose a business card with your gift, or have packaging with the company's vital information that can be removed, so just the gift remains.

An inexpensive but impressive way to give numerous gifts without breaking your bank account is to accumulate little figurines or craft items at any time during the year when you are traveling. If you spend a week in the Outer Banks of North Carolina and you have the foresight to buy examples of local balsa wood carvings for under $10 you will be set for holiday gift-giving. All you may need are boxes and wrapping paper. (If you wait until right around the holidays it will be harder to come up with such a unique and attractive gift for under $10. You will probably end up spending a lot more money or getting something trite or cheap looking.)

Here are just a few of the many inexpensive gift items that are appropriate as business gifts:

- Photo album (especially for wedding, birth, anniversary, or retirement)
- Picture frame
- Reference (dictionary, thesaurus, etiquette guide) or other books (especially if you know the hobbies or interests of the recipient, such as cooking, fishing, interior design, or detective stories)
- Illustrated calendars
- Cooking supplies
- Coffee mug
- Desk accessories such as paperclip dispenser
- Engraved stationery
- Gag gifts (upon leaving company or getting a new job; select carefully)
- Drinking glasses (for engagement, wedding, or anniversary congratulations)
- Decorative or serving bowl
- Jewelry
- Pen
- Pencil
- Perfume
- Photograph (framed)
- Prints (framed)
- Scarf
- Travel items (for a new job requiring travel or an upcoming major trip)
- Watch (retirement, departmental gift to secretary at holiday time)

If you wish to emphasize the advertising and promotion aspect of the gift you give, you can have any of the above-mentioned gift items engraved or imprinted upon. Several mail-order companies specialize in doing just that, and some of their products are inexpensive yet useful and attractive. Products that are especially popular as business-promoting gifts as well as being useful to your clients or customers include:

- Calendar

- Calculator

- Golf balls or golf tee

- Luggage tag

- Key ring

- Mug

- Napkins

- Pads

- Pen or pencil

- Playing cards

- Pocket magnifier

- Ruler

- Sports cap

- Teddy bear (with imprinting on removable shirt)

Flowers, instead of a plant, may be a more appropriate gift for a new mother or someone who is convalescing, since plants may require too much care for someone who is facing new responsibilities or health concerns. Flowers make the same point and can be left behind for other patients in the hospital or be brought home.

Some etiquette experts suggest that times have changed, so that men may receive flowers as a gift, not just women. It is my observation, however, that flowers may be provided for a male executive's desk on a steady basis for decorative purposes, but a gift of flowers would still make most men uncomfortable. A way to avoid embarrassing the male executive you are sending flowers to, or having your giving flowers backfire, is to ask his secretary if he ever received flowers as a gift and, if so, what his reaction was. The best advice about flowers for men, however, is that when in doubt, give something else.

Some individuals may prefer a donation to a favorite charity in lieu of flowers at the time of bereavement. Check with the executive's secretary to find out what the executive or his or her family prefer before you automatically send flowers.

Another gift that has to be given with caution is any type of liquor. First of all, you want to be sure that the person you are giving liquor to does in fact drink and drinks whatever liquor you choose, whether it is scotch, gin, vodka, or wine. Not only should you give the kind of liquor someone drinks, but it should be his or her favorite brand, if possible. Once again, a call to the executive's secretary may provide you with the information you need. If you know you will be giving an executive liquor for an upcoming event or for the holidays, and you dine together beforehand, make a note of what he or she orders, or somehow get a conversation going about different brands of favorite drinks to determine what the executive in question favors.

GIVING OF ONESELF

It is also important to note that some of the best gifts are the ones you give of yourself, rather than the ones you buy in a store. These gifts should be valued and acknowledged by those to whom you have given them. If they are not treated in the same way the recipient would treat a wrapped present, then you are wasting your valuable time and talents on the wrong people. For example, say you are an expert in office management. You might provide someone who just got a new job with a half-hour of your valuable time, advising him or her on how to set up a new office. This gift could be volunteered by you or in response to a request for help. In any event, such time and effort should be treated as a present and acknowledged in the same way you would acknowledge receiving a sugar bowl for a wedding present.

You might be in a time crunch and someone else's secretary types up your report. That too is a gift and you should acknowledge it appropriately. It is especially important to ask those we refer to a business associate to express gratitude appropriately, for their poor manners reflect upon us. The niece of a business colleague, for example, called me and asked if I could help her find a weekend house at the beach. I gave her the name and phone number of someone I knew who was looking for additional house members. A few weeks later I heard from the man that she had, indeed, become part of their household for the summer. But the woman never called to thank me for my suggestion. A few months later, when I saw her aunt at a business function, I commented on her niece's behavior and she said she would say something to her about it. The point is that we all want to avoid being commented about in a negative way. When someone helps beyond the call of duty, show gratitude.

Visiting someone sick in the hospital is another example of giving of oneself. However, you should be certain that your visit is appropriate.

Male bosses may feel uncomfortable visiting a female employee at the hospital because of the bed clothes or bathrobe she might be dressed in, just as a female boss might feel uncomfortable visiting a male employee in the hospital. Use your judgment about when such visits are appropriate and when they are not. (You should also make sure a sick or hospitalized employee wants visitors.) It might be better to send flowers to the hospital, or wait to visit the employee at home. If the situation might be a compromising one, another possible solution is to visit the hospital or the home with one or two other co-workers or employees, or to send another employee as your representative. Sometimes a thoughtful phone call will go a long way in such situations; the employee might actually prefer it to being visited by co-workers, superiors, or subordinates.

THANK-YOU NOTES

Presents require a thank-you note or a phone call of thanks—notes or greeting cards do not—so let us consider what makes for an effective thank-you note.

You may recall in the executive communication chapter that we distinguished four criteria of effective writing—thought, readability, correctness, and appropriateness. Thought, the content of your writing, is what you say in your thank-you note. If possible, avoid clichés like, "Thank you for your lovely gift"; be as original as possible. Try also to be specific in what you write. Say something about the gift—what is means to you, why you are pleased with it—or about the gift-giver. Avoid flowery language, or exaggerations, like "This is the most fantastic pen-and-pencil set I have ever received," unless, of course, it is the truth.

Readability, or clarity, is best accomplished using short words, sentences, and paragraphs. A few well-chosen words about the gift is what is called for. For overall length of the note, use your discretion. Your best friend who is also your client might be miffed by just two lines, whereas a distant business acquaintance you rarely interact with might find two well-chosen lines about his wedding present just fine.

The correctness of your thank-you notes refers to the grammar and spelling you use. As noted before, use whatever aids you need—dictionaries, thesaurus, grammar texts, on-staff or freelance communication editors or experts—to make sure your thank-you note is as correct as any other piece of executive writing that bears your name.

Appropriateness, the tone of your writing, requires that you tailor the tone of your thank-you note—your choice of words, how informal or intimate a style you follow—to fit the person to whom you are writing as well as the occasion that the gift denotes. A thank-you note for a promotion present to a close co-worker will have a different tone than one for a donation on behalf of a deceased relative made by the chairman of the board.

The best way to judge the effectiveness of any thank-you note is to ask yourself: "If I received this note, how would I react?" Is it interesting? trite? thoughtful? exaggerated? Good writing often means rewriting, so feel free to make notes, and even drafts, before writing the final one.

If you and other family members, such as a fiancé (or fiancée), spouse, or child (in the case of graduation gifts), have jointly received a gift, you must decide whether you alone will write the thank-you notes or whether the others will help you. In a business situation, it may be more appropriate to write on behalf of the other recipients and sign the note, "Carol Konrad and family." If the other person is willing, he or she could write a second, short note.

You have to decide if you will use imprinted thank-you cards, small-size stationery imprinted with just your name, or illustrated cards (with paintings, flowers, or other decorative images) for your thank-you note.

KEEPING TRACK OF GIFTS RECEIVED OR GIVEN

Keeping track of when you acknowledge a gift is an efficient way to make sure you have fulfilled this part of the gift-giving process. Consider purchasing a book, such as *The Lifetime Book of Gifts and Invitations* by Richard Borah (North Woodmere, New York: Leichester House, Ltd.), which provides a place to record every gift received (or given), the date, from or to whom it was given, the occasion, a description of the gift (if given, where bought and cost), and if an acknowledgment was received or sent.

Or, if you like, you can create your own gift-giving and receiving master list by creating master sheets that you then photocopy. A prototype appears on the next page that you can photocopy and reuse.

In the next chapter, we will look at the practice of giving or receiving cards, especially Christmas cards, or notes for special occasions or events.

Gifts Given

Given to	Date	Reason	Gift Description	Cost	Where Purchased	Thanks Received

Gifts Received

Received From	Date	Reason for Gift	Description of Gift	Thank You Sent

Chapter 11

Giving or Receiving Cards or Notes

If you are afraid that even a modest gift of under $10 could be misconstrued as an attempt at influence-peddling, if you are on a tight budget, or if gift-giving is simply not your style, consider sending cards or notes as a way of fostering goodwill and promoting yourself and your business. Cards or notes keep your name, or your company's name, out there and visible.

The most common time cards are exchanged in a business setting is during the annual Christmas or holiday season—so pleasant on a personal level and so necessary in the business world.

There are, however, other reasons that cards might be exchanged, including all the reasons for gift-giving stated in the previous chapter, but especially:

- Thanking someone for a business referral

- Birthday or anniversary of a close friend in business *or* of a more casual business associate celebrating a special birthday or anniversary, such as the 21st, 30th, 40th, 50th, 60th, or 75th (for birthdays) *or* the 5th, 10th, 15th, 20th, 25th, 40th, 45th, 50th (for anniversaries)

- Promotion
- Graduation
- New job
- Marriage
- Thanking someone for any kind of exceptional help
- Condolences
- Get-well soon

Consider keeping a stack of cards that fall into the most typical categories—birth, marriage, congratulations, anniversary, condolences—available to you so you can send one at a moment's notice. In sending cards, as in sending a gift, immediacy enhances the impact of the gesture.

CHRISTMAS OR HOLIDAY CARDS

Keeping track of the occasional card that you exchange in business is not as monumental a task as the Christmas card list you should be maintaining.

Consider a master list, maintained by a computer, if possible, in which you note all the names, addresses, affiliations, and cards sent and received, on a yearly basis. This master list could contain all your business contacts, whether or not a Christmas or holiday card is exchanged, or it could be just for Christmas card recordkeeping.

Even if you use a computer file, however, it is less appealing even in business to send a card in an envelope with a computer-generated address label than a handwritten address. But the computer file will make it that much easier to have up-to-date and accurate records and also to turn the master file over to someone else for addressing the envelopes.

You should maintain your list throughout the year, updating it with changes in addresses, affiliations, and phone numbers. However, if you have not done that kind of recordkeeping throughout the year, preparing the list for the holidays is a good time to enter all those changes and get your address files in order.

Follow a system for keeping track of names and addresses that works best for you. The most obvious style would be alphabetical—by the last name of the person involved, regardless of where he or she works. Another system is to alphabetize by category, either the type of business or its name, with individuals' names listed beneath that entry. Make sure all entries are up-to-date, including any changes in name, address, or affiliation, by entering any changes you have been keeping on scraps of paper or on your Rolodex.

Here is a sample of a purely alphabetical listing:

Ms. Beverly Anthony
Vice President
Department of Communications
Wilburt Company
47-01 Culver Street
Paradise, Connecticut 08475

Mr. Carl Becker
Account Executive
Raymond, Kelly, and Brown
47 Willoby Lane
Columbus, Ohio 47302

Ms. Beverly Parker   see Beverly <u>Anthony</u>

Here is an example of the category master-list system:

Raymond, Kelly, and Brown
47 Willoby Lane
Columbus, Ohio 47302
    Mr. Carl Becker, Account Executive
    Mr. Wayne Reynolds, Chairman of the Board
    Ms. Grace Winkler, Public Relations Associate

I use an alphabetical system with annotated Christmas or Hanukkah card exchanges. After each name, I indicate whether a Christmas or Hanukkah card was sent, the year sent, whether one was returned, and, if it was a special kind (or design) of card, what it was, so as to avoid duplication in the future. That a card was also received or returned by that person is indicated with an asterisk (*). Here is a sample:

Rosemary Wilkins
Manager
Communications Department
Triad Personnel Agency
333 Westwood Boulevard
Los Angeles, California 90046
'88 Xmas sent 12/16/88*
'89 Xmas sent 12/19/89 (Boy-snowman drawing)

Some companies have adopted strict policies regarding holiday card exchanging because of the time, effort, and expense involved. Some try to limit the length of the lists (one company of 100 employees limited the total number of names to 1,000 that the employees in this firm could send cards to); others make card-sending an individual responsibility so that the cost is borne by the executive.

One executive came up with this solution to whether or not he should send holiday cards to each of his two hundred employees: for the last three years, he has sent an interoffice memo to all his employees notifying them that he has made a donation to his favorite charity in all their names, in lieu of sending them holiday cards, and that he suggests (albeit somewhat presumptuously) they do the same.

Other companies see sending holiday Christmas cards as a necessary business expense and they try to create or buy cards that will advance the company in its public relations efforts. On the opposite page are two holiday cards sent by two different companies. The first one, from John S. Sturges of Siebrand-Wilton Associates, Inc., a consulting firm, has a typical inside message; the promotional aspect of the card was contained in the business card, which was enclosed with the card.

The second card is one I received a few years ago from the *National Business Employment Weekly* newspaper, a Dow Jones publication, which was sent to authors and others affiliated with the paper. It is witty, original, and the theme pertains to the contents of the newspaper, job hunting-related information.

Try to select your company card and have it imprinted by November 15 to avoid a last-minute rush. Address and mail cards by December 15 so you can get the most mileage out of your efforts. (If you send your cards so that they arrive too close to December 25, it is unlikely you will receive a card in return, thus eliminating the possibility of the two-way communication that exchanging cards provides.)

Even if a card is inscribed—with your name or that of your company—

"YOU GET FREE MEDICAL, DENTAL AND PAID VACATIONS, BUT I'M AFRAID THAT USE OF THE COMPANY SLED IS OUT OF THE QUESTION."

sign each card you send. If possible, write a short note even if all you say is "Best wishes for the New Year." Sending an imprinted card without a personalized greeting, or even the name of the addressee written inside the card, defeats the goodwill sentiment that is behind the sending of the card.

If you or your firm are trying to conserve energy or time in any given year and you want to send a minimum of cards, consider these three approaches:

1. Send cards only to those who send to you.

2. Send cards only to those you sent to last year: do not increase your list this year.

3. Prune your list from last year by eliminating anyone with whom you have not done business and make the list reflective of your actual business needs rather than of years of back-and-forth exchanges that have become meaningless.

Once again, a card, whether it is an occasion card or a holiday card, should be appropriate and in good taste. Avoid funny cards if there is any possibility that the humor will either be missed or misunderstood. Avoid cards with any sexual connotation. For holiday cards, if your business deals with both Christians and Jews, consider a card with a winter theme and a more nonsectarian greeting, such as "Season's Greetings." If you deal only with Christians, a more religious card is acceptable; and if only with Jews, a Hanukkah card is perfectly all right.

Instead of a traditional Christmas card you might consider simply using attractive photographs, drawings, or landscape scenes that are blank inside, or with "Happy Holiday" imprinted. (See sample on next page.)

If your card will be used for business associates, reconsider the appropriateness of sending a photograph of your family or your children. This is fine as a personal holiday card for family and friends, but it is far too personal in a business context.

Observe the policy at your company about displaying Christmas or other cards. Some may find it festive to have all their holiday cards displayed on or around their desks. Others may find it tacky or causing too much competition among workers as to who has more cards. Cards taped to desks or overhanging storage areas may also be viewed disdainfully. If cards are to be displayed, more tasteful ways can be considered, such as creating a collage with the cards on a piece of green construction

Holiday business card: Original drawing with message written with press-on letters. Local artists may charge an affordable fee to create a master drawing for your company's holiday card.

paper cut into the shape of a Christmas tree; running a string that cards can be hung over; or simply keeping the cards in a stack or in a basket on your desk.

CONDOLENCE CARDS AND NOTES

One of the hardest notes to write, but one of the most important in terms of extending your goodwill when it will mean the most, is the note written at the time of sympathy. Even if you send a commercial condolence card, a personal note should be added to it.

Whether the condolence note is to a family member about your direct loss of a valued customer, client, or co-worker, or you are consoling your business associate about his or her loss, it is difficult to express sympathy in words. Many people tend to avoid dealing with the situation for fear of appearing unbusinesslike, or become so frozen by their emotions so that they seem rather cold and insensitive.

A useful way to improve any condolence note is to avoid such clichés as, "Words are inadequate to express my sadness." Instead, just use words as best you can to express your sadness.

If you knew the person who died, write even a brief line or two about the deceased, appropriately sharing a positive memory that will give the family something to add to their store of memories. This is not the time or place to air your gripes.

If you are consoling a business associate who has lost a family member, avoid clichés about what they must be feeling and avoid trying to compare losses, such as "I still remember how *I* felt when my grandmother died five years ago." Instead, simply express your sorrow at the death of your business associate's family member. If you have made a donation in that deceased person's name, it may look less self-serving to have the organization that received your donation send a separate notice to that effect to your business associate. Leave that information out of your condolence card; otherwise it may look like you are trying to take advantage of the sad circumstances by playing the good samaritan.

In the next chapter we will examine end-of-the-day and weekend behavior that will enhance your career.

Chapter 12

End-of-the-Day and Weekend Concerns

If you start your workday with a smile, you most certainly need an even bigger, more positive smile at the end of the day: it may be the last image of the day that your employees, co-workers, boss, clients, or customers will have of you. You want to avoid looking overwhelmed, tired, bedraggled, or depressed, as though the day-to-day pressures are too much for you to cope with, and you need the evening and a good night's sleep to replenish yourself. Instead, you want to look as if you had a productive day and are in good shape, mentally and physically.

WHEN AND HOW TO LEAVE

It may be considered good etiquette to leave after your employees, but before your boss. You want to look like the leader and the hard worker of your group, but you do not want to upstage your boss. (Of those answering this question in my survey, 54 wrote it was good etiquette to leave after their employees, and 29 wrote it was not; 43 wrote it was proper etiquette to leave before their boss, and 39 wrote it was not.)

Upon getting a new job, it is important to be very observant about what

179

leavetaking habits work best at your company, and in your specific situation, since you do not want to step on anyone's toes; nor do you want to create schedules and habits that are wrong for you.

The issue of when to leave a job each day, however, has important implications for you and your career as well as others at your level. I recall a job I was offered in the advertising industry as a copywriter. I was shown the office where I would work and was told, by another copywriter who had recommended me for the job and who would be at my level, that the copywriters had a certain amount of work they were able to accomplish each week and that I too was expected to meet that quota—no more, no less. It was also expected that I stay in the office until everyone else at my level left, around 5:30; I could not leave before, even if I had finished my work, or later, because it would have made the others look bad. I could do other things at my typewriter, but reading a newspaper, which might look as though I was goofing off on the job, was frowned upon (even if the newspaper reading had been job-related for background research!). I turned down the job, partly because being prohibited from staying late and finishing my work, if need be, was as unreasonable and restrictive to me as being told I had to stay late each day.

WHAT TO LEAVE BEHIND

Try to leave the office carrying only one object (beyond a pocketbook, if you are a woman), namely an attaché case. If you have to bring additional magazines, newspapers, papers, or reading materials home, as noted earlier in the chapter on business dress, try to use a carryall that is of executive quality, rather than a plastic shopping bag.

If there are grooming aids that you use all the time, consider keeping a second set in a locked desk drawer or closet so you need not carry those supplies back and forth each day. Similarly, an extra pair of shoes for rain or snow or an additional umbrella in your closet will cut down on how much you have to carry out of the office. You want to look as dignified as possible at all times, whether you are arriving in the morning or leaving at the end of the day for home or for a dinner appointment.

If you are going to an appointment that requires a change of clothes, do it at your destination, rather than in the office. It looks better to leave at the end of the day wearing the same clothes you arrived in that morning. Your office should not look like a wardrobe trailer on the set of your movie role as a "rising executive." Changing into other clothes brings unnecessary attention to the nonwork-related aspects of your life, blurring the line between business and personal concerns.

Similarly, if you are going away for a personal trip at the end of a workday, especially on a Friday, avoid bringing your suitcase to the office, if you can. Check it at the train station on your way to work, if possible, or keep it in the trunk of your car. Once again, you want to avoid the impression that your job is just a weigh station between personal destinations and commitments. You also want to avoid making those around you jealous that you are going away, or make them want to watch your leavetaking time (and your arrival time the following Monday) to see if you are taking advantage of the company because of your weekend trip commitment.

PARTING WORDS

In leavetaking as in the rest of your company interactions, you want to show good etiquette by showing interest in the others you work with. You can accomplish this by using parting words that focus on those you are saying goodbye to, rather than on yourself. Combine that concept with the belief that people like to hear their names, and you have the perfect parting words—"Enjoy your weekend, Margaret," you might say to a co-worker, or "I'll look forward to hearing how your son's birthday party went, Carl," to another.

It is fine to be somewhat personal in your parting words without being too intrusive or inappropriate. If mentioning anything of a personal nature feels uncomfortable to you, stick to more general comments while still addressing the person's name, such as "Have a nice weekend, Marilyn" or "See you Monday, George."

Leave at a time that is best for your career. Do not sneak out as early as possible and hope no one will notice. Being visible, as *Fortune's* Walter Kiechel III points out in *Office Hours* in his essay, "The Importance of Being Visible," is a key to success today, because being a good, hard worker is expected of you and is not enough to get you to the top. Use the leavetaking part of the day as another chance to enhance your visibility.

LEISURE TIME

Except for the occasional dinner party or game of golf with a boss or co-worker who is both a friend and business associate, you may find spending leisure time with work associates who are not close friends more stressful than helpful. Your behavior is under scrutiny and there are stricter rules about what you should say or hear if you are among business colleagues. Although keeping up your guard is counterproductive to developing close friendships, in all but the most unusual co-worker situations, where the two are very good friends, it is best to spend leisure time with people other than those with whom you work. You will not have to watch everything you say and you will also have a respite from "talking shop"—a necessary break for you and those close to you. The weekend should be a time to talk about sports, current affairs, politics, your hobbies, and anything else beyond job.

You need time to unwind. You cannot be "on" all the time. If you are to look and act your best Monday through Friday, it is not unreasonable to want the weekend so you can "be yourself." If you do have a work-related dinner party on the weekend, try to make it a Friday night, since you will still be in a business frame of mind, going right from work to the dinner. If the dinner is Saturday night, you would have to unwind just to gear back up again into your business etiquette style.

In the next chapter we will look at job changes and etiquette.

Chapter **13**

Job Changes
and Etiquette

Knowing business etiquette will help you get ahead faster, but you also need to know the etiquette of getting ahead. This covers everything from how to go about advancing at your current job to getting a new one at another company. There are also business manners to be considered if you become a consultant or a freelancer, or if you have to work with consultants and freelancers at your salaried job.

ADVANCING AT YOUR CURRENT JOB

We know it is polite to present yourself as a team player who talks in terms of "We are working on our sales presentation" instead of "I am working on my sales presentation." But if *you* want to get ahead, how may you stand head and shoulders above the other employees if you are always talking in terms of "we"?

Presenting yourself and acting as part of a team does not conceal individual achievement. For example, you are part of a team of three vice-presidents, but in reality there is a hierarchy, with you at the bottom, someone over you, and someone over all three of you. There are some

183

projects you do together, but most of the time you each have your own responsibilities. Furthermore, how often you stay late, how willingly you do whatever the boss asks, how often you work on weekends, how often you are on time, how few days you are out sick—these are all ways in which you may stand out without making a point of telling your boss "I did this" or "I did that."

At times someone, perhaps even your boss, might try to further his or her own career by violating one of the basic etiquette rules, namely failing to give credit where credit is due and trying to take credit for your work. (This was, after all, the basic plot of the movie *Working Girl* and we know who won in the end—not the conniving boss but the brilliant underling.) If your boss tries to take credit for something you have done, you could tell your boss about his or her error but then you place your fate in his or her hands. Will a bad evaluation be in your folder before you turn around? Will your boss get defensive and accuse you of lying? If you go over your boss's head, will you look like a disloyal employee and will you suffer more by "turning in" your boss?

This is a complicated situation without any easy answers. But remember that whatever happens in this one instance, if your boss has a pattern of taking credit for an employee's work, he will probably not go very far anyway. At some point, his lack of original ideas will catch up with him; then you will be waiting in the wings to replace him or you will already have gone on to a bigger and better opportunity—talent *does* usually win out.

If your boss's ego is in tact, he or she will be thrilled with your achievements and be pleased to let those upstairs know about them. After all, your success reflects well on your boss's own management skills.

So, in summary, work as part of a team but make sure the right people know what your particular achievements are. Be on time. Take as few sick or personal days as possible. Get to know those directly above you so they will immediately think of you if there is a new job or promotion available.

When a Co-Worker Becomes the Boss

This is one of the hardest changes to deal with when someone is promoted. Having a former co-worker become your new boss means that you must now attach more status and competence to someone who used to be on an equal level. For example, it might be easier to accept a co-worker's becoming a boss if he or she has recently completed an advanced degree, such as a Master's of Business Administration, which might set him or her apart from the former co-workers. Participating at a management training seminar or program, for even a week or more, might give some justification to the promotion as well. What co-workers need is something to hang on to that sets a new boss apart from them that does not make them look bad. If there is reasonable justification for the former co-worker's becoming a boss, it becomes less an issue of personality or luck and more one of competence. It enables the co-workers who are now on a lower level to retain their self-esteem and feelings of self-worth.

If you become a boss to your former co-workers, you might even consider having a meeting with the men and women who now report to you. Talk about the changes that have occurred and how it makes everyone feel. Consider dressing in a more professional manner, if you have been dressing in a more casual one, to help make the new distinctions. For women, that might mean more business suits and dresses and no pantsuits. For men, it might mean only white shirts and dark suits instead of colored shirts and light suits. It might even be useful to take a day or more off between your job change; this will allow some time to pass and make way for an easier transition once you return.

WORKING WITH CONSULTANTS
OR FREELANCERS

There are numerous reasons for your company to use outside consultants or freelancers. Because of the downsizing at some companies, there simply may not be enough employees, with specific skills, to complete all the work at hand. Especially if a company has seasonal tasks, such as an annual report, there may be times when it will hire consultants or freelancers to complete vital tasks instead of bringing a full-time employee onto the payroll. Outside consultants may be necessary because they bring an objectivity to certain jobs that staff employees may lack.

It will help your own staff position if you work effectively with consultants or freelancers, extending to them the same courtesies you would to a fellow employee. Too often staff personnel and freelancers feel a big gap between their worlds; this poor understanding may perpetuate untrue stereotypes about each other. For example, a freelancer may be falsely believed to work in her bathrobe all day long; a staffer may be perceived as simply mouthing company policy on every issue and lacking his or her own professional views.

"If I stayed home and worked, I would watch TV all day," a bank executive says to a freelancer. But freelancers rarely watch TV all day—or they would not get any work done. That is why the bank executive is not a freelancer! Her view of what she might do if she were a freelancer does not match the work reality of those who are.

Mutual trust and respect is the key to staff and freelancers working effectively together. Not only do freelancers rarely watch TV all day, they often impose even harsher schedules than the eight A.M. to six or seven P.M. that most managers work, working fourteen-hour days and throughout the weekends and holidays. Freelancers, who do not get a steady pay-check and are usually paid either by the project or by the hour, know better than most time truly is money.

You should be aware of just what a consultant or freelancer is able to provide to your department or your company. Check their references or review their past, related projects. If the project you are asking them to complete is new for them, do not force them to act as if they have done it before. Allow them to take on a new task, but let them tell you they are new at this but will learn what is needed to successfully complete it, and before the deadline.

Give deadlines that are realistic and fair. Try to give an interim deadline and a final one, but if the consultant or freelancer works best with just one final deadline, respect that. But make sure the final deadline—of sub-mission by the consultant or freelancer—is not *your* final deadline for doing whatever you have to do with the project or material. For example, if you need to review the annual report and add an introduction or make any necessary editorial changes, make sure the freelancer's deadline for submission of the final draft allows you enough time to complete your part of the project—perhaps another two to four weeks beyond that deadline. If you are on a tight schedule, you might call the freelancer a week or two before the deadline, just to chat and see how things are coming along. Instead of pressuring the freelancer, or making him or her feel you doubt the deadline can be met, be positive and open-minded. Say something like, "You know we are all really looking forward to reading your annual report. The other companies you have done this for have been so pleased that we know we will be satisfied with your efforts. Are there any facts or quotes you still need that someone on our staff might help you to obtain?"

Make sure the consultant or freelancer understands your objectives. A written letter of agreement may help to avoid problems down the road caused by a misunderstanding about what exactly was expected. Always provide feedback to your freelancers or consultants since you may be their only link to your company. They lack the day-to-day supports that you have. Give praise freely and criticism carefully and quickly.

Make it clear when the freelancer will be paid. If it will be two to three months after the work is accepted, say so. Do not give the impression that the payment will be within a week or two, causing the freelancer to make numerous verbal or written inquiries as that time period passes. You might even give a date for him or her to mark down on the calendar: "If you do not get a check by March 14, give me a call and I'll look into it." This may avoid a lot of frustration and back-and-forth exchanges between you and the freelancer.

Prompt payment will be appreciated by your freelancers, so try to get your accounting department to process its invoices quickly. If you have to fill out forms to facilitate payment, attend to them as soon as your freelancer's work has been accepted. (It is embarrassing when freelancers call to say that a payment has not been received and you realize that is because you never forwarded their invoices to the payroll department.)

Even though a freelancer works on a project-by-project basis, it is in your best interest, the company's, and your freelancer's to develop a long-term relationship with each other. Even if you use the same freelancer just once a year, or once every other year, you will be developing a solid working relationship based on trust and a knowledge of each other's abilities, personality, and skills. Consider even taking a freelancer to lunch, whether or not you are currently working on a project together, with the idea that you might be working together again in the future.

Keep in touch with each other, through holiday cards, occasional keeping-in-touch letters, or phone calls. Get to know your freelancers as well as they should be getting to know you.

LOOKING FOR A NEW JOB

Not everyone leaves a job because he or she is unhappy. Sometimes you want to get a new job because you have discovered that your talents lie in directions your current job is unable to fulfill. You might want to move to another part of the state or country or you may have worked long enough at one company and believe a change would be stimulating and challenging.

In any case, you should have a good reason for trading the security of your old job and the relationships you have formed for the uncertainty of the new job and the strangers you will initially meet.

Of course the real reasons why you want to look for a new job—a higher salary, different co-workers, or an alternative kind of work—may very well differ from the reason you give your co-workers, boss, human resources manager, and employer. As we discussed in the section in

Chapter 4 on letter writing, in your resignation letter you keep the reason for leaving the wish for a new opportunity; be positive and praise the company, your former co-workers, and boss. You want to sing the praises in what you say verbally as well, whether on a daily basis with your co-workers or if you are asked to talk about your career move with those in personnel or at the top of the company. You may decide, of course, not to talk about your wish to get another job with anyone at your current job until you have a new job and have two weeks to go. Even then, be careful what you say about your current and future jobs. This is not the time to speak disdainfully or critically of your co-workers, boss, or company, even if you have a new job. First of all, you may continue to do business with some of the people you are leaving since most people move to a similar job in the same field, and in some fields everyone seems to know everyone, like publishing, personnel, high tech, teaching, decorating, and others. Furthermore, your former co-workers, boss, and company may be your best source of recommendation letters and possibly even future job referrals.

Get in the best shape you can when you look for a new job. Everyone you meet in your new job search will probably be seeing you for the first time and judging you within the first ten seconds on all the obvious things—your clothing and appearance, your voice, your language. Only after they assess your professional image will they begin to consider the content of what you say—your past accomplishments, your skills and strengths, what you want out of your next job, and what you will give to your new company.

The Right Way to Ask for Help

Anyone you know or have ever known is fair game when you are looking for a job. But there is a tactful way to go about talking to a friend, or the friend of a friend, and finding out if he or she wants or is even able to help you with your job search. Some people are unable to help because the kind of work they do, such as being a government employee, might make it less acceptable to make referrals for openings. Others, such as companies with employee-referral incentive programs, may actually welcome your request for assistance since it makes them look good to their boss if they do, indeed, help you get a job at their company.

When you call a friend, an acquaintance, or a friend of a friend about helping you get a job, *listen* carefully to what he or she says even before you say you are looking for a job. Ask them questions about themselves to try to determine what situation they are in—whether this is a positive or negative time in their career—so you know if they have the time or ability to help you. If Sally tells you she just got a bad evaluation and her three kids are all having a tough time in school, maybe Sally has her hands full and does not need to be more burdened. But Bill's therapy practice is thriving, he has more free time than before, and his one daughter is doing just fine. Bill would welcome a chance to help you; he even offers to read over your resume and any cover letters you write. Bill suggests talking with one of his friends who owns a company and is looking to add another employee with just your skills.

I have observed that friends of friends are often better sources of new jobs than immediate friends. One reason might be that a friend of a friend is once removed from the subjectivity that often exists when a friendship is involved. The other reason is that we all have a handful or two of true friends, but each of our friends may have lots of friends, and their friends may have other friends or acquaintances as well. As you continue the snowball, a few friends could open up possibly hundreds of contacts for your job search.

What to Do If You Are Fired

Once again, it is best not to ventilate your feelings in public about your being fired. Of course you may share the details of your firing with the few close people in your life whom you trust—such as your spouse, sibling, best friend, or parent—but be careful not to tell too many people. Not only might what you say get back to the very people you wish not to know your thoughts, but you might someday work again in another capacity for the very person you now want nothing to do with.

You might also try playing down the firing with everyone but your closest loved ones by using euphemisms, such as "They had to let me go," "There was a downsizing," or "My position was phased out."

Unlike the person looking for a new job who is taking control of his or her life, the fired person has had the control taken away. There is anger and rage. There is fear about the future and sadness about the lost relationships and the work itself. There is the need for resolution, as in all unexpected trauma, resolution that often does not occur until there is a new job with the new network, commitment, financial benefits, and renewed self-esteem that accompanies it. That some fired people find jobs that are less desirable or pay less money than their previous jobs may fan the flames of anger over the firing.

The Job Search and Etiquette

Well-meaning friends and acquaintances may offer the fired person *any* job without realizing that if it is not a good opportunity, their suggestion might backfire. "*That's* what he thinks I'm worth!" the fired employee might exclaim as he rejects a job offer that pays a third of what he was earning.

Companies today, especially at the executive level, will offer a fired employee a somewhat attractive severance package, so at least there is financial compensation to help offset the psychological shock. They may also suggest or pay for the services of an outplacement firm. Some outplacement firms help fired executives with every aspect of job hunting, from writing their resumes, helping them develop new skills to replace outdated or outmoded ones, or videotaping job interviews and critiquing the executive's performance, to advising them to attend cocktail parties where they might meet prospective employers.

Be grateful for the help you are receiving. It is hard to say thank you when your ego has been damaged, but the help is appreciated all the more because of the circumstances.

The Job Interview

Whether you voluntarily leave your job or are fired, the success of your job interview will determine whether or not you will be hired. This is your time to shine: show your best manners, dress appropriately, and arrive on time. Do not criticize your interviewer if he or she is late. Of course tardiness is impolite, but you are the one who is supposed to be making the good impression. Criticism, especially of your job interviewer, is bound to ruin your chance of getting the job.

What are you trying to accomplish during that all-important initial meeting, that first job interview? "Basically look the part," suggests Larry Marshall, President and CEO of Marshall Consultants, Inc., of New York, which has conducted searches and placed executives in corporate communication positions for at least half of the Fortune 500 companies. "Look like you're a successful executive and that you are able to play that role in both your business and personal life," Marshall continues.

Do not be surprised if your interviewer takes calls while you are being interviewed. Of course it is impolite but once again, you are the one who must be patient and nonjudgmental.

Sit up straight and tall in the sofa in the waiting room or in the chair in the interviewer's office. If the interview is conducted during a meal, observe all the rules of good manners that we have emphasized in this book, such as not talking with your mouth full, waiting until after you order to begin talking about business (as a courtesy to the waiter), eat familiar foods that you are comfortable with, eat slowly, and do not do any grooming at the table. Avoid smoking during a job interview, whether in an office or restaurant setting. If the job stipulates a nonsmoker, and the interviewer asks you if you smoke, you have to tell the truth (unless you can definitely quit, and stay a nonsmoker, before you get the job).

By now you know it is polite to say thank you, even if you do not get the job, since you never know when you might cross paths with the interviewer or the executives with whom you met. Write a simple thank-you note such as this one:

Dear Mr. Carter:

It was very kind of you to take the time to personally call me the other day and explain why I was not selected for the job of assistant manager. I know you had a large number of qualified candidates to choose from, and it must have been a difficult decision.

Although I will not be working for your company, I want to thank you for the opportunity to interview for the position. I enjoyed meeting you and talking with you about our mutual interest in the stock market.

Sincere regards,

Name

You should also be considerate in the way you decline a job offer. If you decline over the phone, you still might want to follow up with a courteous letter, thanking the company for the opportunity and repeating your regret that you are unable to take the position. Keep in mind that someone has spent a lot of time and effort considering you for a position, and that effort should be acknowledged.

A simple note like the following would be acceptable:

Dear Ms. Peters:

This is just a brief note to thank you and your staff for all the time and trouble you took in selecting me for the employee benefits manager position. Unfortunately I already accepted another position a week before I even received your offer.

I am sorry I will not be working for your firm, but I did appreciate meeting you and your fine staff.

Sincerely,

Name

FROM CORPORATE TO FREELANCE: MAKING THE TRANSITION

You may decide to become a consultant or a freelancer on a permanent basis, or until you find a new full-time job. Of course it is better if you make this decision for yourself, rather than being forced into it because you have been fired or laid off.

If you decide to become a freelancer or consultant, plan on one to three years to implement your new job style. If you are forced into it, of course you will have to quickly put into effect all the suggestions that are best done in a more gradual fashion.

Some basic questions to ask yourself if you are considering freelancing: What do I do better, faster, or differently than others? Will I be a generalist or a specialist?

Here are steps to take *before* leaving your current job, if possible:

1. Begin building up your freelance business in your spare time— evenings and weekends. In addition to having good skills, demonstrating excellent business manners will serve you especially well in the highly competitive freelance arena. Thank anyone who gives you a referral with a phone call, note, or nominal gift, such as a book, flowers, or fruit.

2. Seek out a steady arrangement with one or two clients so some or all of the "house nut" will be covered once you are completely on your own.

3. Save enough money to live on for six months to a year *plus* enough for the extra expenses of running your own business—postage, purchasing a fax machine, printing, photocopying or purchasing a photocopy machine, travel, office supplies, entertainment, paying the salaries of a secretary, administrative assistant, or other help you might need.

4. Have business cards and other office supplies that you will need ready for doing business even before you go out on your own. Remember

if you plan to do business internationally, you may have your business cards printed in English on the front and the other language, such as Japanese, on the back.

5. Make your exit from your company work for you. Too often, those who leave a company to become a freelancer fail to notify current clients or customers of that fact. Of course, if your company has a policy of not taking business away from them when you leave, you have to handle telling clients or customers of your departure in a very diplomatic way. But you should still be able to bring those relationships full circle, and help to keep the door open, in some appropriate manner. If possible, finish up any projects or negotiations that are in midstream before you depart. If your company allows it, perhaps a simple letter is in order:

Dear Mr. Smith:

It has been a pleasure doing business with you during the past two years. I will be leaving R & B Company this Friday, but a fine replacement, Mr. Jones, has already been chosen.

Sincerely,

Name

Once on your own, here are some tips for your freelance or consulting business:

1. Try to develop good relationships with clients with whom you hope to do continued business. Spend as much time and money as possible on business breakfasts, lunches, dinners, or entertaining as you would if you were on salary and the tab was being picked up by your boss. It is money well spent if it leads to strong business relationships and repeated business or assignments.

2. Network informally and formally through professional associations or annual meetings, conferences, seminars to improve your skills, or any industrywide parties or conventions.

3. Use promotion, publicity, advertising, and an annual holiday greeting card to generate and keep business.

4. Make a list of the important dates for your key customers— anniversaries or birthdays—and send a congratulatory card or make a keeping-in-touch phone call.

5. Attach yourself to services that might get you work, such as organizations that use freelancers or consultants to fulfill assignments for their business.

6. Keep up with the literature in your field—about your craft as well as about freelancing, becoming a small business, entrepreneurship, and so forth.

7. Carefully consider how your office should be set up—whether it is based at home or is a rented, outside space. (Refer to all the points raised about an office in Chapter 5.)

8. Learn and use as many time-management techniques as possible since time is money especially for the freelancer, who rarely receives a steady paycheck. The faster you can complete projects (while still doing quality work), the more work you can handle.

9. Turn work down only if the fee is unreasonably low or the work is too far afield from your specialization. If possible, accept all appropriate assignments, staggering deadlines or subcontracting the work, if allowed, so your business keeps booming.

10. Be the best boss you have ever had—to yourself as well as to any of your employees.

ACCEPTING A NEW JOB

Accepting a new job usually requires a formal resignation letter to the old job, a formal acceptance letter to the new job, and verbal or written letters to clients, customers, or colleagues about the change in your work life. It may be inappropriate to let your old customers, clients, or colleagues know how to get in touch with you, or what your future plans are, but it is certainly appropriate and polite to say "I enjoyed working with you and even though I will be working at another firm, I value the business relationship we have had. Perhaps we will work together again in the future."

The idea of leaving your old job with everyone happy is an important one since you never know what may happen if you allow bad feelings, opinions, or experiences to get "played out in the press" of gossip, so to speak. You want to leave without burning any bridges. Save the "true story" material for your confessions or memoirs; be a lady or a gentleman when you leave a job. Even if you feel the words gluing your teeth together as you say them, part on nice terms with your boss, co-workers, and employees.

Assuming a New Job

What should you do when you first take on a new job? Resist the impulse to show off and display all your knowledge or skills too quickly. Be cautious about setting up unrealistic performance levels that will be hard to live up to once your initial enthusiasm and energy subside. *Pace yourself* and keep your eyes open as you observe the new work rules and the management style of your boss.

If you are a new manager or supervisor, you should observe and listen to what your predecessor did so you know what your employees are used to. Avoid being too authoritarian and demanding; even if this is done out of nervousness, it may set up a fearful and unpleasant work environment that might be hard to undo in the months or years to come.

Implement your own ideas slowly and carefully. Put your energy into establishing positive relationships with your new employees, relationships that will enhance your team effort throughout your management experience.

Avoid criticizing the manager you have replaced. If necessary, simply point out that you have a different way to do things than your predecessor. Neither way is right or wrong, just divergent.

One of the most important early efforts you should make, in addition to establishing a good rapport with your staff, is to allow for effective critique and feedback mechanisms for the way your group performs—your own performance as well as that of each individual. Will you have daily, weekly, or monthly face-to-face meetings? Is a weekly memo sufficient? Will there be a procedure for providing feedback on an ongoing basis? Will you have an "open door" policy or should employees make appointments to see you?

Just as you should resist working unrealistically long hours or creating hard-to-match production schedules, be careful not to schedule feedback sessions too frequently. Once again, you are aiming for consistency, and the intensity you initially think is necessary may no longer be needed once you get your feet wet. It is easier to increase meetings than to decrease them.

Most of all, keep any promises you make to other employees. Your credibility is one of the most important behavioral traits to demonstrate to your employees in these initial weeks. Set good examples for punctuality, responsiveness, and diligence, and you will reap the rewards for the duration of your management experience with those employees.

In the next chapter we will examine whether there is a connection between etiquette and ethics.

Chapter 14

Etiquette and Ethics: Is There a Connection?

Etiquette deals with what is considered *acceptable* by a society or within a given company; ethics is what is considered moral. Sometimes there is overlap: it is both proper and morally correct to tell the truth, but being nice to people is a rule of etiquette, not of ethics.

Both etiquette and ethics are codes of conduct that business workers have to consider. It is poor etiquette to use foul language, but it is not unethical. It is poor etiquette to misuse company property, and it is also unethical.

Although ethics and etiquette sometimes overlap, ethics issues tend to be larger than the offense caused someone in business by failing to say "thank you," "please," or sending a congratulatory note upon learning of a colleague's promotion.

Let us look at the following real-life ethics/etiquette examples:

- An employee goes on a popular business news talk show and talks about good stocks, hyping her own company's product as the best one to buy. The etiquette mistake is that of excessive bragging, but the ethics breach is that of plugging one's own product.

- Robert Osborne, the *Hollywood Reporter's* "Rambling Reporter," wrote that the late George Cukor said of MGM superstar Norma Shearer: "Norma is absolutely unbearable. You ask her how she is, and she tells you. . . ." Providing more personal information than is appropriate in a business setting may be poor etiquette, but sharing too much information about what top secret projects are going on at your company is a breach of ethics.

- An executive misrepresents the probable profits on a project; because of those inflated projected sales figures, two professionals plan to allot several years of their lives to completing that project. The executive, who gets a salary, has possibly placed the families of her contractual professionals in jeopardy since the projected income may not be forthcoming. Unfortunately, inflating sales figures and making unrealistic promises is all too common; it is more than poor etiquette, it is unethical.

Every etiquette issue, from bragging to gift-giving, has to be examined in light of the ethics guidelines of a company. What may be etiquette, appropriate, and acceptable for a profit-making chain of employment agencies may be unethical and suspect for a government agency or a financial services institution. (As a human resources manager at a manufacturing company in California wrote: "As a government contractor we have a specific code of conduct and policies relative to our relationship with customers and vendors.") It may be considered poor etiquette to vent your criticisms of one employee to another, but it would be considered unethical for a company psychologist to critique a client/patient/employee before another, much less mention clients at all.

Often in business it is necessary to say things about a product or project to get someone to invest their time or money into a new venture. When is it ethical to give figures that are inaccurate and when is it not? The key is whether you know the information you are providing is "iffy" or downright untrue. If you innocently repeat false information, that is one thing. If you willingly relay false information—information that helps someone decide to proceed with this venture or that purchase—you are behaving unethically.

An insurance broker articulates how some brokers may behave unethically by misrepresenting certain basic financial issues to their prospective clients: "In insurance, there are projections of what dividends will be, which are only projections. For example, in permanent whole-life insurance, there is a certain guaranteed cash accumulation portion and that is absolutely guaranteed. That might only be four or five percent. But the balance is not guaranteed and it depends on how efficiently the insurance company manages itself. They may do very well and they may do only okay or they could do outright poorly. It is not necessarily common to stress this to the client. It's very important to make clear to clients that some of that is only a projection with no guarantee attached. Indeed, a few companies have exceeded projections."

One of the best ethics protections for a worker is to be employed by a top company. They will have less of a need to lie to workers or customers than poorly rated companies, or those with inferior products. As the insurance broker, who works for one of the top American companies, explains: "I see a lot of people selling second-rate products. I don't know what the management tells their people about the company and their strengths and whatever. I'm taking an insurance course and meeting a lot of people from other companies. One company is very weak. It is clear that one of the salespeople there has no idea how bad the company's ratings are. Every now and then she finds out about their ratings and she just cringes. Obviously you don't tell your sales troops the bad news. There are only eleven insurance companies out of about seventeen hundred to two thousand in the United States today that have all the top ratings."

Business schools are starting to recognize how important it is to teach ethics to their students. As reported by Joel Kurtzman, when the *New York Times* got three deans together from the graduate business schools of the J. L. Kellogg Graduate School of Management at Northwestern University, Darden Graduate School of Business Management at the University of Virginia, and the Columbia Business School of Columbia University, Meyer Feldberg of Columbia University said: "We are asking ourselves a number of questions: . . . What is the correct mechanism for introducing morality and ethics into our curriculum, not just at the beginning, but all the way through?"

John W. Rosenblum of the University of Virginia pointed out that his school has had a center on ethics for almost twenty-five years, but they decided to add a required course on ethics to the curriculum. "But not a course that says this is right and that is wrong," said Rosenblum. "It is a course that says you are going to face certain decisions where you are not sure of the consequences of your actions on other human beings—where the consequences are favorable for some individuals and unfavorable for others. Responsible managers, at all stages of their careers, need to be equipped with ways to think about and resolve those dilemmas."

The Ethics Resource Center in Washington, D.C., is helping companies to revise and update the ethics guidebooks that were developed in the late 1970s, mainly in response to Watergate and other business and government scandals. A handbook entitled "Creating a Workable Company Code of Ethics" is available that is based on a decade of research into company ethics. As Lydia Schindler, Director of Communications of the Ethics Resource Center, explains:

> *Since its establishment in 1977, the Ethics Resource Center has been working with businesses to help strengthen and clarify standards of ethical conduct. What the Center sees as the challenge to business today is incorporating ethics into the daily fabric of everyday decision making. In order to maintain an ethical work environment, the Center believes, companies should supplement codes of conduct with ongoing training programs that strive to enhance employees' awareness of ethical issues and conflicts. A recent survey the Center conducted among two thousand U.S. corporations reveals that while ninety percent have written codes of conduct, only forty-four percent have ethics training programs in place.*

A human resources administrator at a steel company based in North Carolina expressed strong sentiments about ethics in my etiquette survey. He wrote:

> *The key is* not to have policies *but rather to hire people of high* honor, integrity, *and good* character. *If the majority of those you hire meet this standard, the minority who don't will fall in line to a point where they will not be a significant problem to your business. Believe me this is true. Don't worry about business ethics. Just spend your time and energies concentrating on hiring honorable people.*
>
> *It is not hard. It is easy. We try to "over-manage" it [ethics] and make it complex and hard. Businessmen do not need textbooks and classes on ethics. They just need to consistently practice behaving honorably in their business affairs/relationships. In the long term their customers/clients will guarantee them success and continuing consideration for market share according to the quality of their product or service and their overall customer responsiveness.*

Both ethics and etiquette deal with doing the right thing. Just as a company has its own standards of etiquette, it also has its own corporate culture about ethics. Does this company encourage absolute honesty, bending the facts, or outright lies in how they conduct business? I am not saying that a company says to its employees, "We're going to lie to our clients," but new employees quickly learn if that is, indeed, what is done as they overhear conversations or observe their supervisors in day-to-day situations. Every single employee that is hired should be an advocate of that company's ethics standards. Today one of the biggest problems in merging companies is the merging of corporate cultures that clash.

Lying rarely serves you or your company well since it is likely you will get caught in your lie, which will hurt you and your employer's personal credibility. For example, a realtor makes comments to try to encourage a sale. When the customer says, "Those bedrooms are too small," the realtor, trying to make a sale, says, "Don't worry. Children don't stay in their bedrooms, they are always outside." A few days later, when the same customer complains that the property that went along with another house is too small, the realtor says, "Don't worry. Children don't play outside. They tend to entertain in their bedrooms." That realtor's credibility has been damaged by those conflicting statements; her customer will undoubtedly deal with her more cautiously from now on.

Camille Lavington, a New York-based international communications consultant, polishes and packages business executives. Lavington comments about ethics and etiquette:

> One of the main things I reassure clients is that I will do nothing to change their ethics or morality, but some of their values may need modifying. This is based on the need to be considerate of another person's values. I believe in the premise that to make another person comfortable, you must do so in an appropriate fashion.
>
> Ethics and etiquette go hand in glove. Your manners reflect your ethics. Decency and concern for others indicate a desire to live by high standards, to the benefit of everyone. Empathy and understanding humanize any relationship. By setting an example for others to follow, you subliminally encourage better behavior and ethics.
>
> American corporations have gone through a low period on the scale of behavior. Wall Street is still reeling from the lack of ethics of a few bad apples. International competition and "Old World" values are going to force us to change our behavior. If United States corporations want to be respected by the international community, their executives must embrace some of the time-honored rituals and etiquette practiced abroad. Unpolished behavior is totally passé.
>
> A "code of ethics" is the quality of standing behind your word. It's your reputation. One way to build a negative reaction is to bend the truth. An example: Corporations delay

payment for services, and then fib about mailing the check.
They are practicing one of the three biggest lies known to
man. It makes you wonder if they are unethical about other
business practices.

Protocol and etiquette expert and trainer Dorothea Johnson was hired by a law firm to teach table manners to one of their rising young star attorneys. Johnson trained the young man in how to eat properly, polished him up, and sent him back to his promising career. A few months later, she inquired how the lawyer was doing. "Oh, we had to fire him," a partner told her. "What?" exclaimed Johnson. "But he was doing so well." "We caught him double billing," the lawyer explained, "and our firm won't tolerate unethical behavior."

If your company issues a company code of ethics or business guidelines, memorize it so you have some specific rules for a range of situations, eliminating the agony of pondering over each and every circumstance; for example, what the maximum worth of a gift is from a customer or client that an employee can accept without being accused of influence peddling. Some companies even make such business codes *mandatory* reading of their employees. As one company adamantly states at the end of the introductory letter to its business conduct manual: "We cannot, and will not, tolerate unethical or illegal actions undertaken either for personal benefit or misguided attempts to achieve gains on behalf of the Firm. No one's bottom line is more important than the reputation of the Firm." This firm's business conduct booklet covers these areas: conflicts of interest, outside business connections, public office, gifts, use of information, regard for the company's assets, relationships with clients, competitors, governmental authorities, and employees, using your own judgment, and reporting misconduct.

- Avoid criticism of the company, especially in public.

- Keep your promises—to your boss, to your clients, to your employees, and to yourself.

- As noted in the chapter on gift-giving and receiving, be cautious about accepting any gift that is more than a nominal one, like an imprinted calendar, basket of fruit, bottle of wine or liquor, book, pen, or flowers.

As Elena Jankowic points out in *Behave Yourself!*: "A purchasing agent who accepts gifts like a VCR or a trip to Las Vegas is guilty of serious misconduct which could lead to blackmail or dismissal. If a supplier offers a gift that is out of line with professional standards, you should report it immediately to your superior so that there is no doubt about your integrity."

The *values* of a company are one of the most important of the eight criteria for excellence isolated by Thomas J. Peters and Robert H. Waterman, Jr. in their bestseller, *In Search of Excellence*. Based on a sample of sixty-two American companies, the authors write about the fifth attribute of excellence of being "hands-on, value-driven":

> *Let us suppose that we were asked for one all-purpose bit of advice for management, one truth that we were able to distill from the excellent companies' research. We might be tempted to reply, "Figure out your value system. Decide what your company stands for. What does your enterprise do that gives everyone the most pride? Put yourself out ten or twenty years in the future: what would you look back on with the greatest satisfaction?"*

What would you do with the following ethical/etiquette dilemma? You are using someone's services and decide he is not as committed or as competent as you had hoped. (He was a referral—a co-worker suggested him. They are either friends, or the worker is the friend of the friend's friend.) Example: You set up a meeting. Two weeks later, when you call to confirm, he says he will not be able to make it because of a family reunion out of town, but he will have his colleague help you out. You decline, saying you will wait for him to return, because you would rather not deal with someone with whom you have not had any prior dealings nor do you plan to use in the future.

What angers you is that this reunion is certainly not something he *just* heard about. Why didn't he tell you right away, two weeks before, that that date was not a good one?

A week after you decide not to use his services, his boss, the president of the company, writes a long letter saying that his company stands for service and that he wants to personally know if the agent is doing a good job. He also states that the president and everyone else in the company has your best interests at heart and will be glad to help you out as well.

Enclosed in the letter is a recommendation card for you to fill out. Do you fill it out honestly, knowing it might get the employee fired, and that your negative remarks might even get back to the employee and even your co-worker who recommended him? Or do you simply ignore the request for a recommendation or reaction, as well as never call the agent again, and continue to look for someone else who will fill your needs?

In the next and final chapter, we will review how business etiquette will help you succeed in the business world today, as well as summarize key business etiquette principles that help to enhance each workday.

Chapter 15

Conclusion

Protocol is a tool for you to use to help you to succeed. Yet protocol alone will not ensure success for the job candidate who is poorly trained or ill-suited for a job. You will not get a job just because you wear nice clothes and write a memorable thank-you note following an interview. But by simply following the rules of etiquette, the qualified candidate increases his or her chances of success. The rising executive who combines business protocol with excellent people skills and superb work performance will rise faster than those who breach etiquette by using unacceptable language, being discourteous, and failing to follow acceptable rules of conduct in terms of dress, business stationery, executive communication, treatment of superiors, co-workers, or subordinates, among other etiquette issues.

The work experience of someone with excellent business manners is different, and usually richer, than that of someone without them. Barbara Chizmas became an etiquette expert because she had just that kind of richer experience when she worked as a salesperson for a computer company. Chizmas explains: "I realized there were often a lot of functions that the branch manager could take different people to, and I went to most of them. I asked why, and they said, 'Most of the people we have taken, frankly, have embarrassed us.' " Chizmas knows that being success-ful in business today requires a lot of entertaining and the taking out of clients. You have to know what to do in those situations so as to not feel awkward or commit too many faux pas.

As sociologist George C. Homans pointed out, every interaction be-tween two or more people is an exchange of material or nonmaterial goods. Etiquette enhances that exchange, ensuring that one or both per-sons will want to continue the interaction over a period of time. Studies of groups have found that *cohesiveness* attracts individuals to a particular group; observing and following the etiquette standards within a company will make that company more cohesive and membership in that group (employment at that company) more rewarding, predictable, and rein-forcing of each individual's behavior.

Observing the business protocol at a particular company is one way to ensure that company behavior is a recognizable and consistent entity. If what is expected is predictable, it is possible to get down to the business of doing business more easily than if what is expected has to be deter-mined in each and every instance. If a man need not stand for a woman who enters his office, it makes it easier for a boss to know that he is not insulting his secretary if he stays seated when she appears, that he is observing the rules of etiquette at work (quite different, perhaps, than those in his social circle). By contrast, it is easier for everyone involved if a business lunch or dinner follows the etiquette rule set forth in *Debrett's Etiquette and Modern Manners:* the principle guest sits to the host's right, and the second most honored guest to his left. If there are women present, they are to be seated at equal intervals among the men.

In working your way up the corporate ladder, manners are essential. Executives are expected to be positive representatives of their companies. The freewheeling sixties, seventies, and even eighties have been replaced with the more staid and image-conscious nineties. Training for etiquette usually begins at home, when parents teach a toddler to say "please" and "thank you," and should continue throughout the school years through family and educational institutions. But finishing or charm schools disap-peared decades ago, and college and graduate schools have been slow to take up the slack. Rising executives and professionals of every kind have the onus on them to get the business protocol training they need from whatever sources are available. That means etiquette training for ev-eryone—from a management trainee who needs good business manners, to a doctor needing a polished bedside manner, to consultants needing to present themselves in an impressive way. For some, that training will be obtained by reading books and articles that convey vital information about etiquette. For others, books will be the start, but they will also need personal trainers or image consultants, or will have to enroll in etiquette seminars or courses to brush up on such things as proper table manners, ways of walking and sitting, and even how to dress. What works on a Saturday night at a fast-food restaurant is not going to go over on a Wednesday afternoon at the Four Seasons.

Etiquette training is essential, if you want to rise to the top . . . beyond your present level. You may be comfortable with the manners you now value, but as etiquette expert Camille Lavington points out:

> Many people enjoy making subordinates, or peers, feel
> comfortable, but have no idea how to treat superiors. They
> simply don't know what's appropriate, because they're
> unaware of the rituals and value systems of this group. Often
> these values are unspoken, and quietly instilled through
> superior education and cultural advantage. In addition,
> international travel broadens a top executive's perspective,
> beyond regional idiosyncracies, and once exposed to
> sophisticated mores, refinement follows. Smart young
> executives are finding out that brains are not enough. They
> soon learn it's also essential to have ethics and etiquette for
> success. Without these qualities, they're going to lose their
> jobs.

Ethnic or racial slurs against groups of people as well as individuals can get you fired, or certainly damage your reputation. A New York journalist was suspended for two weeks without pay for responding to a criticism of one of his columns as "sexist" with a comment that was an ethnic slur.

If he had observed the etiquette rule against making disparaging comments, he would have avoided compromising his professional image of an objective reporter who should be above such conduct.

In a corporate or business situation, talking against someone or negative gossip is very dangerous because it usually gets back to someone with all the ramifications you might predict.

Paul Critchlow, Senior Vice President for Communications at Merrill Lynch, explains how business manners help a company to function better. Says Critchlow:

> Successful executives learn if you extend someone a bit of
> kindness, a little interest, even if junior to you, that comes
> back in kind. The executive world of any given company is an
> echo chamber. Sooner or later that junior person will cross
> paths with you again and it really creates the proper aura. If

*you're basically a confident person, but also seen as a good
and caring person, it adds a dimension that many folks don't
have.*

This book has laid out some of the fundamentals of business protocol
that will help you to get a job, keep it, and facilitate your rise to the top.
Here is a summary of some of the key ideas put forth in this book, as well
as additional ones to consider:

1. Being courteous, polite, and pleasant will take you far in the business world just as being critical, negative, or maudlin will hamper your
success.

2. Saying "please" or "thank you" should be part of your everyday
behavior in the business world unless it is a life-and-death situation
where time is of the essence, such as a physician opting to say "Get me
another pint of blood" rather than "Please get me another pint of blood."
In most situations, however, *please* and *thank you* will promote goodwill
and are the way to behave whether you are the superior, co-worker, or
subordinate.

3. Avoid criticizing anyone—subordinate, co-worker, superior, client,
or customer—especially in the presence of others. If you must unfavorably review someone's performance, do it privately. It is also better to
begin with praise and follow with criticism (feedback is a more neutral
way of describing this process), and end with additional praise. For example, "Ms. Hansen, you are doing an admirable job with the volume of work
that I have demanded of you lately. However, I have noticed an occasional
typographical error slipping into some of the correspondence. I know,
because you are so reliable and conscientious, that you will take care of
this now that I have pointed it out to you. You are an asset to this
department and I hope you will accept this feedback in the spirit in which
it is given."

4. Dress according to examples of others at your level and function in
your company. For a job interview, it is better to be a little overdressed
than too casual. When in doubt, go to the company in advance of your
interview and observe workers entering and leaving the building, or try to
contact any friends or acquaintances who might already be working at
that company for inside tips.

5. There should be consistency in how individuals are addressed at
your company. If your secretary is required to address you as Mister
Jones, he or she might prefer to be called Mr. or Ms. Clark. It is up to the

senior person to let the rules of address be known to the employees. Introduce yourself with your complete name, "I am Mister Gordon Jones," and, if you wish to be called by just your first name or a nickname add, "But you can call me Greg."

6. Ms. is easier to use than Miss or Mrs. since it eliminates having to check on a woman's marital status before writing a letter or addressing someone. In that way, Ms. is equal to Mr.

7. If a company office party is going to include a spouse or fiancé (or fiancée), it is polite to allow single persons to ask a guest along, if they wish, so they are not discriminated against.

8. Write a thank-you note to the host of any company dinner or party immediately after you attend it. However, if you see the host the next day in the office, you should also mention in person what a good time you had and what a splendid dinner or party it was.

9. Observe the guidelines on gift-giving that your company provides. You should give or receive gifts only if it is considered appropriate.

10. Be aware of and respect the etiquette standards of other cultures if your business has international dealings. For example, if you deal with a Muslim, the month of Ramadan requires Muslims to fast from dawn to dusk; party-giving is to be avoided during the first month of the Islamic year. Arabs might find it hard to deal with a woman in business. The Japanese first exchange business cards, and meet to discuss topics other than business, while slowly moving into a business relationship based on a sense of trust. Presents are expected to be mutually exchanged.

11. You are judged by the *following up* of your actions, not just your initial contacts. If you call someone, follow up to see if whatever you talked about has been accomplished. If someone writes to you, follow up with an answer. And always return phone calls.

12. Beware of being silent merely because you feel uncomfortable rejecting someone. Remember: you are rejecting the project or situation, *not* the person. This policy of saying nothing rather than a simple no is rampant is some industries, such as Hollywood, where some screenwriters will simply not hear from a producer, agent, or studio—not even a phone call or short note saying, "Not for us." (This is a generalization, of course; some producers, agents, and studios are very polite, getting back to a writer with any answer very quickly.) To those who cowardly prefer silence, remember that the person you are afraid to say no to today, who now sees you as impolite, might be the person you want to say "yes" to

next month, next year, or in ten years. People do not forget impoliteness. Be polite and give an answer to a submission or inquiry—if not for today, for the future.

If you have trouble saying or writing "no," have a secretary do it for you. If you are too busy to do even that, the least favorable alternative, but an action more courteous than silence, is to have a printed or photocopied short statement sent, along with any material to be returned, to the effect that:

> We are sorry we cannot reply personally to you, but we receive hundreds of inquiries each week about possible jobs at our company.
>
> We are returning your resume, since all executive level jobs are handled on a referral basis only.
>
> Thank you for your inquiry. We wish you the best of luck in your job search.

13. New York copywriter Don Hauptman advises including a note or letter with everything you send, even an article or news clipping. Comments Hauptman: "It's been said that if you omit a note or a letter, it's like walking into someone's office without an appointment. Quite often the envelope will be thrown out, and the recipient doesn't even know the identity of the sender, unless there is a personal communication." Hauptman suggests that a simple "Hi" or "For your information," on your note or letterhead stationery, will often suffice.

14. Immediately attend to such polite gestures as sending a congratulatory card when a business associate gets a new job or a promotion. It will take less time to send a card as soon as possible after the event than it will take adding it to your "to do" list and then ruminating over finding the time to do it. Furthermore, if you keep a stack of cards suitable for business for various occasions—congratulations, condolences, get well—right in your drawer at work, it will be easy to translate your good thoughts into the good deed.

15. Do not assume because someone calls you through a referral that your services are presold. You still have to work hard, perhaps even harder, to prove yourself, to live up to their recommendation, and to retain the business. If business comes to you through a recommendation, rather than a cold call, you may have to work more diligently, since the potential client or customer's expectations may be higher. Such referrals may actually be easier to get the initial business, and harder to keep it.

16. Corporate spouses should know business manners so they help (not hurt) their partner's career. With the development of the two-career

family, some corporate spouses may be unable or unwilling to place their partner's career before their own. A spouse may be reluctant or unable to take time off from work to accompany a spouse on a trip. A partner who teaches evening classes, for example, may be unable to accompany her spouse to business dinners. That should be a decision the couple makes, and one that is kept between them. When a spouse *must* attend a business function—because the boss has requested it—and it is proper for the spouse to be there, the corporate spouse should try hard to do so. Once there, he or she should let his or her spouse shine. This is not the time for the spouse to talk nonstop about his or her achievements, or to bring up controversial topics that may embarrass the spouse or the employer. As hard as it may be for the corporate spouse, this is the time to defer to the spouse and the spouse's career for the few company-sponsored business functions, such as the company picnic, dinner, or out-of-town trip. Corporate spouses will reap the rewards in helping the employed partner to advance and to be known at his or her company as an asset to their spouse's career.

However, if there are problems at home, it may be wise to make polite excuses why a spouse cannot attend a company function, or to avoid inviting business associates to any personal functions, such as a child's wedding. If a spouse's behavior is in any way unpredictable, keep corporate and personal affairs separate. I am reminded of the embarrassed doctor who invited a few associates to his son's bar mitzvah only to have his ex-wife make a fool of herself—by drinking too much, saying the wrong things, and dancing erotically—in front of hundreds of business and personal guests.

If corporate spouses are not pursuing a career of their own, try not to make them feel less valuable or important than the spouses who have their own careers in addition to family and household duties. One way to avoid insulting a corporate spouse in this area is to let them volunteer information about their families and activities rather than asking the questions, "What do you do?" or "Where do you work?"

17. Keep kissing for social occasions; a handshake is more proper in business settings.

18. Keep promises in business.

19. Take the long view in business. Don't be shortsighted about your efforts. If a business relationship does not immediately seem to lead to a sale or deal, work as hard at that relationship as the ones that do. Not only may it *someday* come to fruition, the name of the game in business is *referral*—if you cannot help someone, maybe you know someone who

can. *Old business gets you new business.* Someday, the person to whom you have referred the business may reciprocate and send business your way. Too often when a business deal fails to ensue, someone who was polite and courteous during the courtship becomes distant and even rude when a sale or transaction fails to materialize. Remember that practically every executive in every business—from propane gas to insurance—is ultimately in a people business based on relationships.

20. Make sure you are polite at all levels of a company. First of all, proper etiquette includes being deferential to age, seniority, and authority but also being kind to those at your level or below it. Second, you never know what person under you today, or on the way up, may be your co-worker, superior, employee, or client tomorrow.

21. Make people feel welcome—to enter your office, to have a phone conversation with you, to do business with you, to work with you, to want to be around you.

22. Remember, and put into everyday practice, the six basic principles of business etiquette:

        1. Be on time.
        2. Be discrete.
        3. Be courteous, pleasant, and positive.
        4. Be concerned with others, not just yourself.
        5. Dress appropriately.
        6. Use proper written and spoken language.

It is important to practice good business manners because others will mirror your example. I am reminded of the anecdote told to me by Richard Zeif, a New York lawyer. He is well aware of the mirroring effect in behavior; it is even part of the nonverbal communication portion of the course in negotiating that he teaches. Mirroring refers to the way in which someone copies the behavior of someone else. Zeif was involved in a negotiation and every day he would see an accountant, who would be smiling, even though he heard that the accountant's mother was dying. The accountant was absent for a few days and Zeif learned it was because his mother had died. When he saw the accountant, who still had a smile on his face—it must have been a nervous gesture—he mirrored the accountant and committed the gaffe of smiling at him as he said, "I'm so sorry to hear your mother died."

Good etiquette, like a college degree, is only noticeable in its absence. It is vital to learn about appropriate etiquette in general as well as what is specifically expected of you in whatever profession, industry, company, or situation you work in so you can get on to the other issues of competence that everyone today must face.

The truth of the business world today is that if you have a choice between employing the services of one individual over another, you will probably pick the kind, considerate, appropriate, and well-bred one over the abrasive, coarse, inappropriate one. A gentle polishing will guarantee that you will always shine in your profession.

Selected Bibliography

ADIA. "Companies Say 'Bottoms Up' With Eye on Bottom Line: Ho, Ho, Ho!" Press release, Menlo Park, Calif., December 4, 1989.

Allen, Jeffrey G. *The Perfect Job Reference.* New York: John Wiley & Sons, 1990.

Axtell, Roger. *Do's and Taboos Around the World.* Compiled by The Parker Pen Company. 2nd edition. New York: John Wiley & Sons, 1990.

Bacon, Mark S. *Write Like the Pros: Using the Secrets of Ad Writers & Journalists in Business.* New York: John Wiley & Sons, 1988.

Baldrige, Letitia. *Amy Vanderbilt's Everyday Etiquette.* New York: Bantam Books, 1981.

———. "Business Manners 1990." *Boardroom Reports,* April 1, 1990, pp. 13–14.

———. *Letitia Baldrige's Complete Guide to Executive Manners.* Edited by Sandi Gelles-Cole. New York: Rawson Associates, 1985.

———. *Letitia Baldrige's Complete Guide to a Great Social Life.* New York: Rawson Associates, 1987.

———. *Letitia Baldrige's Complete Guide to the New Manners for the '90s.* New York: Rawson Associates, 1990.

Barkas, J. L. See *Jan Yager.*

Barringer, Felicity. "The Dress for Success a Second Time Around." *New York Times,* January 11, 1990, p. A18.

Becker, Franklin. *The Successful Office.* Reading, Mass.: Addison-Wesley, 1982.

Bixler, Susan. *The Professional Image.* New York: Perigree Books, Putnam, 1984.

Blanchard, Kenneth, and Spencer Johnson. *The One Minute Manager.* New York: Morrow, 1982.

Bowman, David, and Ronald Kweskin. *Q: How Do I Find the Right Job? A: Ask the Experts.* New York: John Wiley & Sons, 1990.

Brown, Patricia Leigh. "The Business of Etiquette." *New York Times Magazine Entertaining,* Part 2, May 21, 1989, pp. 8, 9.

———. "Making Over an Image with an Expert's Help." *New York Times,* January 18, 1989, pp. C1, C6.

Caplow, Theodore. "Christmas Gifts and Kin Networks." *American Sociological Review,* vol. 47, June 1982, pp. 383–392.

Carnegie, Dale. *How to Win Friends and Influence People.* New York: Pocket Books, 1936, 1964.

Cypert, Samuel A. *Writing Effective Business Letters, Memos, Proposals, and Reports.* Chicago: Contemporary Books, 1983.

Deal, Terrence E., and Allen A. Kennedy. *Corporate Cultures.* Reading, Mass.: Addison-Wesley, 1982.

Deutsch, Claudia. "To Get Ahead, Consider a Coach." *New York Times,* January 14, 1990, p. 29.

DeVries, Mary A. *The Complete Office Handbook.* New York: Signet, 1987.

Donald, Elsie Burch, editor. *Debrett's Etiquette and Modern Manners.* New York: Viking Press, 1981. (Written by Sybilla Jane Flower, Judy Allen, Anna Sproule, Jane Abdy, Jonathan Abbott, Jo-An Jenkins, and Iain Finlayson.)

Dorman, Michael. "Making the Perfect Executive." *Newsday,* February 7, 1988, pp. 8–11, 26, 28, 29, 32.

Ethics Resource Center. *Ethics Resource Center Report,* vol. 5, no. 1. Washington, D.C., Fall 1989.

Fanning, Deirdre. "It's 6 a.m., So That Must Be the Hairdresser." *New York Times,* April 15, 1990, p. 25.

———. "Out With Wire Hangers, and Death to Tired Togs." *New York Times,* Sunday, Section 3, May 13, 1990.

Flesch, Rudolf. *How to Say What You Mean in Plain English.* New York: Barnes and Noble Books, 1972.

Flippo, Chet. "Samurai Businessman." *New York,* June 29, 1981, pp. 29–31.

Freedman, Howard S. *How to Get a Headhunter to Call.* New York: John Wiley & Sons, 1986.

Gibson, Richard. "Personal 'Chemistry' Abruptly Ended Rise of Kellogg President." *Wall Street Journal,* November 28, 1989, pp. A1, A9.

Girard, Joe, with Stanley H. Brown. *How to Sell Anything to Anybody.* New York: Warner Books, 1977.

Godin, Seth, and Chip Conley. *Business Rules of Thumb.* New York: Warner Books, 1987.

Goffman, Erving. *Behavior in Public Places.* New York: Free Press, 1963.

Goodman, Gary S. *Winning by Telephone.* Englewood Cliffs, N.J.: Prentice-Hall, 1982.

Gouldner, Alvin W. "The Norm of Reciprocity: A Preliminary Statement." *American Sociological Review,* vol. 25, no. 2, April 1960, pp. 161–178.

Hackett, Larry. "Trading Places." New York *Daily News,* November 21, 1989, p. 35.

Hall, Edward T., and Mildred Reed Hall. *Hidden Differences: Doing Business with the Japanese.* Garden City, N.Y.: Doubleday/Anchor Press, 1987.

Homans, George C. "Social Behavior as Exchange." *American Journal of Sociology,* vol. 63, no. 6, May 1958, pp. 597–606.

Horton, Thomas R. *What Works for Me.* New York: Random House, 1986.

Hughes, Kathleen A. "Businesswomen's Broader Latitude in Dress Codes Goes Just So Far." *Wall Street Journal,* September 1, 1987, p. 33.

———. "The Corporate Kiss." *Harper's Bazaar,* November 1988. (Reprinted from *The Wall Street Journal.)*

Inwald, Robin G. "Profile: Hilson Research Inc." Press release. Reprinted June 28, 1988.

———. "Success Quotient Theory." Jan. 1988.

Jankowic, Elena, with Sandra Bernstein. *Behave Yourself!* Englewood Cliffs, N.J.: Prentice-Hall, 1986.

Kanter, Rosabeth Moss. *Men and Women of the Corporation.* New York: Basic Books, 1977.

Kiechel, Walter, III. *Office Hours.* Boston: Little, Brown and Company, 1988.

Kurtzman, Joel. "Shifting the Focus at B-Schools." *New York Times,* December 31, 1989, p. F4.

Lurie, Alison. *The Language of Clothes.* New York: Vintage Books, 1983.

Mackay, Harvey. "Image: Cast a Tall Shadow." *Success,* June 1988, p. 26.

———. *Swim with the Sharks Without Being Eaten Alive.* New York: Morrow, 1988.

Mager, N. H., and S. K. Mager. *The Complete Letter Writer.* New York: Pocket Books, 1957, 1968.

"Manners Count on the Corporate Ladder." *New York Times,* April 24, 1985, p. C12.

Martin, Judith. *Miss Manners' Guide to Excruciatingly Correct Behavior.* New York: Warner Books, 1983.

McCarthy, Michael J. "Are Office Romances Unfair to Others?" *Wall Street Journal,* August 17, 1988, Section 2, p. 23.

Molly, John T. *New Dress for Success.* New York: Warner Books, 1988.

Morrison, Ann M., Randall P. White, Ellen Van Velsor, and the Center for Creative Leadership. "Women with Promise: Who Succeeds, Who Fails?" *Working Woman,* June 1987, pp. 79–82, 84 (from *Breaking the Glass Ceiling: Can Women Reach the Top of America's Largest Corporations?* Reading, Mass.: Addison-Wesley, 1987).

Moore, Martha T. "When in Rome . . . or Jeddah . . . or Oman." *USA Today,* March 19, 1990, p. 6E.

Ono, Yumiko. "There's an Old Saying: Never Look for a Gift, of Course, in the Mouth." *Wall Street Journal,* December 13, 1989, p. B1.

Osborne, Robert. "Rambling Reporter." *The Hollywood Reporter,* December 11, 1989, p. 4.

Phillips, Linda and Wayne, with Lynne Rogers. *The Concise Guide to Executive Etiquette.* Garden City, N.Y.: Doubleday, 1990.

Pincus, Marilyn. "Mastering Business Etiquette and Protocol." New York: National Institute of Business Management, 1989.

Peters, Thomas J., and Robert H. Waterman, Jr. *In Search of Excellence.* New York: Harper & Row, 1982.

Pettus, Theodore T. *One on One: Win the Interview, Win the Job.* New York: Random House, 1981.

Phillips, Stephen, and Amy Dunkin, with James B. Treece and Keith H. Hammonds. "King Customer: At Companies That Listen Hard and Respond Fast, Bottom Lines Thrive." *BusinessWeek,* March 12, 1990, pp. 88–91, 94.

Posner, Mitchell J. *Executive Essentials: The Complete Sourcebook for Success.* New York: Avon Books, 1982, 1987.

Printing News. " 'Mind Your Manners,' Artise Advises SAGA Members at Luncheon Meeting." *Printing News,* April 20, 1989, pp. 17, 19.

Redeker, James R. "Code of Conduct as Corporate Culture." *HR Magazine,* July 1990, pp. 83, 84, 86, 87.

Reuter. "Ethics Make Good Business." *Newsday,* January 17, 1989, p. 43.

Roel, Ron. "On-Job Manners Matters." *Newsday,* December 8, 1987, p. 55.

Rossman, Marge. *When the Headhunter Calls: A Guide for Women in Management.* Chicago: Contemporary Books, 1981.

Rossman, Marlene L. *The International Businesswoman: A Guide to Success in the Global Marketplace.* New York: Praeger, 1986.

Rowland, Diana. *Japanese Business Etiquette.* New York: Warner Books, 1985.

Schwartz, Barry. "The Social Psychology of the Gift." *American Journal of Sociology*, vol. 73, no. 1, July 1967, pp. 1–11.

Sell, Shawn. "Office Party Etiquette: Holiday Dress for Business Success." *USA Today*, November 30, 1988, p. 4D.

Sobel, Dava. "Social Phobia." *New York Times Magazine*, January 1, 1989, pp. 24, 25.

Solomon, Julie. "The New Job Interview: Show Thyself." *Wall Street Journal*, December 4, 1989, pp. B1, B7.

Spikol, Art. "Expletive Deleted." *Writer's Digest*, May 1985, pp. 61, 62, 64.

Stewart, Marjabelle Young, and Marian Faux. *Executive Etiquette*. New York: St. Martin's Press, 1979.

Strunk, William, Jr., and E. B. White. *The Elements of Style*. New York: Macmillan, 1979.

Tarrant, John. *Stalking the Headhunter*. New York: Bantam Books, 1986.

Thompson, Jacqueline. *Directory of Personal Image Consultants*. Staten Island, New York: Image Industry Publications, 1990.

Thourlby, William. *Passport to Power*. New York: Forbes/Wittenburg & Brown, 1990.

Wall Street Journal. "Business Schools Seek More Polished Students." December 4, 1989, p. B1.

Wallach, Janet. *Working Wardrobe*. Washington, D.C.: Acropolis Books Ltd., 1981.

Wassmer, Arthur C. *Making Contact: A Guide to Overcoming Shyness*. New York: Dial Press, 1978.

Werne, Jo. "The Comfortable Office." *Chicago Tribune*, August 27, 1989.

Westoff, Leslie Aldridge. *Corporate Romance*. New York: Times Books, 1985.

Williams, Lena. "Social Studies: The Christmas Lunch and the Office Party." *New York Times*, December 10, 1989, p. 74.

Wyse, Lois. *Company Manners*. New York: McGraw-Hill, 1987.

Yager, Jan (aka J. L. Barkas). *Creative Time Management*. Englewood Cliffs, N.J.: Prentice-Hall, 1984.

———. "Getting the Message Across." *New York Newsday*, April 5, 1988.

———. "Holiday Stress: Coping With Year-End Crush." *Newsday/New York*, December 15, 1987, p. 5.

———. *How to Write Like a Professional*. New York: Arco, 1985.

———. *Making Your Office Work for You*. Garden City, N.Y.: Doubleday, 1989.

———. "The Power of 'No!' " *National Business Employment Weekly*, Fall 1988, pp. 40, 43.

———. "The Uniform Trend Makes Its Mark Across America." *Chicago Tribune*, September 8, 1980.

A p p e n d i x 1

Research Methods and Survey

To get a multifaceted picture of business etiquette in corporate America today, I followed a three-level approach to researching this topic. After background research, extensive original interviews and observations in a variety of companies enabled me to develop hypotheses about business etiquette, which were then incorporated into a questionnaire. The survey was then distributed to randomly chosen members of the Society for Human Resource Management. Of the 450 who were sent the anonymous survey, 108 replied. (Because I promised that the survey was anonymous, a coding of names and addresses was not kept. For that reason, follow-up was impossible to try to prod questionnaire recipients to fill out and return their survey.) Of the 108 respondents, 30 provided their name, address, and phone number for either follow-up interviews or having survey results sent to them.

Revised or new hypotheses, based on an analysis of the objective questionnaire results, were then retested through additional in-person or telephone interviews, discussions, or observations with additional managers, human resources administrators, executives at various levels in a range of businesses, or other business etiquette experts.

The cover letter I sent to members of the Society for Human Resource Management as well as the final questionnaire are reprinted below.

Cover Letter Sent to Survey Respondents

I am asking members of the Society for Human Resource Management (chosen by a random probability sampling plan) to complete and return a confidential (and, if you wish, anonymous) survey on business etiquette issues. I am sure you will agree that this is an area of importance to all workers, especially rising executives; input from those "in the field" is vital to the book I am writing on this topic.

A copy of an article from the *Chicago Tribune* that you might find useful—it highlights some of the key findings from my recent book, *Making Your Office Work for You* (Doubleday, 1989)—is attached for your perusal.

Thank you for your valuable time and interest. I would appreciate receiving your completed survey as soon as possible.

Sincerely,

Jan Yager

encs.

RESEARCH SURVEY

Private and Confidential

Sex: *Female* _____ *Male* _____
Age: *Under 40* _____ *40 or older* _____
Type of company: _____
Company size: _____ (number of employees)
Your job title: _____
Number of years with company: _____

Written Guidelines

1a. Does your company have written guidelines on business etiquette?

Yes _____ *No* _____ *Other* _____

1b. If yes, what format do these written guidelines take?

Booklet _____   *Typed sheet* _____
Spiral notebook _____   *Other* _____

Violating Company Policy

2a. Has anyone been fired in the last year for violating a company business etiquette policy?

Yes _____ *No* _____ *Other* _____ *If yes, how many?* _____

2b. Check off any of the reasons for those firings that apply:

	Percentage
Violating dress code	_____
Using foul language	_____
Inappropriate romantic relationship at work	_____
Excessive drinking	_____
Drug abuse	_____
Inappropriate behavior at a company function	_____
Misuse of travel and entertainment privileges	_____
Saying the "wrong thing"	_____
Other (list) _____	_____

Looking the Part

3a. How strongly do you agree that employees at your company have to dress according to a particular company image?

Strongly disagree	*Somewhat disagree*	*Somewhat agree*	*Strongly agree*
_____	_____	_____	_____

3b. Are employees ever reprimanded for the way they dress?
Frequently ____ *Sometimes* ____ *Occasionally* ____ *Never* ____

Doing the Right Thing

4a. At your company, which of the following are correct etiquette?

Man opening the door for a woman   Yes _____   No _____
Woman opening the door for a man   Yes _____   No _____
Man standing if a woman enters his
office   Yes _____   No _____
Keeping business confidences   Yes _____   No _____
Being on time   Yes _____   No _____
Exchanging Christmas gifts   Yes _____   No _____
Leaving at the end of the day:
   before your boss   Yes _____   No _____
   after your employees   Yes _____   No _____
Extending your hand to greet a man   Yes _____   No _____
Extending your hand to greet a woman   Yes _____   No _____
Addressing superiors by their complete
name   Yes _____   No _____
Addressing superiors by their first
name   Yes _____   No _____

4b. How much money does your company recommend spending on a Christmas gift for an employee?
$10 or less ____ $11–$25 ____ $26–$50 ____ $51–$75 ____
Other ____

Friendship at Work

5a. Is it company policy to hire a friend? Yes _____   No _____

5b. Which statement do you agree with?

My company encourages becoming friends with clients _____
My company discourages becoming friends with clients _____
My company does not have a policy one way or the other _____

Socializing at Work

6a. How much time do you spend socializing with co-workers at work?
Less than 30 minutes ____   Between 2–3 hours ____
31 minutes to 1 hour ____   Between 3–4 hours ____
Between 1–2 hours ____   Over 4 hours ____

6b. How much time do you spend socializing with your boss outside of work?

Less than 30 minutes ___   *Between 2–3 hours* ___

31 minutes to 1 hour ___   *Between 3–4 hours* ___

Between 1–2 hours ___   *Over 4 hours* ___

6c. Where/when does this socializing with your boss occur?

On a weekday ___   *On a weekend* ___   *Over lunch* ___

Over dinner ___   *At sports event* ___   *At cultural event* ___

Playing tennis ___   *Playing golf* ___   *Other* ___

The Office

7a. Does the company dictate what you can hang on your wall?

Yes ___   *No* ___

7b. Are there rules about clutter on the desk?

Yes ___   *No* ___

7c. Is it etiquette to offer a chair to a visitor?

Yes ___   *No* ___

Business Breakfasts, Lunches, or Dinners

8a. What is the etiquette about picking up the tab?

Senior person always does it   *Yes* ___   *No* ___

Person who did the inviting   *Yes* ___   *No* ___

Other ___

8b. How are RSVP's to business dinners handled?

In writing ___   *By phone* ___   *Other* ___

9. What is the key business etiquette concern at your company?

___

10. List below any further comments about business etiquette. If you wish, also list how to contact you for possible follow-up and/or to notify you of the survey results. _____

_____

_____

_____

_____

_____

_____

_____

Appendix 2

Essential Equipment for a Home or Office Bar

Ice bucket
Tongs (for ice bucket)
Strainer
Squeezer
Bottle opener
Corkscrew
Ice pick
Sharp knife
Jigger
Muddler
Bitters bottle with dropper-type
    top
Heavy glass cocktail shaker
Martini pitcher
Bar spoon
Utensils or machine for converting
    ice cubes into crushed ice or a
    heavy canvas bag and wood
    mallet or cloth-covered hammer

Lemon peeler
Juicers
Bitters
Carbonated water
Lemons
Oranges
Limes
Olives
Small onions
Cherries
Assorted glasses: whisky,
    champagne, cocktail, daiquiri,
    sour, wine, beer, tall

Appendix 3

Sample Menus

Here are a few sample lunch, brunch, and dinner menus. If you are using a professional caterer, or a restaurant, you might create a similar menu from the range of dishes available to you. Creating a written menu, even if you decide not to give copies out to your guests, will be useful to you in planning this and future meals. However, most guests will appreciate a copy of the menu as a keepsake, especially if it is for a special dinner, such as for Christmas or the holidays, or a lunch to celebrate a promotion.

Happy Holidays

DINNER PARTY
Friday, December 15th, 1989

M E N U

Appetizer:
Fresh Fruit Cocktail

Salad:
Tossed Green Salad with Choice of Dressing

Entrees:
Veal Française
Chicken Marsala
Fillet of Sole Stuffed with Crabmeat
Surf & Turf

Baked Potato   Rolls   Vegetable

Dessert:
Pineapple Sherbert

YULETIDE HORS D'OEUVRES/APPETIZERS

Party for 40–50 Guests

Cheese Fondue with French Bread or Bagel Bits

Meatless Meatballs in Tomato Sauce

Swedish Meatballs

Potato-Eggplant Paté

Coconut-Banana Applesauce

Applesauce

Coleslaw

Citrus Avocado Salad

Assorted Hard Cheeses

Potato Chips, Dry Roasted Peanuts, Popcorn, Marshmallows

Coconut or Chocolate Chip Drop Cookies

Cranberry Fig Bar Cheesecake

Coconut Cheesecake

Chocolate Spice Cake with Yuletide Icings

Apples

Red or White Wine

Assorted Hard Liquors

Soft Drinks, Orange Juice, Tomato Juice

Hot Apple Cider, Coffee, Tea

For Christmas Eve or New Year's Day

HOLIDAY SEASON OPEN HOUSE
ITALIAN MEAL

Thursday, December 30th, 8 o'clock

Cheers!

ITALIAN ANTIPASTO
Provolone, Bel Paese, Gorgonzola, Parmesan, Eggs,
Marinated Eggplant, Romaine Lettuce,
Olives, Artichoke Hearts, Radishes, Celery, Peppers, Carrots

Olive Oil and Wine Vinegar
Italian Salad Dressing with Basil Leaves

GARLIC BREAD

RICE MILAN STYLE WITH PINE NUTS, FRUIT, AND PARMESAN CHEESE, CASSEROLE STYLE

SPAGHETTI WITH TOMATO SAUCE

ITALIAN CHEESECAKE MADE WITH RICOTTA

ASSORTED HOLIDAY COOKIES

RED OR WHITE WINE

COFFEE OR TEA

LUNCH MENU

Assorted Hard Cheeses

Celery and Carrot Slices

Chicken Kiev

Rice

Mixed Vegetables

Assorted Rolls and Breads

Cinnamon Coffee Cake with White Glaze

Fresh Fruit in Season

Coffee, Tea, Cold Drinks

BRUNCH MENU

Crunchy Salad

Creamy Italian or Thousand Island Dressing

Welsh Rarebit

or

Quiche Supreme

Sauteed Carrots

Yellow Cake with Double Fudge Chocolate Frosting

Fresh Fruits in Season

Coffee, Tea, Cold Drinks

BRUNCH: MENU FOR EIGHT TO TEN GUESTS

Beverages

Orange or Tomato Juice
Beer, Scotch, Vodka, Bourbon, Gin, Red or White Wine
Assorted Soft Drinks
Tea, Coffee, Milk, Skim Milk, Hot Cocoa

Appetizers

Mystery Paté Served on a Bed of Lettuce with Sliced Tomato
Easy Coleslaw
Health Slaw
Avocado and Citrus Salad on Romaine Lettuce
Assorted Cheeses: Muenster, Provolone, Cheddar, Gouda, and Edam

Condiments

Cranberry Sauce
Applesauce
Banana-Coconut Applesauce
Sour Cream, Cottage Cheese, Farmer's Cheese, Cream Cheese,
    Margarine, and Butter
Peach Preserves, Orange and Grapefruit Marmalades, Raspberry Jam

Main Dishes

Cheese Blintzes
Saucy Eggs and Creamed Spinach Casserole

Desserts

Banana Cake with Vanilla-Flavored Icing
Cranberry-Topped Fig Bar Cheesecake
Frozen Yogurt or Ice Cream
Fresh Apples, Fruits in Season

Breads

Pumpkin Bread
Assorted Rolls and Bagels

DINNER PARTY FOR FOURTEEN
Menu

Party Punch

Light Fluffy Eggnog and Hot Cider

Deviled Eggs

Fresh Vegetable Platter with Cottage Cheese Dip

Dogs in a Blanket

Fresh Breads

Walnut Chicken and Rice

or

Meatloaf with Mashed Potatoes

Brownies with Chocolate Frosting

Oatmeal and Chocolate Chip Cookies

Fruit Salad Supreme

Appendix 4

Mail-Order Guide for Gift-Giving*

Note: Although mail-order (or phone-order) companies make it especially easy to charge and send all kinds of gifts, most stores in your local area will take orders over the phone or, if you shop in person, will wrap and send a gift for you.

Contact any of the companies listed for their catalogs as well as for information about ordering their products. Note that some companies may charge a small fee for a catalog, so be sure to ask if it is free or not.

Books

Book Call
New Canaan, CT
800-255-2665
800-ALL-BOOK (outside Connecticut)

Food

Davidson of Dundee, Inc.
Dundee, FL
(813) 439-2284 (fruit)
(813) 439-1698 (candy)

---

* Neither the author nor the publisher assumes responsibility for the up-to-date accuracy of the names, addresses, or phone numbers contained here. Since information might change, please check any listings before using.

Harry and David
Medford, OR
800-547-3033

Hickory Farms
Maumee, OH
800-222-4438

Pinnacle Orchards
Medford, OR
800-759-1232

The Swiss Colony
Monroe, WI
(608) 324-4000

Wisconsin Cheeseman
Sun Prairie, WI
(608) 837-4100

Garden Supplies

Park Seed
Greenwood, SC
800-845-3369

Kitchen Items/Glassware

J. C. Penney
Scranton, PA
800-222-6161

Spiegel
Chicago, IL
800-345-4500

Williams-Sonoma
San Francisco, CA
(415) 421-4242

Miscellaneous/Gadgets/Hardware

Brookstone: Hard to Find Tools
Peterborough, NH
(603) 924-9541

Gump's
Desoto, TX
800-334-8677

Leichtung Workshops
Cleveland, OH
800-321-6840

San Francisco Music Box
Company
San Francisco, CA
800-227-2190

The Sharper Image
San Francisco, CA
800-344-4444

Smithsonian Catalogue
Washington, DC
(703) 455-1700

Luggage/Attaché Cases/Leather Goods

Lands' End
Dodgeville, WI
800-356-4444

Outdoor Clothing

L. L. Bean
Freeport, ME
800-341-4341

Toys

Constructive Playthings
Grandview, MO
(816) 761-5900

The Disney Catalog
Lakewood, NJ
800-237-5751

FAO Schwartz
New York, NY
800-426-TOYS

Just for Kids!
New Brunswick, NJ
800-654-6963

Pleasant Company (Dolls)
Middleton, WI
800-845-0005

Lillian Vernon
Virginia Beach, VA
(914) 633-6300

Toys to Grow On
Long Beach, CA
800-542-8338

The *Great Catalogue Guide*,
published by The Direct
Marketing Association (DMA), lists
400 catalogs in more than twenty-
nine categories. It is available only
by mail for $3 from DMA at
11 West 42 Street,
New York, NY 10163.

*Mail-Order Companies That
Imprint Business Gifts*

Amsterdam Printing Company
(pencils and pens)
Amsterdam, NY
800-342-6116
800-833-6231 (outside New York
State)

The Business Book
Oshkosh, WI
800-558-0220

Where to Find Business Etiquette Consultants

The Directory of Personal Image Consultants, edited by Jacqueline Thompson (Staten Island, New York: Image Industry Publications, 1990), lists over three hundred consultants in a range of areas. Some of the consultants on etiquette, interviewed for this book, or whose written works were consulted, include:

Letitia Baldrige Enterprises, Inc.
2339 Massachusetts Avenue, N.W.
Washington, DC 20008
(202) 328-1626

Susan Bixler
The Professional Image
1000 Parkwood Circle
Suite 425
Atlanta, GA 30339
(404) 953-1653

Barbara Chizmas
Chizmas Business Etiquette International
700-U East Redlands Boulevard
Suite 335
Redlands, CA 92373
(714) 797-9595

Dorothea Johnson and Company
Metropolitan Square
655 Fifteenth Street, N.W.
Suite 320
Washington, DC 20005
(202) 828-1966
(703) 803-9263

Camille Lavington
160 East 38th Street
New York, NY 10016
(212) 490-0389

Linda and Wayne Phillips
The Executive Etiquette Company
48 Duffy Drive
Taunton, MA 02780
(508) 823-6003

Randi Freidig
The Freidig Group
1300 Dexter Avenue North
Suite 200
Seattle, WA 98109
(206) 284-3833

Diana Rowland
Rowland and Associates
6920 Miramar Road
Suite 308
San Diego, CA 92121
(619) 578-9994

William Thourlby Ltd.
250 West 57 Street
Suite 1527
New York, NY 10107
(212) 969-0467

Here are additional related resources:

The BCIU Institute (Business Council for International Understanding)
American University
3301 New Mexico Avenue, N.W.
Suite 244
Washington, DC 20016
(202) 686-2772

BCIU offers executive training to managers and executives at their Washington, D.C., headquarters (as well as some overseas locations) in the etiquette issues of 147 different countries. This training prepares executives for overseas assignments or for doing business with people from other countries. Fees are usually paid for by the corporate clients.

Ethics Resource Center, Inc.
600 New Hampshire Avenue, N.W.
Suite 400
Washington, DC 20037
(202) 333-3419

The Ethics Resource Center is a private, nonprofit organization established in 1977, "working to strengthen public trust in business, government and other institutions in our society." Literature and audiovisual materials, such as videotapes, are available.

NAPO (National Association of Professional Organizers)
3824 Ocean View Boulevard
Montrose, CA 91020
(818) 957-1658

Membership organization of professional organizers who will provide help in reorganizing your office, on a fee basis. National association maintains an annual directory of members and their specialties (office design or organizing, space planning, or time management).

Index